Measuring America

U.S.A.

MEASURE OF A NATION

A Graphic Presentation of America's Needs and Resources

By

Thomas R. Carskadon
and Rudolf Modley

TWENTIETH CENTURY FUND

Measuring America

How Economic Growth Came to Define
American Greatness in the Late Twentieth Century

ANDREW L. YARROW

University of Massachusetts Press
Amherst & Boston

Copyright © 2010 by University of Massachusetts Press
All rights reserved
Printed in the United States of America
LC 2010018921
ISBN 978-1-55849-835-8 (paper); 834-1 (library cloth)
Designed by Jack Harrison
Set in Monotype Dante with Futura display typography
Printed and bound by Thomson-Shore, Inc.

Library of Congress Cataloging-in-Publication Data
Yarrow, Andrew L.
Measuring America : how economic growth came to define American greatness
in the late twentieth century / Andrew L. Yarrow.
    p. cm.
Includes bibliographical references and index.
ISBN 978-1-55849-835-8 (pbk. : alk. paper) —
ISBN 978-1-55849-834-1 (library cloth : alk. paper)
1. Economics—United States—Sociological aspects. 2. Public opinion—United States.
3. Nationalism—United States. 4. United States—Economic conditions—20th century.
5. United States—Social conditions—20th century. I. Title.
HB119.A2Y37 2010
330.973'092—dc22
                          2010018921

British Library Cataloguing in Publication data are available.

To my wonderful son, Richard, who has tremendous curiosity about America, the world, and so much else; and to the memory of my parents, Marian Radke Yarrow and Leon J. Yarrow, scholars who taught me that scholarship means little if it does not in some way seek to make ours a better world.

Contents

Acknowledgments

I would like to thank Clark Dougan, Carol Betsch, and the University of Massachusetts Press for so ably helping me bring this book to completion and publication. There are many people, particularly at George Mason University, whom I wish to thank for their varied contributions, including the late Roy Rosenzweig, Hugh Heclo, Zach Schrag, the late Larry Levine, Rosie Zagarri, Peter Stearns, Alison Landsberg, Sharon Bloomquist, Mack Holt, and Jack Censer; Dan Rodgers at Princeton University; Robert Griffith at American University; the students in my seminar on this subject at American University in 2007; editors at *Journalism History, The History of Education Quarterly,* the *Journal of Cold War Studies,* and *The Encyclopedia of Postwar America,* which have published parts of this work; as well as James Ciment at M. E. Sharpe, all provided valuable assistance.

I am grateful for generous grant support from George Mason University, the Harry S. Truman Library Institute, and the John F. Kennedy Presidential Library.

Among the many archivists who led me to relevant sources are Dwight Strandberg at the Dwight D. Eisenhower Presidential Library, in Abilene, Kansas; Randy Sowell and Lisa Sullivan at the Harry S. Truman Library Institute, in Independence, Missouri; Steve Platkin and Sharon Kelly at the John F. Kennedy Presidential Library, in Boston; Faith Davis Ruffins, Deborah Richardson, Susan Strange, and Ruben James at the National Museum of American History Archives Center, in Washington, D.C.; Marge McNinch, Chris Baer, and Carol Ressler Lockman at the Hagley Museum and Archives, in Wilmington, Delaware; and Sally Kuisel and other archivists at the National Archives, in Washington, D.C., and College Park, Maryland. In addition, Colleen Healy at the Joint Economic Committee of Congress provided me with access to JEC records; Everett Ehrlich and Van Ooms at the Committee for Economic Development provided me access to CED materials; and George Diez at the National Library of Education, in Washington, D.C., helped me with access to K–12 educational materials from throughout the twentieth century.

Many players in this period of American history gave of their time, memories, and perspectives to enrich this study. They include three former chairmen of the President's Council of Economic Advisers—Raymond Saulnier, Charles L. Schultze, and Martin Feldstein. Charles Schultze, now a Senior Fellow at the Brookings Institution, also kindly read and commented on chapter 2. A number of CED leaders, including Bob Holland, Sol Hurwitz, Van Ooms, and Charles Kolb, offered perspectives on that vital business organization. Leading practitioners in the economic education movement who gave of their time and perspectives include Stowell Symmes, Mark Schug, Bob Highsmith, and Leon Schur. Three former *Fortune* magazine journalists—Carol Loomis, Dan Seligman, and Todd May—offered invaluable insights about business journalism in the postwar period. Prominent economists and presidential advisers—in addition to the CEA chairmen mentioned—who provided recollections and ideas include Paul Samuelson at MIT and former Truman aide Lincoln Gordon.

Finally, to the many friends, family members, and students, particularly Emily Anstaett, who have supported me, provided insights, and challenged me to think in different ways, my heartfelt appreciation.

Measuring America

Introduction
A New Measure of America?

This is the richest and most powerful country which ever occupied the globe. The might of past empires is little compared to ours.
LYNDON JOHNSON, 1965

A nation is more than a political entity; it is a state of mind.
BENEDICT ANDERSON

The central conservative truth is that it is culture, not politics, which determines the success of a society. The central liberal truth is that politics can change a culture and save it from itself.
DANIEL PATRICK MOYNIHAN

On the eve of America's entry into World War II, social scientist Lee Coleman wrote a short essay ("What Is American?") in which he analyzed "alleged American traits" and ideals most often mentioned in books, articles, and speeches throughout the country's history. Coleman listed America's democratic tradition, republican form of government, pioneer and frontier spirit, individualism, and belief in liberty, equality, and mobility. Secondarily, in a darker vein, he noted Americans' conformism and materialism.[1]

The United States has always fancied itself as a nation apart—an "exceptional" nation, and, with more than a touch of hubris, the world's greatest nation. Tom Paine famously wrote in *The Rights of Man* that "the case and circumstance of America present themselves as the beginning of a new world." Yet most leaders from the eighteenth century until World War II focused on the idea that America and American identity were the unique products of a liberal idealism rooted in the thought of John Locke and articulated by Jefferson, Madison, and the other founders. As Louis Hartz argued in his influential Eisenhower-era book, *The Liberal Tradition in America,* America was conceived from a platonic, liberal ideal whose intellectual progenitor was Locke. The founders were lionized as demigods who had crafted a "new order of the ages." The United States—according to Hartz, Daniel Boorstin, and other commentators hearkening back to

1

Alexis de Tocqueville—came into being through a moderate and measured revolution, was deeply pragmatic, and was concerned with constant improvement of the technical means of achieving progress.[2]

However, when Coleman wrote—and before—many commentators also offered variations on the theme that America was a land of plenty. The United States stood head and shoulders above other countries in its abundant resources, productive capacity, economic opportunity, and potential to achieve unimaginable wealth. America had long seen itself as the land of opportunity, defined by individuals' ability to start anew and not be hindered by entrenched political, social, and economic barriers. Americans also had long boasted about the nation's productive powers—from the Lowell mills to the 1876 Centennial Exposition in Philadelphia to Ford's River Rouge plant in the 1930s. Such ideas of America as a Silverado of riches had been paired with and supported by a Jeffersonian/Jacksonian faith in liberty and equality, as well as by a geographical frontier unbounded at least until the end of the nineteenth century. It was in this more timeless sense of "plenty" and potential abundance that dreamers and promoters believed—as far back as Coronado's quest five hundred years ago for the Seven Cities of Gold and the seventeenth-century Virginia Company's promises of gems hanging on trees— as did sophisticated commentators from Tocqueville and Frederick Jackson Turner in the nineteenth century to Brooks Adams and David Potter in the early to mid-twentieth.[3]

Within a few years of World War II's end, however, abundance was no longer a timeless, abstract idea but rather a dynamic, measurable concept of rising economic output and living standards. Opportunity and the chance to escape old world (or third world) poverty were quite different from an emerging belief that America's purpose was ineluctably to produce and provide its people with more goods. Likewise, abundance was no longer so much a neutral description of plenitude as a patriotic celebration of much that was right with America. Prosperity, the pursuit of economic growth, and national greatness went hand in hand. The United States was quantitatively rich and had been made rich by its economic system, which—people were told—distinguished the United States from other countries and was central to its identity.

Beginning in earnest in the postwar era, opinion-shaping elites in politics, business, academia, media, schools, and public diplomacy gloried in America's ever-growing economy as the "measure of the nation." Thanks to new national income accounting and other economic data-collection and analysis techniques the concept of American plenty was now measurable. One could tally up production and, increasingly important, consumption of an ever-expanding universe of goods and services. And one could measure Americans' income, extrapolated from the queen of postwar statistics, the gross national product. American greatness and identity were linked with a quantitatively defined prosperity, presented in the language of a newly influential economics profession. As economics assumed a significantly more prominent role in American thinking, opinion shapers' ideas about what were valued and core qualities of "Americanness" increasingly emphasized economic virtues such as the country's high, rising, and broadly diffused standard of living and its economic dynamism and growth. This new way of thinking developed as economic ideas and an economic style of thinking were popularized, and economics increasingly became a principal language and lens through which the United States understood and defined itself. Economists got much of the credit—and took credit—for America's postwar growth and prosperity. This change went hand in hand with the rise of an economic nationalism, or patriotic consumerism, which helped unify the nation, as "economic freedom" and "free markets" began to replace the more generic "freedom" in political and popular rhetoric.

But as we will see in the many, almost poetic paeans to prosperity first articulated between the late 1940s and mid-1960s, this "measure" was not so much statistical as cultural. It was about what it meant to be American and what America itself meant. After World War II, the United States, culturally, became first and foremost an "economy." America's democratic ideals and its geopolitical power still very much mattered, but culturally the most important metrics of American success were ever more economic.

Thus, we have two parallel, interlocking stories—of how economic ideas came to have vastly greater influence on American culture and how these ideas dovetailed with an outlook expressed by opinion-shaping elites that the meaning and value of the United States increasingly resided in its growing, quantifiable abundance. This book examines the relationship among culture, social psychology, economics, and politics to explore how after World War II Americans increasingly were told to think about themselves and their country in economic terms, and how—even in the changed economic and political environment of the late twentieth and early twenty-first centuries—this thinking has affected the nation and its people. This book is not about the emergence or endurance of pro-growth economic politics or policies, or about the nature of economic growth or the "consumer culture" in U.S. history. Much has been written about "growth liberalism" and the Keynesian "liberal consensus" of the mid-1940s to the late 1960s, and what has become of it.[4] Rather, this book explores how ideas seeped into Americans' thinking about the nature or "identity" of their nation—what they should be proud of as patriotic Americans, and what their aspirations for themselves and their country should be. This changed idea of what it meant to be "American" is examined by looking at messages conveyed to Americans by key voices in the economics profession, business, politics, print journalism, K–12 education, and U.S. cold war propaganda.

The focus of my arguments will be on congruent patterns that speak to how Americans were guided to define themselves during the decades after World War II and beyond. Elite conceptions of Americanness have changed in the course of American history, and they changed dramatically in the postwar decades. Measuring the "reception" of elite messages is extremely difficult, as polling questions and social-science research designs skew answers, and opinions collected at any time may be overwhelmingly influenced by very recent events or other short-term concerns. Ideas also are "overdetermined," as Freud said, and are fluid. While subnational group identities are always meaningful, in the postwar era, American culture was ever more nationalized—extending beyond middle-class white males to embrace much of the population—making ideas about Americanness increasingly more important than ones highlighting class, ethnic, or other identities.

The Measure of America, a 1947 report from the nonpartisan research foundation the Twentieth Century Fund, heralded the new belief that America's principal raison d'être was to ensure affluence and continuous growth, and that America should be depicted as a rich, new nation. Over and over, it was repeated—with copious economic statistics and in the serious-sounding argot of economics—that the country had the highest standard of living in the world and a level of abundance unprecedented in human history. Thanks to wise business leaders, a helpful but not overreaching government, productive but cooperative workers, the expertise of economists who were close to solving all economic problems, and the technological benefits of applied science, Americans could have it all. They could have more and better products. They could end poverty and solve any domestic problems. They could maintain the global U.S. strength and leadership that were essential to win the cold war. This combination of factors—enlightened business, responsible government guided by economic experts, technology, and productive workers who were really happy consumers—made for a "new America" and a new and improved version of capitalism.

This new view of America included a belief that American supremacy and exceptionalism were founded in the country's wealth, productive capacities, and economic growth; economics, wealth, and consumption were the principal measure of social value; optimism, idealism, and thinking about the future were defined in material—rather than moral, political, or geographical—terms; increasing abundance was advanced as the preeminent national objective; the language of growth, prosperity, free enterprise, and consumption increasingly replaced the language of political liberalism and religion as the vernacular for talking about the nation; and individual psychological fulfillment and meaning were to be found in prosperity, growth, and consumption. This perspective—of thinking of America's and Americans' lives and worth in economic terms—had antecedents in the late 1920s and early 1940s, began to gain traction in the late 1940s, but only came into its own as a leading vision of America from the end of the Korean War to the Great Society.

Certainly, it was not hard to sell Americans—deprived for a decade and a half by the Depression and wartime rationing—on the virtues of mass consumption and economic growth. The abundance that flowed from American production beckoned like a candy store even to the most progressive labor leaders. "The enormous quantity production per man employed will be greatly increased in the postwar years," United Mine Workers president John L. Lewis said. "We are living in a marvelous age when genius and science are performing modern miracles. . . . We are abolishing work as such."[5]

The remarkable performance of the U.S. economy during and after World War II fueled these beliefs. As commentators Murray Shields and Donald B. Woodward glowingly proclaimed in 1945:

> This nation has unprecedented resources for prosperity. If, with such resources, it experiences any significant period of considerable unemployment and want, it will be the shame of history. . . . If prosperity is attainable upon this earth, it is attainable here and now. . . . In material things, who can doubt that we have just learned Aladdin's formula and that plastics, electronics, synthetics and innumerable other magic procedures of our scientists and production men will, within our very lifetime, give to us more than any Christmas tree of our childhood promised in our fondest expectations? Never has a nation stood in the midst of so much solid attainment, so much promise of the future, so much justification for expecting to realize that promise.[6]

A widely quoted Twentieth Century Fund report added in 1955: "The United States has not merely climbed to a new plateau, but is ascending heights whose upper limit is not yet measurable, and at an accelerated speed. . . . Of all the great industrial nations, the one that clings most tenaciously to private capitalism has come closest to the socialist goal of providing abundance for all in a classless society."[7]

Polls during the boom years of the mid-1950s and the 1960s regularly found that virtually all Americans believed that the good times would just keep on rolling. They also believed that government was a prime and trusted agent of economic progress. In 1956, for example, only 8 percent doubted that these "good times" would continue, and a mere 3 percent even questioned whether the times were "good." When asked three times by the Gallup Poll over a decade and a half (in 1951, 1961, and 1966) about their standard of living, by margins of three to one to six to one they said it was going up. The Institute for Social Research, a University of Michigan–affiliated laboratory for interdisciplinary research in the social sciences, found similar optimism. Throughout the late 1950s and 1960s, polls showed rising levels of happiness.

For example, a 1951 poll found that Americans over age fifty believed in good times ahead by a 56–25 margin, whereas twenty-one to twenty-nine-year-olds expected them by a 62–19 margin. In 1959, most Americans expected their living standards to double by 1980. Likewise, a February 1965, poll found that three of four Americans held expectations of rising living standards, with business and professional workers believing five to one, white-collar and manual workers three to one, and farmers divided evenly on the prospect of good times ahead. A July 1967 poll found that African Americans were evenly divided about their economic outlook and prospects, while whites—by a five-to-one margin—believed that economic prospects were improving for blacks. The Institute for Social Research found that Americans under sixty-five and men were most optimistic; surprisingly, African Americans were slightly more upbeat about their personal prospects than whites but less optimistic than whites about the nation's economic outlook in 1965. And in 1966 six times as many Americans were optimistic about their economic futures as compared to those in other countries such as Canada, the UK, and Europe. Among the citizens of eight countries surveyed, Americans were consistently the most optimistic about their futures, as compared to a roughly two-to-one positive ratio in the next most positive European countries.[8]

The United States always had been rich by global standards and had beckoned to the world with its promises of opportunity. Popular perceptions of American plenty had existed since Colonial days, but in actuality poverty had been widespread for much of U.S. history. Most Americans lived short lives, in decrepit housing, with poor nutrition (which apparently worsened during the nineteenth century), worked long hours at low pay, had few conveniences or accoutrements of leisure, and had neither discretionary income nor security should they be disabled, lose their jobs, or manage to live into old age. In 1914 dollars, wages averaged $338 in 1865, $705 on the eve of World War II, and $2,181 in 1969. Life expectancy in 1855 was less than forty, only four years higher than it had been in 1790, and the average American attended school only five hundred days in his or her lifetime.[9] Even with the ephemeral and ill-distributed "prosperity" of the 1920s, the Depression hardly suggested that the economy was a good barometer of American success. At the end of the 1930s, the conventional wisdom was that the U.S. economy was "mature" and that the economic pie would no longer grow. Thus, the reality and prospect of ever-rising living standards after World War II was new. The great post–World War II boom saw real U.S. GNP and average household consumption double, following a doubling of national output during the war. The U.S. economy grew by an annual average of about 4 percent between 1947 and the late 1960s, with the fastest growth from 1947 to the mid-1950s and 1961 to 1968. Per capita output, on average, rose annually three times faster between 1950 and 1973 than the yearly average of the previous 130 years. By comparison, annual per capita growth between 1790 and 1860 is estimated to have been only 1.3 percent. Unlike earlier periods of rapid growth such as the 1840s, the turn of the twentieth century, the 1920s, and much of the post-1973 era, when incomes rose but inequality was increasing, America's rising incomes were now more broadly shared. Most Americans were getting richer together, poverty rates were cut in half between 1960 and 1968, and the black poverty rate fell from 90 percent in 1940 to 41 percent in 1966. Inequality declined modestly for the only sustained period during the last century, and consumption levels appeared to equalize. College attendance and graduation rates soared between the late 1940s and late 1960s. By the 1960s, at least five out of six Americans had televisions, telephones, cars, refrigerators, and running water, and about three-fifths of the population owned their own homes.

The "revolutions" of "rising expectations" and "rising aspirations" described by 1950s commentators were well founded. Moreover, whereas previous periods of high growth had been interrupted by severe, prolonged, and/or frequent downturns, during the postwar era, the business cycle seemed to have been vanquished through the wonders of Keynesian economic management, making postwar recessions short and mild. What John Kennedy referred to as the "rising tide" was lifting all boats in the postwar era: In 1947, 27 percent of white families had income under $3,000 in 1965 dollars, while 65 percent of nonwhite families did; by 1966, these percentages had fallen sharply to 13 percent of whites and 32 percent of nonwhites.[10]

Yet if a sense of national success significantly predicated on abundance and the conception of America as an economy were generally accepted, what was its significance? What was the driving force behind the new faith in America as a great and growing economy providing benefits for all? Why did it emerge when it did, and why did it become so potent? What were the components of these beliefs? How were they conveyed? What older conceptions about America did they challenge? Why did this change occur when it did? Did business, government, and other elites introduce these ideas purposefully to change public thinking, or did these ideas emerge through an interaction between elites and the broader population? How did the economics profession—its ideas, its language, and its social power—affect this emergent identity? What was in it for the messengers who articulated it? And what were, and have been, the consequences of these changes?

This was more than just a new way of conceptualizing what the United States was and what distinguished it from other nations. It provided explanations of what propelled America, what its goals should be, and what the country's destiny would be. This cluster of beliefs and the ways in which they were expressed also were a means of instilling patriotism and popular commitment to the nation. Even though the fight against godless communism united the United States during this period, this new vision of an abundant, growing, and middle-class America was put forth to unify the population by providing a secular, lowest-common-denominator national identity and agenda. It could be almost universally appealing in a way that more abstract ideas about freedom, more overtly religious ideas, more militaristic beliefs, or more ethnically or socioeconomically limited conceptions were less able to accomplish by the second half of the twentieth century. It was a perfect set of beliefs for a presumably classless, melting-pot society that was overwhelmingly urban and suburban, and increasingly conditioned to respond to the clarion calls of consumerism.

It was ostensibly an apolitical and upbeat message that could bring Americans together, patching over the bitter social divisions not only of the 1930s but of the preceding half century, as well as lingering post–Civil

War geographical divisions. It was the answer to the "social question" that had plagued the United States since the early days of industrialization, from the 1877 railroad strikes to the Flint sit-down strikes of the 1930s. It was not only the answer to socialism but was really socialism turned on its head. The rising incomes of the postwar mixed economy showed that the social needs of most Americans could be met, and promised that remaining social problems such as poverty could be solved. For the business community, the image of a prosperous, growing America helped it reinstate the power and esteem that it had lost during the Depression. For cold warriors, the idea that the United States had beaten the Soviets at their own game—providing "classless abundance for all"—was far more palatable to all but the Dr. Strangeloves than talking about superior throw-weight in nuclear arsenals. Postwar opinion leaders may have spun the message, but they were not making up the story of America's upwardly arcing abundance. Most Americans benefited tremendously.

If this alignment of a more capitalism-friendly New Deal liberalism, a more Keynesian and consumer-oriented business, and popular desires for the good life provides one explanation for the change in American culture, other factors also played a part. The new influence of economists in U.S. politics and culture was of critical importance. No longer a small, marginal profession with little influence on public policy, much less on the American public, the economics profession, its expertise, its ideas, and its language were enthusiastically embraced by government policymakers and Americans during the decades after World War II. For economists, and those in thrall to their presumed omniscience, the suggestion that economic growth could be managed and facilitated was extremely seductive. Economists influenced America through books, popular articles, and their closely heeded advice to political, business, and other leaders. This new influence was part of broader trends that celebrated technical expertise and elevated the prestige of the social sciences. Yet economists came to occupy a particularly vaunted place among "experts" and social scientists, as their efforts and pronouncements seemed key to assuring rising income and profits. Economic concepts and terms, such as *economic growth, GNP, living standards, purchasing power, per capita income,* and *demand,* were popularized by politicians, journalists, business, and educators, and were invested with almost mystical meanings. "The words 'economic growth,' previously unknown to most economists much less to ordinary Americans, entered the national consciousness," in the postwar era, according to authors Robert Heilbroner and Aaron Singer.[11]

The rise of economists and the faith in expertise able to solve "technical" problems also reflected a historically new optimism that people were not subject to the vagaries of an uncontrollable economic fate. Instead, Americans believed that they, and their leaders, were masters of their economic destiny, and that perpetually increasing abundance could be provided for all, solve all problems, and bring about wondrous tomorrows. They also believed that their leaders, and the experts who advised them, had their best interests at heart. Americans had faith in the "system," political and economic.

Rising incomes and consumption contributed to a powerful, free-floating optimism. This is all the more striking given the dark cloud of thermonuclear war that hung over the nation, particularly in the early 1950s and early 1960s. Many economists since publication of Richard Easterlin's 1970s cross-cultural studies have posited that happiness rises with incomes—up to a point, after which there is little change, as aspirations also rise with income. Perhaps, the postwar ascent in living standards represented the rise to this plateau, as Americans reported greater satisfaction with their lives in the late 1950s and early 1960s than at any other time between the beginnings of scientific polling in the 1930s and the early twenty-first century. The American Institute of Public Opinion (AIPO) and the University of Chicago–affiliated National Opinion Research Center's Structure of Psychological Well-Being and General Social Surveys found that the self-reported happiness of lower-income groups rose from 1957 to 1972, converging with the happiness levels of higher-income Americans, whereas the same surveys have found a general decline in happiness since 1973.[12]

On the other hand, thinking about America as an economy—rather than as a society, a polity, or a community—has myriad implications for how people view themselves as citizens and their responsibilities and rights vis á vis their compatriots. For one, an economy is more impersonal, leading people to interact through market mechanisms. Such thinking suggests that compassion, neighborliness, and a civic outlook may be less important in dealing with others than competing in terms of income or consumption, or letting market forces define one's interactions. Seeing the nation as an economy rather than a polity or a civic sphere also may diminish the importance placed on obligations of democratic citizenship, including engagement in public affairs. It may encourage retreat from the demos or any non-economic public arena. Moreover, it may recalibrate what rights are important—from free speech and equality under the law to the "right" to rising incomes and consumption. Notable indeed is the shift in how Americans were characterized—from "citizens," "workers," or "producers" to "consumers."

Politically, this identification of America with growing, measurable abundance meant that policies to support economic growth and expanded consumer choice tended to assume greater importance than policies to secure and expand political and civil rights, enhance less economically quantifiable aspects of well-being, or promote conceptions of justice beyond ensuring procedurally equal access to markets rather than more equal distribution of resources or power. Even in the civil rights movement of the 1950s and 1960s, and the other rights movements that it spawned, calls for social equality often blurred into desires for fuller and equal participation in American abundance.[13]

This set of beliefs shifted the country to a center-left consensus that largely held from Harry Truman to the 1970s. In party-politics terms, most Republicans accepted a limited welfare state, a federal budget five to seven times larger as a percentage of national income than it had been before the Depression, and a mixed economy more generally. Likewise, Democrats largely accepted an essentially capitalist economy and the cold war defense buildup. Business gained in social and political power, and organized labor—at the apogee of its power during the Truman and Eisenhower years—accepted the wage increases and private welfare state codified in the "treaty of Detroit" between General Motors and the United Auto Workers in lieu of power in the workplace or significant political power. The "growth consensus"—borne of a mind-set conditioned by aspects of the New Deal (full employment, planning, Keynesianism) and the World War II perspective that Americans, working together, could lick any problem—also may have contributed to an acceptance that all Americans, not just the wealthy, should benefit from prosperity and economic growth. The postwar decades were the heyday not only of New Deal liberalism but also of liberal Republicanism and what some called "corporate liberalism."

Many Americans on both the left and right increasingly worried about their nation's devotion to freedom and individual liberty. The anticommunism crusades of the late 1940s and McCarthyism in the early 1950s led many liberals and others to wonder about the nation's commitment to free speech, due process, and other basic civil liberties. The Birmingham bus boycott, lunch-counter sit-ins, the 1957 Little Rock confrontation, books such as Gunnar Myrdal's *An American Dilemma* (1944), and the brutal response to early 1960s freedom riders led growing numbers of whites to realize that America's professed commitment to "freedom and justice for all" was an empty promise for African Americans and, perhaps, others as well. The rise of "second wave" feminism, with Betty Friedan's *The Feminine Mystique* (1963), only added to this sense that some Americans were freer and more equal than others. At the same time, by the late 1950s, as Daniel Bell and others spoke of "the end of ideology," the attempt to define America by its traditional, abstract ideals either seemed dated, overly intellectual, or too burdened with caveats or commonplace among Western nations.

At the same time, a small but influential number of conservatives questioned whether the United States remained true to time-honored principles of individual liberty. The growth of government since the New Deal led some to wonder if the nation was en route to a *1984*-like, big-government, "big brother" socialism, or what economist Friedrich von Hayek suggested in 1944 was a *"road to serfdom."* The idea that "American freedoms," including free enterprise, were threatened became an increasingly insistent theme among conservative intellectuals, business leaders, politicians, and popular commentators from Ayn Rand to Barry Goldwater.

These converging worries about America's lost commitment to what were seen as its historic "freedoms" necessitated an alternative, consensual national identity and belief system. Into this vacuum stepped America's vaunted and supposedly unique politico-economic system and "way of life," predicated on the nation's unparalleled, measurable, and growing economy. Virtually all could agree on America's signal achievement in generating economic growth and prosperity. Democratic and Republican politicians celebrated America's abundance and wrapped it in the mantle of soaring idealism. Freedom, free enterprise, and a prosperous American way of life became indivisible. This consensus was embraced by Truman and Kennedy Democrats as well as Eisenhower Republicans, and even enticed many further to the left. As Eisenhower said, government's purpose was "the maintenance of a strong and growing economy. The American economy is one of the wonders of the world. This Administration is determined to keep our economy strong and to keep it growing."[14]

Internationally, while America justly could celebrate its leadership in defeating fascism, promoting democracy and stability in postwar Japan and Western Europe, and defending freedom in early cold war confrontations in Greece, Berlin, Korea, and elsewhere, the broader record appeared more mixed. Sensitive to European and third world criticisms—stoked by Soviet propaganda—of "American imperialism," some Americans began to wonder whether their country was truly on the side of freedom in Latin America, Southeast Asia, and elsewhere. Worries increased about why other peoples disliked the United States. In addition, for some liberals, the "national liberation" and decolonization movements of the 1950s and 1960s had usurped U.S. claims to be at the leading edge of world freedom.

By virtue of its GNP and panorama of consumer abundance, however, the United States could hold itself up as a model to the world and differentiate itself from its erstwhile Western allies. The nation used its growing, broad-based affluence and the system that created it as a chief selling point in its global ideological battle against communism. Economic growth, as Truman economic adviser Leon Keyserling, Lyndon Johnson, and others argued, allowed the United States to have guns *and* butter—to expand its military capabilities and fight a global battle against communism, and fund domestic social and infrastructure programs. It also provided funds and political support for foreign-assistance programs ranging from the Marshall Plan and Truman's Point Four initiative to JFK's Peace Corps and other aid programs, all designed to enhance U.S. international prestige and power and export American-style prosperity and the beliefs that came with it. Most important, given the USSR's relentless drumbeat about its economic "achievements," the United States—using similar economic measures of success—could rightfully claim that it was beating the Soviet Union by its own metrics.

American "Identity"?

Ideas about a nation's identity and how its people or its leaders see their land are slippery concepts. Like any generalizations about millions of people and their leadership elites, they can too easily simplify complex realities that are irreducible. They run the risk of caricature and of offending many whose beliefs are far different. Just like saying that the United States is a "conservative" nation, or a religious or optimistic one, such labels too easily applied deny the many countervailing tendencies. Even if one can tentatively make general statements, trailing a string of caveats, statements about a nation's identity, belief system, or values can be a tyranny of the majority in cultural terms. Of course, culture is never monolithic, and conflicting—or, simply, differing—ideas always coexist.

Moreover, much discussion of America's, or any nation's, identity or values often comes with an agenda lurking not far beneath the surface. Commentary about national identity frequently takes the form of heroic hagiography, such as the cultural puff pieces that celebrate admired and "common" traits that are hardly true of an entire population. A more critical tradition often has viewed national culture psychologically and even anthropomorphically, dissecting and analyzing its neuroses and other purportedly common problems. Even more "neutral" studies such as Lee Coleman's, or most famously Tocqueville's *Democracy in America* (1835), have tended to be laundry lists of defining historical experiences and qualities.

In all cultures, but particularly in U.S. history, many scholars, political leaders, and observers have wrestled with the concept of national identity or "character," with Americans from J. Hector St. John de Crèvecoeur in the 1780s to Ronald Reagan two hundred years later emphasizing U.S. "exceptionalism." The heyday of "American identity" studies was from the 1940s to the 1960s—drawing in writers such as Margaret Mead, David Riesman, and David Potter, yet scholars and armchair analysts have pondered the idea from the eighteenth to the twenty-first centuries. As noted, many hypotheses have been advanced about the essence of Americanness and the key factors defining it. These purportedly essential—and contradictory—qualities (and causes) have included individualism, Puritanism, the lack of a feudal past, the frontier, abundant resources, liberalism, practicality and pragmatism, America's democratic tradition, the "melting pot," materialism, and a belief in liberty, equality, and mobility.[15]

Arguments about a discernible American identity and exceptionalism have become more academically suspect since the 1960s. Many scholars have highlighted the similarities and cultural continuities between the United States and other cultures, while others have emphasized that subnational, transnational, and other group identities—including those of gender, class, race and ethnicity, and even the "Atlantic world"—are more real than national identity.[16] Many have argued that national identity tends to diminish individual agency or various forms of group identity. Some see it as expressing the views of economically or politically powerful white male elites. Still others see it as something of a quicksilver concept—intellectually seductive but prone to vanishing under close analysis.

Nonetheless, culture is not entirely chaos. National, ethnic, and religious cultures would not be distinct if they did not display identifiable qualities and beliefs that are at least normative—held by the preponderance of the population and instilled by influential elites. Indeed, anthropologists and other cultural observers are right to focus on how elites interact with the general population in defining the broad contours of a culture. Some left-ist twentieth-century theorists such as Antonio Gramsci, Georg Lukacs, Herbert Marcuse, and Raymond Williams have contended that a domi-nant social class or elite shapes popular beliefs, values, and the ways that people see their world. As Marcuse said: "We can imagine no other tune, since our consciousness is limited to the factuality of the contemporary commodity world and we have lost the capacity for critique." Williams spoke of "a saturation of the whole process of living . . . to such a depth" that the social structure "seems second nature." Historian T. J. Jackson Lears, following Gramsci, has argued that elites do not so much force be-liefs on people as set the terms of debate and establish what is accepted as "second nature," or what economist John Kenneth Galbraith called "con-ventional wisdom."[17] But even elites hardly speak with one voice and must compete for cultural saliency.

Certainly, cultural meaning—how people come to see ideas as true and second nature—emerges through a dynamic process. Ideas presented by those with cultural, political, or economic power are not automatically accepted as true or conventional wisdom. As historian Thomas Bender has said, ideas and "meanings move back and forth" between elites and the general population.[18] It is important to recognize that people are cre-ators of their culture and the meanings in it, as anthropologist Clifford Geertz has argued, but also are shaped by broader cultural, political, and economic influences. At best, Americans—like all peoples—select values, beliefs, and ways of thinking from a cultural menu served by elites, and hold (or reject) those beliefs to differing degrees.

Although one must tread gingerly in drawing conclusions about the nature or identity of a culture from elite messages, people do "imagine" themselves as part of a larger community, as social scientists Ernest Gellner and Benedict Anderson contend. These imaginings do not emerge from thin air, and most people are hardly averse to seeing themselves, proudly or patriotically, as part of a national culture. Gellner and Anderson have argued that national identity is constructed—by the state or related opin-ion-shaping elites. To Gellner, nationalism "invents nations where they do not exist," while to Anderson, a nation "is a state of mind." National identity and nationalism are related concepts, and Gellner and Anderson illustrate the fine line between supposedly descriptive and value-neutral national identity and prescriptive, celebratory, and hortatory nationalism.

Both constructs exist for domestic as well as international consumption, defining the United States in comparison to other nations and cultures.[19] Indeed, a key feature of most Americans' understanding of themselves is that they are American, as well as white or black, "middle class," Southern, female or male, or any other label that people use to identify themselves. In fact, Americanness—however defined and whoever helps define it—is far from unimportant to most Americans' identity.

Unlike many commentators on American identity, I argue that—caveats in mind—it is not timeless and unchanging. Although some cultural historians have tried to characterize a particular era's zeitgeist, most writing on American identity has been more transhistorical. To Potter, Hartz, Boorstin, and other "consensus" historians of the 1950s and 1960s, national identity was largely unchanging. On the other hand, the zeitgeist literature has tended to ignore the relationship between the "spirit of the times" and cultural identity. To these authors, the "spirit of the times" hovers like an aura, perfuming sectors of the population but generally not defining how they think of themselves or their culture.

Instead, I argue that ideas about American identity are historically rooted—conveyed by particular elites in particular eras—and thus are subject to change with other changes in a culture. Images of the nation and its people, and visions of the nation's "meanings" and most salient and valued characteristics change over time. Examining the views of articulate leaders and opinion-shapers, and the patterns revealed by the ideas and messages they transmit, can provide an extremely useful understanding of what beliefs are important among the broader population. The messages that elites convey, and how they change over time, not only say something about what beliefs elites value but also what they assume is appealing to the general population.

Intimations of a New Vision of America

There are nuances to the new postwar idea that American greatness could be calibrated economically. Many Americans, as far back as the Colonial era, believed that theirs was a land of unrivaled plenty. Potter argued this in the 1950s, Tocqueville observed this in the 1830s, Turner in the 1890s made the "frontier" emblematic of America's absence of material limits, and Brooks Adams and other Gilded Age observers hailed American economic "supremacy" at the turn of the twentieth century. Historian T. H. Breen has pushed the putative dawn of an American consumer culture to the eve of the Revolution, arguing that the colonists' experience of a flood of British imports in the eighteenth century gave them "the cultural resources" to protest British rule through boycotts; yet economic historians believe that per capita economic growth in the eighteenth century was minuscule.[20]

The problem with these views—and the crucial difference with the postwar era—is that before the 1940s (or, perhaps, briefly, the late 1920s), American abundance was seen in abstract terms of limitless land, resources, opportunity, and potential for wealth, not actual, quantifiable, steadily growing abundance for the mass of Americans. It was also a producers' vision of abundance, not a consumers' reality for the vast majority of the American people. Moreover, it could not be honestly touted as widely shared, "classless," and rising abundance, as it was so effectively after 1945. Consumer goods and a consumption mentality may have surfaced in the eighteenth century, and the United States may have become the world's preeminent economic power around 1900, yet the vast majority of Americans did not share in this abundance, and few, if any, thought to quantitatively and culturally measure the worth of their nation by it. They may have been thankful for the abundant land provided by settlement policies from Jefferson through Lincoln, marveled at the inventions displayed in the 1876 and 1893 world's fairs, and been awed by the railroads and industrial blast furnaces of the late nineteenth century, not to mention the nascent consumer culture appearing in mail-order catalogs and department stores by the late 1800s. By the turn of the twentieth century a modestly comfortable, though small, middle class had emerged—but they were the exception. Despite the bravado of industrial moguls such as John D. Rockefeller and Andrew Carnegie, or the commentaries of Brooks Adams and others, American "wealth" c. 1900 was that of a producing elite. At best, Americans shared a hope, and believed in a potential, for abundance to be realized someday.

In addition, wealth and consumption hardly were unchallenged values in America's early history. It was not just Puritans who railed against the sins of avarice, indolence, and consumption. The idea that accumulating wealth and consuming ever-growing quantities of goods was wicked only died a slow, lingering death by the early twentieth century. Well into the late nineteenth century, popular magazines such as *Godey's* criticized consumption as frivolous and extravagant.

Nonetheless, it is worth considering ways in which American opinion-leaders thought about wealth and economic expansion before the early twentieth century. By the 1830s, writers such as Daniel Webster and J. A. Etzler recognized America's "unprecedented augmentation of general wealth" since the Revolution and its potential to achieve more. Etzler's utopian tract *The Paradise within the Reach of All Men, without Labour, by Powers of Nature and Machinery* (1833) concocted an American future in which technology could provide unlimited power to create all manner of things. By the 1851 Crystal Palace Exhibition in London, the "American System" of manufacturing, based on interchangeable parts, was touted as a revolutionary wonder that would make the United States the economic wave of the future. In the wake of Edward Bellamy's 1888 best seller, *Looking Backward: 2000–1887,* dozens of late-nineteenth and early-twentieth-century utopian novels such as H. G. Wells's *A Modern Utopia* (1905) predicted a coming society in which technology married to a quasi-authoritarian social organization would produce enough to satisfy everyone's needs. Bellamy wrote: "The Golden Age lies before us and . . . is not far away."[21]

Nineteenth-century ideas about America's material promise pivoted off of two broad premises—the country's technological capacity and its "conquest of space." The faith in technology stemmed from both cultural factors that date to Benjamin Franklin and before, as well as the labor shortages that drove technological innovation and high productivity growth in early U.S. history. The sense of natural, physical abundance, of course, stemmed from the obvious geographical fact that the nation and its territories had expanded to more than 3.5 million square miles by the 1860s. Exploration, pioneers,; the Homestead Act, and the westward expansion of the railroads, and the purchase and seizure of territory from France, Mexico, Native Americans, and Russia all contributed to what Turner famously described as America's "frontier" mentality. This sense of America's dynamic physical growth was captured in Josiah Strong's 1885 best seller, *Our Country,* and his 1904 *Social Progress: A Year Book and Encyclopedia of Economic, Industrial, Social and Religious Statistics.*

The post–Civil War decades were, despite a few major "panics," an era of tremendous economic growth and technological innovation, witnessing the birth of graduate science and technology education, a revolution in capitalism characterized by the rise of large corporations and a managerial elite, and the beginnings of advertising and mass marketing. Steam-powered factories helped vastly expand production. The modern business enterprise, run by professional managers, established efficient, vertically integrated entities for production and distribution. Railroads, the steamship, the Western Union telegraph, and an improved postal service facilitated mass distribution. Advertising agencies such as N. W. Ayer & Son and J. Walter Thompson emerged after the Civil War to structure and stoke consumer desires. New department stores such as Montgomery Ward, Sears, Woolworth, and Wannamaker's also were born between the 1870s and 1890 to cultivate and serve a new market for consumer goods.

Many of these technological and economic triumphs were celebrated at the various world's fairs held in the United States during the forty years after the 1876 Centennial Exposition in Philadelphia. The Philadelphia fair—whose spectacular Machinery Hall exhibited Alexander Graham Bell's telephone, the Corliss steam engine, and mechanical refrigeration, among other new products—was an encomium to technical progress seen by 10 million visitors. Contemporary observers said that the centennial fair boosted American self-confidence, though it came during a dark period of economic depression, the Grant-era scandals, the collapse of Reconstruction, and the stolen election of 1876.

The World's Columbian Exposition in Chicago in 1893 was one of the most spectacular fairs, drawing 21 million visitors in six months to its White City and Midway, where gas turbines, kinetoscopes, elevators, and other mechanical wonders uneasily vied for attention with exotic dancing girls, the "streets of Cairo," and trained animals. Once again, the fair came at an inauspicious time to celebrate American abundance, given that year's economic collapse and Turner's melancholy over the "closing of the frontier." Nonetheless, many undoubtedly saw the Chicago fair, as well as later fairs such as the 1904 St. Louis Louisiana Purchase Exposition, as "timekeepers of progress," as President McKinley said, or fantasy worlds of what Americans could expect in their future.[22]

Some post–Civil War Northerners saw the new wealth as God's reward for their righteousness. Exponents of a "gospel of wealth" such as Andrew Carnegie and minister Russell Conwell spoke a harsh, social Darwinian language of "survival of the fittest" and of the "duty" to get rich. Carnegie, writing in 1889, saw his era's problem as "the proper administration of wealth," acknowledging that most were poor and deserved "moderate" compensation, cooperative work arrangements, and charity. At the same time, Horatio Alger novels famously peddled a rags-to-respectability fantasy to millions.[23]

Henry George, in his 1888 classic *Progress and Poverty,* saw a tale of two Americas—on the one hand, "a marvelous era" in which "the enormous increase in the power of producing wealth would make real poverty a thing of the past," and on the other, a society in which "these gains are not shared" and poverty and inequality were a curse upon the nation. The Populists, while espousing the laborer's right to a fair share of the era's prosperity, railed against a society in which "the fruits of the toil of millions are boldly stolen to build up colossal fortunes for a few." Radical labor leaders sounded similar alarms.[24]

In short, many recognized the new wealth of late-nineteenth-century America, but few saw abundance as the common experience of most Americans. Instead, commentators saw a nation bitterly divided between economic plutocrats and masses of poor workingmen. These observers—from Carnegie and Alger to Bellamy, George, the Populists, and the new union movement—believed that there was a way out, a future in which plenty, albeit a relatively fixed quantity of it, could be shared. Many believed that the answer was in the redistribution of existing wealth, not the sort of economic growth that in the postwar era promised a bigger pie with bigger pieces for all. But most such ideas were an inchoate hope for the future—not a reality that could be pointed to and celebrated in the present.

Indeed, late-nineteenth-century skies were filled with more economic clouds than the new corporate gentry and their spokesmen could handle. Severe depressions hit in 1876 and 1893, poverty was widespread, social inequality was growing, and bitter labor-management confrontations were widespread, as an estimated thirty-seven thousand strikes occurred between 1881 and 1905. While the robber barons may have smugly expounded on the—or, their—new wealth from their Newport mansions, many more Americans failed at business or struggled as low-paid workers in often-dangerous jobs working sixty hours a week. Turn-of-the-twentieth-century America was not a land of widespread prosperity, and beliefs in a broad-based, quantitatively measured abundance could have no reality in these circumstances. Beyond a few moguls and utopians, in a society on the threshold of modernity, in which even high school and news were the province of a small fraction of the population, few Americans systematically thought about their nation's economy.

Glimmers of change appeared during the Progressive Era. The National Civic Federation, founded in 1900 but whose influence peaked several years later, sought expanded government and social cooperation among business, labor, and government to expand prosperity. In his 1909 book, *The Promise of American Life,* Herbert Croly, who influenced Teddy Roosevelt, argued that America needed a democratic Hamiltonianism in which the good society would be shaped through concerted government and social action.[25]

During the mid to late 1920s—with arrival of the Model T, radio, Hollywood movies, widespread electrification, and the first home appliances—a consumer society began to emerge, aggregate national output increased 39 percent, profits doubled, and the stock market soared. Political leaders and businessmen, riding high in public esteem, hailed the dawn of a "new era." *Prosperity* was a popular buzzword of the era, and Coolidge's Wall Street advisers assured him that it could be maintained indefinitely. Coolidge himself celebrated the "new era" of prosperity and wondrously spoke of "the enormous capacity for consumption of all kinds of commodities which characterizes our country." Herbert Hoover, a more complicated, transitional, and widely misunderstood figure, said in 1928: "We in America today are nearer to the final triumph over poverty than ever before in the history of any land." Even four years later, after the Wall Street crash, he said: "During the last 30 years . . . we have secured a lift in the standards of living and a diffusion of comfort and hope . . . such as have never been seen in the history of the world," ignoring the precipitous economic decline of the preceding three years.[26]

Other voices of the 1920s hinted at what was to come. The French commentator André Siegfried said in 1928 that Americans treated their standard of living as sacred, and Paul Mazur, in *American Prosperity* (1928), described a new mentality focused on satisfying consumers' desires. Advertising came into its own in the 1920s to sell not only products but also the idea of America providing a "democracy" founded on consumption. By the 1920s, advertising theorists Bruce Barton and Edward Bernays explicated a new psychology in which people were motivated not by mere survival or high-minded ideals but by the desire to consume. Bernays, echoing economist Paul Nystrom, audaciously claimed that democracy itself was now defined by Americans' ability to choose among a pluralism of goods. This theme was developed in the *Ladies' Home Journal* that appeared a month before the 1929 stock-market crash. *Journal* readers were treated to an elaborate discussion of America's emerging "Democracy of Goods." The consumer-engineering movement of the early 1930s also urged attractive product design to lure consumers to spend, seeing consumption as the basis for prosperity.[27]

A few business leaders during the late 1920s—including department store magnate Edward Filene, General Electric chairman Owen D. Young and executive Gerard Swope, Henry Ford, Massachusetts paper manufacturer Henry S. Dennison, and Kodak executive Marion Folsom—became proponents of a "new" or "welfare" capitalism, in which they argued that workers needed good wages and benefits and access to goods at affordable prices to ensure their ability to purchase consumer products. Business also told its story of America at Chicago's 1933 Century of Progress and New York's 1939–40 world's fairs, where such goods as Formica, telephones, and automated freeways portrayed technology as a beneficent, democratizing force that would bring better tomorrows.

If any business effort of the 1930s truly presaged postwar messages about America measured by its economic achievements, it was the New York fair and, particularly, Norman Bel Geddes's Futurama exhibit for General Motors. Like the 1876 and 1893 fairs, the two great fairs of the 1930s were held at a time when technology-driven abundance for all was a cruel joke to tens of millions of unemployed underemployed Americans. Business messages had mixed results during the short, peculiar prosperity of the late 1920s and the Depression, yet the National Association of Manufacturers and the U.S. Chamber of Commerce combined tirades against the New Deal with feeble attempts to highlight the economic benefits of the "free enterprise system" during the 1930s. The chamber's 1936 *American Economic System* booklet incongruously touted America's high standard of living when millions were destitute, on breadlines, or on relief.[28]

While some rhetoric of the late 1920s and early 1930s began to change attitudes about America, the big problem with talking about a genuine "consumer society" or a "prosperity decade" in the 1920s—a phrase coined by *New Republic* editor George Soule[29]—is that the era's prosperity was brief and not widely shared. Most Americans experienced stagnant or falling incomes, attenuated only partly by the rise in consumer credit and the new availability of some cheap, mass-produced goods such as cars and a few appliances. Even Herbert Hoover's pathbreaking 1929 report, *Recent Economic Changes,* concluded: "One can paint a glowing picture of American prosperity which emphasizes the triumphs of mass production in automatic factories, the success of large-scale farming with power machinery, the rapid spread of chain stores, the cooperation of labor unions in enlarging output, the economy of high wages, our new position in international finance. Or one can paint a picture of average and sub-average performance by ordinary men struggling with difficult circumstances and ending in discouragement and failure."[30]

Yet a handful of economists and social theorists began to envision a truly new America defined by its material riches and potential. From Simon

Patten and Walter Weyl in the early twentieth century to Stuart Chase and Mordecai Ezekiel in the late 1920s and 1930s, they may have been visionaries who anticipated an economically conceived America beyond the unforeseen horizons of World War II, but their impact on popular thinking was minimal. Patten, an independent-thinking economist who helped found the American Economic Association, argued in his 1902 book, *The Theory of Prosperity*, that industrialization was solving the problems of production and that conventional economic wisdom about the permanence of "scarcity" would soon be consigned to the dustbin of history. Similarly, dismissing traditional, moral ideas of consumption as a vice, he urged that an "economy of abundance" could be achieved if economists, policymakers, and businessmen focused on distribution and consumption. Patten influenced later thinkers such as Weyl and Rexford Tugwell, and sociologist Lester Ward hailed Patten for seeing the way from "a pain economy into a pleasure economy," but few of Patten's contemporaries agreed with him.[31]

Economist and cofounder of the *New Republic*, Weyl, in his 1912 book, *The New Democracy*, argued that true democracy—which he said the United States had not yet attained—required abundance. Like Patten, he argued that economic development must be planned by an activist state. He said that workers had little on which to unite, given their differing occupations and circumstances, but consumers were truly united by their interests in more material goods. James Truslow Adams, in *Our Business Civilization* (1929), nostalgically yearned for a lost idealism and individualism, yet he also popularized (if not coined) the phrase "the American dream"—of a richer, happier life, which he extolled as "the greatest contribution we have made to the world." Horace Kallen recast the phrase's evolving meaning, saying that "the American Dream is a vision of men as consumers."[32]

This vision also was promoted by Edward Filene, a businessman and theorist who helped pave the road for postwar thinking about Americanism as abundance. Economists William Trufant Foster's and Waddill Catchings's *Road to Plenty* (1928) anticipated the Keynesian revolution to come. They all advanced notions of business-government partnership to create a new economy in which growth would bring widely shared prosperity. Filene, who established the Twentieth Century Fund, frequently spoke during the depths of the Depression of a coming "age of plenty."[33] Of course, the New Deal and the 1940s were times of considerable uncertainty about the U.S. economy's prospects. Harvard economist Alvin

Hansen in the late 1930s was among those who popularized the idea that the U.S. economy was "mature" and unlikely to grow much in the years ahead. Franklin Roosevelt exemplified the era's ambivalence. In his 1941 State of the Union address, he called for "freedom from want" and a "constantly rising standard of living" for all Americans, though he also believed that economic resources were limited and thus not a good measure of American greatness.

Similarly, Stuart Chase—whose 1932 book, *A New Deal,* became FDR's policy moniker—boldly envisioned in his next book, *The Economy of Abundance* (1934), a need for consumers to change their mind-set, from a scarcity mentality that meant a fixed pie where "more for you means less for me" to an "abundance mentality that meant more for all." Mordecai Ezekiel, the architect of FDR's agricultural adjustment legislation, not only popularized the idea that abundance could be achieved but—together with economist Lauchlin Currie, Hansen, and Gardiner Means, a Columbia University economist who briefly served in the Agriculture Department—also popularized John Maynard Keynes's new ideas in books such as *$2500 a Year: From Scarcity to Abundance* (1936) and *Jobs for All through Industrial Expansion* (1939).[34]

Ezekiel, Harvard president Charles Eliot, Henry Dennison, and economists Hansen, Beardsley Ruml, and Luther Gulick were instrumental in the late New Deal's National Resources Planning Board (NRPB), whose 1943 National Resources Development Report called for a nine-point economic Bill of Rights. Government would ensure jobs, economic security, medical care, and other social rights but would collaborate with private enterprise. The NRPB trumpeted the Keynesian line that policymakers now understood that government fiscal and monetary policy could be used to promote an economy that would provide "enough for all . . . for the first time in history." Anticipating postwar economic hubris, the board declared in January 1943: "The road to the new democracy runs along the highway of a dynamic economy, to the full use of our national resources, to full employment, and increasingly higher standards of living. . . . We stand on the threshold of an economy of abundance. This generation has it within its power not only to produce in plenty but to distribute that plenty."

By the mid-1940s, as the NRPB and others were busily planning a postwar economy, U.S. vice president Henry Wallace said, "we live by these ancient standards of withdrawal and denial in a world bursting with abundance." The common man, he told Americans, "need not tolerate less prosperity in time of peace."[35]

1

The Economics Profession and the Changing Discourse

Among the fruits enjoyed by those who live under the fundamental concepts and principles that define our system are an abundance in all that makes a good life, unparalleled in the entire history of tribes and nations and empires.

DWIGHT D. EISENHOWER, 1954

A tiny profession with little public influence in the 1920s, economics became a celebrated key player in Washington by the 1950s. Its ideas and language were enthusiastically embraced by national leaders and policymakers, opinion shapers, and the public in post–World War II America. And many economists were happy to bask in the limelight.

The intellectual fodder was provided by the parallel developments of Keynesian economics, which became orthodoxy among economists and politicians, and national income accounting, with its sophisticated techniques of measuring the nation's income, productivity, and growth. Economists, entering the public sphere en masse for the first time, offered seductive new paradigms that put quantitatively defined abundance at the heart of how Americans thought about their economy and nation. The growing influence of economists on American thinking was both direct, in books and articles, and indirect, through their impact on political, business, and labor leaders, in the press, and through educators.

This influence was part of a more general veneration of technical expertise and social science, but economists clearly were at the pinnacle. Eisenhower, in his Farewell Address, presciently warned that "public policy could itself become the captive of a scientific-technological elite." In 1973 the *Saturday Review* would write: "In a civilization devoted to material fulfillment, the economist has come close to being regarded as the one true oracle, bearer of pragmatic wisdom, guide on the path to a utopia of perpetually expanding prosperity." While physicists and other scientists were lionized for the technological advances they facilitated, and psychology was to become culturally popular in the 1970s (challenging economics as the discipline that could best explain the meaning of Americans' lives), economists had a distinctly profound impact on politics and policymaking, academic research agendas, and popular consciousness.[1]

Economic concepts and language—ranging from economic growth, GNP, living standards, and purchasing power to the mixed economy, per capita income, the welfare state, and economic stimulus—were popularized by politicians, journalists, and business, and invested with new significance. These terms entered the popular vocabulary, and economic statistics and reports were assiduously followed by politicians, journalists, and the public. Gardner Ackley, of Kennedy's and Johnson's Council of Economic Advisers (CEA), remarked: "I sometimes feel that we are becoming a nation of economic hypochondriacs. The pulse-taking and fever-charting in which we engage; the scrutiny of weekly and monthly indicators; the learned and not-so-learned dissections of GNP and industrial production sometimes remind me of a friend of mine who keeps a thermometer in his desk drawer, a calories chart in his vest pocket and litmus paper in his lavatory." Economists may have had differing ideas of what "economics in the public service" meant, but few questioned that economics had decamped from the ivory tower and found a place in the councils of government, in the media, business, education, and the popular mind.[2]

While economists had been brought to Washington by Franklin Roosevelt to help plan New Deal and wartime production initiatives, these largely were seen as emergency actions. Previously, presidents rarely sought economic advice, and when they did they generally turned to bankers and businessmen. Even the tools to measure economic growth and national income did not exist before they were developed and refined by the National Bureau for Economic Research and the Commerce Department between the 1920s and 1940s. A milestone in the ascendance of economists and economic thinking was the Employment Act of 1946, codifying economists' role as both policy advisers and educators of the general public by creating both the CEA within the executive office and a Joint Economic Committee of Congress. The *Wall Street Journal* appropriately called the Employment Act a "Magna Carta for economists," and the CEA's first chairman, Edwin Nourse, spoke of the rise of the "economic politician." The act also created a position for an economist with the congressional joint committee, and the Federal Reserve, which first became a major policy player in the 1950s, hired its first two economists in 1948 and 1949. By the early 1950s, as many as five to eight thousand economists—a sizable chunk of the profession, and a sharp rise from the six hundred of 1929—worked for the federal government.[3]

The ascendance of Keynesian macroeconomics, with its emphasis on government's role in stabilizing and stimulating the economy, went hand in hand with economists' growing influence in Washington and American society. By the 1950s, even non-Keynesians no longer believed that economists should sit on the sidelines. Summarizing a 1955 survey by *Fortune* magazine of ninety-two leading economists, Raymond Bowman, assistant director of the Bureau of the Budget, noted that economists' "philosophy has changed from the view that 'the economy is best served if you do nothing' to the view that 'the economy is best served if you do something.'" As even free-market, anti-Keynesian economist Ludwig von Mises noted in 1949, economics "rivals the legal profession in the supreme conduct of political affairs. The eminent role [economists] play is one of the most characteristic features of our age of interventionism."

Eisenhower's second CEA chairman, Raymond Saulnier, noted that "the notion grew that economists would be helpful, even quite necessary, in achieving the country's economic aspirations." Herb Stein, later Nixon's CEA chairman, said: "Our problem is not so much that the world thinks too little of us. It is more that we have allowed the world to think too much of us. We have allowed the world to think that we know more than we do, or that we know with more certainty than we do."[4]

While CEA chairmen such as Leon Keyserling, Arthur Burns, and Walter Heller became well known, other economists—including Paul Samuelson, John Kenneth Galbraith, Walt Rostow, Sumner Slichter, and Alvin Hansen—attained an unprecedented near celebrity status in the 1950s. Popular magazines and newspapers wrote glowingly of the profession's leading lights. *Fortune,* noting "a bull market for economic theory," said in 1950: "Economics . . . has achieved what to older economists appears as an unexpected popularity." Galbraith, Samuelson, Rostow, and more prominent CEA members were widely revered as the sages who could explain America's remarkable postwar economic expansion, and the "wise men" who could assure that it would continue. A 1949 article in *Harper's* on the CEA was glowingly titled "Truman's Three Wise Men," and *Life* magazine called Eisenhower's CEA "the President's prophets." Presidential historian Clinton Rossiter noted that, even in the anti-intellectual Eisenhower administration, CEA chairman Arthur Burns "was almost a hero." And Samuelson said that: "As bad as we economists are, we are better than anything else in heaven and earth in forecasting aggregate business trends," and noted that "the leaders of this world may seem to be led around through the nose by their economic advisers."[5]

Many economists were keenly aware of, and reveled in, their newly influential status, and contributed to the public's belief in their profession's importance. Samuelson—the Nobel Prize–winning economist whose textbook, *Economics*, first published in 1948, introduced millions of college students to the discipline—popularized Keynesian ideas, extolled the virtues of the mixed economy, and celebrated America's capacity for growth. Robert Heilbroner, a liberal economist at the New School for Social Research, also influenced vast numbers of students and general readers with *The Worldly Philosophers* (1953), a multimillion-copy best seller about economists, economic history, and economic concepts. Many economists—from Henry Hazlitt on the right to Alvin Hansen and Samuelson in the Keynesian center and Galbraith, Leon Keyserling, and Heilbroner on the left—were regular contributors to mass-circulation and opinion magazines. Samuelson wrote that "economists relished their newfound prominence and basked in the glory of public adulation." Others served as presidential speechwriters, including Keyserling for Truman, Gabriel Hauge for Eisenhower, and Galbraith for Kennedy.[6]

The Public Role of Economists, 1885–1933

The American economics profession came into its own in the late nineteenth century, and the American Economic Association (AEA), founded in 1885 by economist Richard T. Ely and Johns Hopkins president Daniel Coit Gilman was one of two hundred learned societies born in the United States during the 1870s and 1880s. While emulating Germanic scholarship, under Ely, Simon Patten, and E. J. James, the AEA focused on the conflict between capital and labor at the end of the nineteenth century, and called on economists to see themselves as agents of social reform, at a time when laissez-faire and social Darwinism were popular among social and business elites. Institutionalist economists such as Thorstein Veblen, John Commons, and Patten argued that the profession should examine the social, historical, cultural, and institutional factors conditioning economic behavior and be wary of ascribing too much rationality to economic action. Reform and Institutionalist impulses soon gave way to a desire to be "scientific" and "objective" and to avoid politics. However, in the early twentieth century, the profession was torn between wanting to be above the political fray yet relevant to policy and business.[7]

During World War I, AEA president Commons urged colleagues to assist federal agencies, and the Washington-based Institutes of Research and Economics were founded in 1916 and 1922 to influence policy by Robert Brookings, a philanthropist and official in World War I's War Industries Board. Economist Wesley Mitchell and Edwin Gay—who helped found the Harvard Business School, the Council on Foreign Relations, and the Social Science Research Council, and edited the *New York Evening Post*—established the National Bureau of Economic Research (NBER) in Cambridge, Massachusetts, in 1920. Like Brookings, the NBER has remained a leading center of theoretical and applied economic research. In the 1910s and 1920s, economics turned away from being a "literary profession," as Martin Feldstein described it, and from "political economy" and a moral science to the more analytical discipline of economics as we know it. While Wesley Mitchell at NBER was beginning the first systematic efforts to gauge national income and study business cycles, Herbert Hoover, as Commerce secretary and president, recognized that economists could be useful to successful policymaking and assist business. Contracting the NBER and hiring economists at Commerce, Hoover oversaw the publication of the new Surveys of Current Business in 1921 and the pathbreaking effort to examine the U.S. economy in toto in the two-volume 1929 report *Recent Economic Changes.* This massive study drew on NBER economists such as Mitchell and Gay to give scientific credence to the impression of an "immense advance in America." Mitchell's and Hoover's review, in the second volume, as noted, was more sober, describing a yin-and-yang economy of "American prosperity . . . [and] high wages" coexisting with "subaverage performance" by "struggling" and often failing Americans.[8]

Reflecting the glimmerings of a consumer society, other economists began to suggest that consumption drove economic progress. At the turn of the twentieth century, Thorstein Veblen recognized that the "satiation" of desires was impossible because wants were determined by emulation, not necessity. And in 1902 Simon Patten suggested that America was moving from an "age of deficit" to an "age of surplus," describing the transition as one from a "pain economy to a pleasure economy."[9] Chase and Tugwell believed that an "economy of abundance" was possible but were less sanguine than business figures such as Edward Filene and Edward Bernays, or economists William Trufant Foster and Waddill Catchings, that only a modified laissez-faire economy could bring it about. Most economists still believed that scarcity defined economic life.

The New Deal, Keynesianism, and National Income Accounting, 1933–45

Despite the Bureau of the Budget's creation in 1921 and Hoover's overtures to economists, economists still had little influence on policymaking or public opinion in the 1920s and the early 1930s. As late as 1931, only six hundred economists were employed by the federal government, a number that increased ninefold during the New Deal. But with millions unemployed and thousands of businesses and banks failing, Depression-era policymakers began to turn to economists to seek solutions to the nation's floundering economy. The trickle of economists who came to Washington under Hoover became a flood after FDR was inaugurated in 1933. Although Roosevelt personally kept most economists at arm's length, the New Deal brought several thousand economists to Washington. Alvin Hansen, Lauchlin Currie, Adolphe Berle, Mordecai Ezekiel, Rexford Tugwell, Gardiner Means, Robert Nathan, Walter Salant, Alan Sweezy, Beardsley Ruml, Jacob Viner, Leon Henderson, and John Kenneth Galbraith were among the best known. In 1934, the AEA for the first time encouraged its members to take government work as a patriotic duty to serve their country in a time of emergency, and in 1941 it established a Committee for Standards for Economists in the Public Service.[10]

However, New Deal economic policies were far from consistent, as some initiatives sought to raise production, while others sought to lower it; some sought to raise prices, while others sought to lower them; and some sought industry consolidation, while others vigorously pursued antitrust actions. Much New Deal thinking was premised on explaining the Depression as the result of insufficient consumer purchasing power and demand, stemming from low wages and social inequality. This focus on the consumer had several important implications: For one, it meant that government policies should be designed to put purchasing power—that is, money—in the hands of the people, whether by creating jobs, creating social-welfare and relief programs, or controlling prices. As "the labor question" receded with World War II and the country became preoccupied with "the American standard of living," more subtly, it meant thinking of civic identity—of Americans' role in their nation as consumers.

This provided an opening for Keynesian thinking to seep into both government policy and popular consciousness. British economist John Maynard Keynes had published the influential *Economic Consequences of the Peace* (1919) after World War I and *The End of Laissez-Faire* in 1926, but it was his 1936 *General Theory of Employment, Interest and Money* that made him the most influential economist of the twentieth century. Although many of his ideas were anticipated by Foster, Chase, the Institutionalists, and others, Keynes's magnum opus systematically took aim at classical economics' belief that capitalism is endowed with automatic mechanisms, of supply creating its own demand that produces full employment. Instead, Keynes postulated that equilibrium was possible at any level of employment and income, which depended on an economy's aggregate demand. Rather than investment leading to employment and consumption, Keynes said that consumption or demand leads to employment, investment, and growth. The best way to stimulate consumption and, hence, investment was through government fiscal and monetary policy, and longer-range economic management, which not only had a multiplier effect but also could serve socially useful ends.

Whereas later Keynesians saw deficit spending as a fiscal stimulus to be used when needed, Keynes argued that policymakers should resort to deficits only during downturns, with governments running surpluses during boom times. Yet as Robert Lekachman said, Keynes "slew the dragon" of a "Puritan outlook that condemned spending and applauded savings. His *General Theory* effected a paradigm shift in economic and social policy after the war. Because of the Depression and the government-led economic success of World War II, economists and policymakers became bewitched by Keynes in the 1940s, 1950s, and 1960s.[11] In the political and economic turmoil of the 1930s, Keynes's triumph was anything but a fait accompli. But it was only World War II that made Keynes into the Einstein of economics and public policy. Wartime public spending created demand for industry's goods—although most demand was from the public sector—which ended the Depression. By 1943, unemployment had vanished in America.

The lessons for peacetime were hardly lost on economists, policymakers, and the public. To economists, it confirmed Keynes's ideas that government spending could stimulate demand and ignite the economy; that markets were not infallible, self-correcting mechanisms; and that equilibrium was possible at higher levels than previously had been imagined. To Roosevelt's administration and some Republicans, it meant that government fiscal policy could play a salutary role in stimulating the economy in peacetime as well as war. And to the American people, it meant that government and economic experts could ensure jobs, if not a better standard of living. Despite business attempts to oppose the New Deal and

Keynesianism, by war's end, few Americans or economists were listening. Instead, economists proclaimed that laissez-faire was the irrelevant relic of an earlier stage of economic development. Samuelson's *Economics* would become not only arguably the most successful college text of all time, going through nineteen editions by 2010, selling more than 4 million copies, and being translated into more than forty languages, but also a primer in Keynesianism for millions of impressionable freshmen and sophomores.

Keynesians were anything but monolithic in their views in the late 1930s, early 1940s, and later, and many economists, policymakers, and business and journalistic popularizers adapted Keynes's ideas to suit their own purposes. Some, like Keynes himself, took the social-democratic view that public spending was not just a stimulus to demand but also a vehicle to achieve greater social justice and support vital public goods such as health, education, and housing. Such ideas were incorporated by Hansen, Galbraith, Ruml, and Lincoln Gordon into reports of the National Resources Planning Board in the early 1940s.[12] The NRPB, an outpost of Keynesian thinking but killed by Congress in 1943, sought to ensure that a depression would not return and to plan for growth. In Britain, where Keynes played an active role in policy, his ideas were a basis for the 1943 Beveridge Report, which became the blueprint for the United Kingdom's postwar welfare state.

Keynes's ideas also won immensely influential converts in Henry Luce's *Fortune* magazine and the Committee for Economic Development, established in 1942 by liberal business leaders and influenced by Keynesian economists such as Beardsley Ruml, Sumner Slichter, and Gunnar Myrdal. The CED's early paper, *The Economics of a Free Society* (1944), by economist Theodore Yntema and ad executive William Benton, described a mixed economy in which "there is a place for private enterprise and there is a place for public enterprise." In addition, government must prevent depression through "fiscal, monetary and other policies" and protect citizens against the hazards of life and set the rules for the economy. Time Inc. vice president Charles Stillman convinced Luce that Keynesian fiscal policies were essential to full employment and growth and compatible with free enterprise. Between 1943 and 1945, *Fortune* published several articles popularizing Keynesian ideas, including a gushing May 1944 piece that asserted that "Baron Keynes" had the brilliance of Madison and Hamilton and had discovered the formula for preventing depressions and creating prosperity.[13]

Another line of economic research contributed substantially to the rising influence and stature of the profession. Although the Census Bureau had attempted to estimate national wealth since before the Civil War, the efforts of Wesley Mitchell and the NBER to study national income began to bear fruit. During the 1930s, Mitchell turned these efforts over to University of Pennsylvania economist Simon Kuznets, who—with fellow Penn economist Robert Nathan—was subsequently called upon by the War Production Board to develop plans to convert the U.S. economy to wartime production. Parallel national income accounting studies were going on in the Commerce Department during the late 1930s and 1940s, under Frederic Dewhurst, who later led the Twentieth Century Fund. Kuznets, who saw the provision of goods and services to citizens as the main purpose of an economic system, defined national income as the sum of wages, salaries, rent, interest, and dividends. He published his work for Commerce as *National Income and Its Composition* in 1941 and his own *summum opus, National Income: A Summary of Findings and National Product since 1869,* in 1946.[14]

The ability to calculate GNP and the year-to-year performance of an economy gave rise to the idea of measurable economic growth. In part thanks to Kuznets and national income accounting—and in part due to wartime and postwar economic performance—"the words 'economic growth,' previously unknown to most economists much less to ordinary Americans, entered the national consciousness, as commentators and Presidents alike projected the current trend into the future."[15] With Keynes providing the paradigm for managing the economy and Kuznets the tools to measure its performance, America and the economics profession by the late 1940s were poised for a long-lasting love affair.

Economics as Queen of the Social Sciences in Postwar America

The role of economists and other academic experts in America's World War II production miracle, and its contribution to America's victory, immeasurably increased their prominence and prestige in Washington and the nation. Postwar and early cold war efforts in the Department of Defense's Office of Naval Research and the research institute Project RAND were instrumental in bringing economists such as Kenneth Arrow and Gerard Debreu to help lead the new efforts at operations research, linear programming, and game theory. By the 1950s, Galbraith and others referred to the rise of a "new class" and technological elite, inside and outside government, entrusted to solve the nation's problems. Daniel Bell popularized the idea that America had only technical problems, and said that the "the liberal temper . . . redefines all existential questions into 'problems,' and looks for 'solutions' to problems." There certainly were antecedents in 1930s Technocrats such as Tugwell, Chase, Means, Soule, and Lewis Mumford, and Herbert Hoover.

This faith in technical expertise was all but unquestioned from the late 1940s to the Vietnam War, including by many leftists. Most Americans, hearing glowing reports of experts' achievements, saw them as the masters of everything from postwar abundance to geopolitical strategy. Other social scientists played a role, but economists ruled the roost. The National Science Foundation, a 1950 offshoot of the Office of Naval Research, provided 46 percent of its social-science funding from the 1950s to the 1980s to economists, and 60 percent of all federal social-science funding went to economists. University funding for social science increased twenty-fold between 1940 and 1980 and foundation funding rose fifteen-fold. The Social Science Research Council reported that academic and private funders "showed a clear preference for economics" throughout this period.[16]

Not surprisingly, the economics profession flourished beyond its wildest imaginings. The number of Ph.D. economists rose sharply in the 1940s to about thirteen thousand in 1951 and twenty-two thousand in 1960, although most academic fields grew rapidly after the war. The most doctoral degrees ever awarded in economics up until that time were bestowed between 1945 and 1960, as seventy universities offered Ph.D. programs by 1952, students flocked to graduate programs, and the annual number of doctorates awarded tripled between 1947 and 1959. As another measure of the profession's growth, the AEA, whose index of all academic economics articles between 1886 and 1939 had been published in a single two-volume work, was by 1966 publishing an index a year.[17]

A handful of universities dominated the profession, with Cambridge and Chicago defining the poles of Keynesian and anti-Keynesian thinking. Harvard's economics department included Hansen, Galbraith, Slichter, Seymour Harris, James Duesenberry, Edward Mason, and Otto Eckstein. MIT's department included Samuelson, Robert Solow, Charles Kindleberger, and Evsey Domar. Yale, which was home to the econometric-oriented Cowles Commission after it moved from the University of Chicago in the mid-1950s, had James Tobin, Tjalling Koopmans, Jacob Marschak, and Eugene Rostow. Stanford had Moses Abramovitz and Kenneth Arrow.

Princeton had Richard Lester and Richard Musgrave. Michigan—with its interdisciplinary Institute for Social Research, founded during the war—included influential economists such as George Katona, James McCracken, and Gardner Ackley. Meanwhile, Chicago had conservatives such as Milton Friedman and Friedrich von Hayek, and moderates such as Theodore Schultz.

By the early 1960s, about half of the nation's economists were employed in academia, one-third in government, and a growing number were on the payroll of large corporations. Reflecting this trend, the National Association of Business Economists was founded in 1959, as employment of economists by financial institutions, corporations, and business associations steadily increased during the late 1950s. Herb Stein, for example, was research director for the CED for many years, Theodore Schultz headed its research and policy committee in the 1950s, Beardsley Ruml did a radio program in its early years, and the organization commissioned many academic economists to write for it. The Conference Board drew on economists such as the NBER's Solomon Fabricant, *Business Week*'s Leonard Silk, and New York University's Jules Backman to write research reports. The Chamber of Commerce hired a chief economist, Emerson P. Schmidt. And the National Association of Manufacturers began contracting economists such as Ray Untereiner at Caltech and *Newsweek* economics writer and Columbia University business professor Ralph Robey. Unions also employed economists such as Boris Shiskin of the AFL in the late 1940s and Stanley Ruttenberg, who was the AFL-CIO's director of research in the late 1950s.[18]

The growing profession did not express a unanimity of views, although Keynesianism was the overarching paradigm through the 1960s, and mathematical model-building and econometrics—seeking to demonstrate the "scientific" nature of economics—increasingly crowded out political economy or Institutionalist economics. The increased reliance on statistical measurement, undergirded by the new national income accounting and the desire to make economics a "science" by developing elaborate mathematical models, were key to the econometric revolution. No figure is more emblematic of these parallel trends than Paul Samuelson. In his regularly revised textbook, his teaching, his advice to President Kennedy and other leaders, his many popular articles, and his *Newsweek* columns from the mid-1960s to early 1980s, Samuelson had an unmatched influence in bringing Keynes's ideas, econometrics, and economics in general to public prominence. The emphasis on the scientific nature of economics—reinforced by ever more technical papers published in the *American Economic Review* and presented by Samuelson, Kenneth Arrow, John Hicks, and others at annual AEA conventions—added to economists' cachet. The message—distilled by journalists and politicians—was that economists could scientifically study a problem, find a solution, and offer it to policymakers and business to build a better, more prosperous America. Reflecting this attitude, *Business Week* headlined its coverage of an AEA convention "7,000 Ways to Cure the Economy."[19]

No problems more engaged economists between the late 1940s and the 1960s than economic growth and consumer behavior. And both fit the Keynesian paradigm and the American zeitgeist par excellence. Growth was a magical word, carried from the economics profession to the broader public. It was a proxy for progress, and the creator of abundance and better living. It was often hard to see where scholarship left off and celebration of growth began. Editions of Samuelson's textbook during this time opened, "America is a prosperous nation. We grow more prosperous each year. . . . All over the world, men have become preoccupied with economic development."[20]

Alvin Hansen, who had argued that America's economy was "mature" in the late 1930s, and Roy Harrod pioneered growth studies in the 1940s. Yet many economists feared depression or, at best, stagnation after the war. Hansen argued that business-government-labor cooperation and government support for research were critical for prosperity. Kuznets's work turned to the study of economic growth before it became faddish in the 1950s, and was the subject of his 1954 AEA presidential address (and later his 1971 Nobel Prize lecture). It was supplemented by historical and theoretical growth studies of economists such as Moses Abramovitz, Evsey Domar, James Duesenberry, James Tobin, Robert Solow, Paul Homan, Walt Rostow, Kenneth Boulding, Paul Douglas, Duane Evans, and others.

The *American Economic Review* was filled with articles about growth, including a 1952 issue devoted to "general" and "theoretical factors in economic growth in the United States." A ten-part 1956 series on growth from the AEA's 1955 convention examined everything from consumption and the length of the work week to innovation and the social goals of growth. Four years later, the AEA and the *American Economic Review* followed up with a series devoted to "the problem of achieving and maintaining a high rate of economic growth." Whereas the leading prewar college economics textbook, Garver and Hansen's *Principles of Economics* (1937), made no reference to growth or national income, Samuelson's postwar blockbuster, by the sixth edition in 1964, referred to economic growth on no fewer than eighty pages.[21]

A JSTOR analysis of the major economic journals confirms, in spades, the sharply increased preoccupation with economic growth among economists. Although overall article production was steadily rising throughout the twentieth century, it is noteworthy that the term *economic growth* was mentioned in just forty-three articles or reviews during the 1920s and seventy-four during the 1930s, appearing in the title of none. During the 1940s, the term's use in articles or reviews rose to 226; it appeared in the title of seven articles; three books about economic growth were reviewed; and a 1947 supplement to the *Journal of Economic History* was devoted to the topic. However, the tidal wave came in the 1950s, as 2,980 articles and reviews addressed the idea of economic growth, with the term appearing in the title of nearly half of them. (This excludes articles in which the kindred terms *economic progress* and *economic development* were part of the title.) The 1960s would see the number of economics journal articles on growth climb to 6,788.

James Tobin, a member of Kennedy's CEA and AEA president in 1971, whose dissertation focused on consumer behavior, carried the Keynesian banner into battle with Milton Friedman of the more conservative "Chicago School." He argued that active government demand management could attenuate short-run downturns and spur long-term growth, although he was a then rare Keynesian to recognize that monetary policy could stimulate the economy, as his criticisms of the tight money policies of the late 1950s indicate. "In recent years, economic growth has come to occupy an exalted position in the hierarchy of goals of government policy," Tobin noted in 1964. "Growth has become a good word. And the better a word it becomes, the more it is invoked to bless a variety of causes and the more it loses specific meaning."[22]

Tobin was right. What had begun with analytical and descriptive efforts to develop national income accounting between the 1920s and 1940s had become a more amorphously defined policy objective during the decades after the 1946 Employment Act and a proxy for the good life that America was providing. Despite political differences over the inflationary impact of growth-inducing policies, there was remarkable unanimity among economists and the policymakers whom they advised that investment, public or private, financed with or without deficits, should be promoted to generate rising national and personal incomes and employment.

Theodore Schultz sought to demonstrate that technology and physical capital were insufficient to explain postwar growth. Introducing the concept of "human capital" in the late 1950s, he argued that growth was partly explained by—and could be enhanced by—increased education and research. Paul Douglas, a University of Chicago economist who later became senator from Illinois and chairman of the Joint Economic Committee, helped develop the Cobb-Douglas production function to analyze and measure potential economic growth. Kuznets, in his 1960 *Six Lectures on Economic Growth,* joined the chorus of optimism, predicting that there was no reason that growth could not go on forever.[23]

The interest in development economics—in how to replicate U.S. growth in the third world—also spurred research and theories about economic growth. Walt Rostow's influential books, *The Process of Economic Growth* (1952, rev. 1959) and the more polemical *The Stages of Economic Growth: A Non-Communist Manifesto* (1960), described the "process of take-off"—when an economy facilitated "a sustained increased in per capita real income." He sought to provide a model of growth that could be exported to developing countries to help win the ideological battle against communism. Rostow, an economic historian, like his brother, Eugene, an economist, was an adviser to both JFK and LBJ.[24]

Economic forecasting—by the government's CEA and other government agencies, as well as business associations and media—was an increasingly popular activity for economists and economic popularizers in the 1950s and 1960s. A raft of studies, articles, books, and commissions published forecasts of U.S. economic growth five to one hundred years into the future. Reports by the Twentieth Century Fund in 1947 and 1955 looked at U.S. income and output, with an eye toward predicting what the economy's capacity would be by 1960. In popular editions of each report, the fund's scholars could not help gushing that the economy is "ascending heights whose upper limit is not yet measurable," giving most Americans "the highest standard of living ever achieved by a great population and the promise that this standard will continue to rise."

Several Brookings Institution studies tried to forecast U.S. growth for the succeeding hundred years, and economists for the CED, Conference Board, and other business groups turned out a host of descriptive, theoretical, and prescriptive papers about growth. Both the Twentieth Century Fund and Brookings forecasts turned out to be remarkably conservative. Brookings predicted that in 2050, the United States would have a $2.5 trillion economy and 300 million people; in current dollars, the nation passed this number in the 1980s, and it hit the population target in the first decade of the twenty-first century. The Twentieth Century Fund was unique in that it also published abridged, popularized versions of its massive 1947 and 1955 reports.

In addition, two blue-ribbon Rockefeller Brothers Fund reports in 1958 and 1961 focused on ways to improve the nation's already strong growth, proclaiming, "A great opportunity confronts the American people. If our economic system lives up to its opportunities, we can achieve an unprecedented degree of well-being for our citizens while making an increasing contribution to world economic progress. . . . The adventure of the American economy is a continuing reality. The dynamism that has produced the present level of well-being holds out the promise of a still more challenging future." As Samuelson wrote in 1960: "The study of economic growth and development is today all the rage, and its voluminous literature testifies that the world's demand for treatment of the subject is met by a copious supply."[25]

Consumption, the other popular theme among postwar economists, also reflected the coalescing of Keynesian theory and the flourishing of an abundant consumer society. Economist George Katona carried out the most systematic focus on consumer behavior, what influenced it, and how it could be forecast to support business and government growth. Also trained as a psychologist, he established the Survey Research Center at the University of Michigan's Institute of Social Research in 1946. During World War II, working for the Federal Reserve, Katona wrote that rising aspirations would fuel economic growth and that experts could chart, if not guide, expectations of consumer sentiment and behavior. For twenty-six years, Katona directed the quarterly Survey of Consumer Attitudes, launched in 1952. He published many books and articles, had a staff of sixty-five plus several thousand part-time interviewers and a thousand-person consumer focus group, and was celebrated by business and the media as a defender of America's abundant capitalist economy. Katona—a perceptive observer of the new mass-consumption economy who claimed to have invented the new field of "psychological or behavioral economics," based on ideas of psychologists Kurt Lewin and Abraham Maslow as much as Keynes—staunchly believed that consumer attitudes were at least as critical as macroeconomic data to understand the economy. He was one of the first to detect consumers' optimism immediately after the war, predicting—against conventional wisdom—that the U.S. economy was headed for a boom.[26]

In *The Powerful Consumer* (1960), *The Mass Consumption Society* (1964), and *Aspirations and Influence* (1971), his many book-length evaluations of consumer attitudes and demand, and the Surveys of Consumer Attitudes, Katona hailed consumers as America's economic dynamo. His basic formula was that abundance depended on sustained high demand, high demand depended on consumer optimism, and optimism did not necessarily depend on income. Contrary to neoclassical ideas of scarcity, and in tune with Keynes's belief that equilibrium could be achieved at ever higher levels, Katona said: "Instead of being driven to avoid hardship and being satisfied with restoring an equilibrium, in an era of prosperity people are spurred by rising levels of aspiration." They continually strive for more and more income and consumption, which "may become cumulative and self-reinforcing." To Katona, capitalism, consumption, and democracy were complementary ingredients to create an abundant society.[27] His survey questions, equating "how well one is doing" with individual and national economic fortunes, buttressed the idea that well-being was best measured in economic terms. Katona's message was like a tonic to the broad postwar consensus that extended, by the mid-1950s, from Eisenhower Republicans such as Arthur Burns and most of the business community to Keynesian liberals such as Leon Keyserling and Walter Heller. Katona brushed aside Galbraith, Vance Packard, and Tibor Scitovsky, who said that consumers were manipulated, or other critics who worried about abundance bereft of social responsibility or higher values. The virtuous cycle of consumer optimism, consumer demand, and growth was what mattered.

Other economists devoted considerable attention to the American consumer in the 1950s and early 1960s. The AEA focused several journals, in 1951, 1957 and 1960, on research on consumers and their role in the economy. James Duesenberry, later a member of President Johnson's CEA, in his 1949 book, *Income, Saving, and the Theory of Consumer Behavior,* echoed or anticipated Katona in his description of a society/economy in which the desire for higher living standards drives spending and growth, thus "[taking] on a life of its own." James Tobin, in his work on growth, declared that GNP growth that did not translate into increased consumer buying power had little intrinsic meaning.[28]

While "growth" and "consumption" were growth industries that consumed the economics profession, other currents were flowing that would become influential later in the profession and American culture. The two most important were the anti-Keynesian, neoclassical, monetarist tradition most associated with the University of Chicago and Milton Friedman and the critical tradition most closely linked with John Kenneth Galbraith.

Friedman, who also had a platform in *Newsweek* from 1966 to 1984, argued that the money supply was the critical determinant of consumption, suggesting that central bankers could exercise greater control over the economy than Keynesian fiscal policymakers. In some ways like Katona, he also argued that lifetime income expectations, not current income—which was more susceptible to Keynesian demand management—played a greater role in determining consumption. In more polemical books such as *Capitalism and Freedom* (1962) and *Free to Choose* (1980), he argued for reliance on price mechanisms to provide public services and counterposed the "cooperation" of free markets with "central direction," saying that government intervention in the United States since the 1930s had been "costly" in terms of economic progress and freedom. Friedman also drew on the Austrian economists, Ludwig von Mises and Friedrich von Hayek, whose 1944 *The Road to Serfdom* served as a cult manifesto to libertarian and many neoclassical opponents of socialism and the mixed economy during the decades of Keynesian ascendancy. A hero to conservatives and a lonely counterpoint to the liberal growth consensus and more leftist economists, Friedman's star rose considerably during the 1970s and the Reagan era, and produced many disciples.[29] Joseph Schumpeter's *Capitalism, Socialism and Democracy* (1942) and other writings also influenced many later conservatives with his defense of capitalism's entrepreneurship and "creative destruction" and his warnings about the growth of state power.

Galbraith's remarkable seventy-year career and best-selling books made him the first celebrity economist. Both *The Affluent Society* (1958) and *The New Industrial State* (1967) spent more than a year on the *New York Times* best-seller list, with well over a million copies of each sold, and even the author's earlier *American Capitalism* (1952) sold 400,000 copies. In addition to his half-century stint on the Harvard faculty and his prolific writings, Galbraith served as FDR's wartime deputy administrator of the Office of Price Administration, a staff writer for *Fortune* during the late 1940s, and a close adviser to John Kennedy and other Democratic Party leaders. A superb stylist who popularized such phrases as "the conventional wisdom," "countervailing powers" and the "new class," Galbraith is best known for his critique in *The Affluent Society* of a nation wallowing in private abundance but suffering from "public squalor." "Increased production is not the final test of social achievement, the solvent for all social ills," Galbraith wrote, urging greater government spending on public needs to redress

America's "social imbalance." Galbraith, who took a dim view of economics as a science, was increasingly marginalized by a profession more and more bent on establishing its scientific credibility and on being the technical managers of prosperity. Yet his ideas were spurs to New Frontier and Great Society liberalism, seeds of a later, more radical critique of America, and endure in parts of economics' (re)turn to moral and cultural concerns since the 1990s, and with the Keynesian renaissance sparked by the financial crisis that began in 2008.[30]

2
Economists Come to Washington

America is a prosperous nation. We grow more prosperous each year, and our present affluence is an outgrowth from the lower standard prevailing in past generations.

PAUL SAMUELSON, *Economics: An Introductory Analysis*

Despite Galbraith's popularity among liberal intellectuals and Friedman's devoted following among neoclassical free-marketeers, it was the "scientific-technological elite," or the "new class" described by Eisenhower and Galbraith, who carried the day. Just as Tom Wolfe called 1980s investment bankers "masters of the universe," economists during the postwar decades became America's masters of abundance. As Samuelson noted, the once "dismal profession" had acquired a decidedly "cheery face," thanks to its promise to deliver ever more prosperity, and "economists relished their newfound prominence and basked in the glory of public adulation." To policymakers and the public alike, economists were wizards who could prevent depressions, ensure an ever-upward progression in living standards, and forecast good times ahead. For many economists, the hubris was palpable. U.S. political leaders were entranced by the idea that economics could solve the nation's problems, enable it to stand tall in the world, and deliver the long-sought dream of abundance for all Americans. The faith that economists could guide America to a better quality of life began during the war, gained steam during the Truman administration, and reached its zenith in the Kennedy and early Johnson years.

As World War II drew to a close, Americans wondered whether their country would falter or continue the war's dizzying economic growth. Similarly, policymakers, business, and workers differed over whether to ramp up New Deal policies to manage an economy of scarcity and instability, or return to more laissez-faire days of minimal government. In late 1944 and much of 1945, during the last months of Franklin Roosevelt's life and the heady days of wartime victory, liberal New Dealers—who feared unemployment yet expectantly hoped for an "economy of abundance"—had the upper hand. For them, the critical postwar question was

43

how to sustain the war's hypercharged economy of full employment, prevent a Depression, and usher in an era of broadly shared prosperity. Into this mix, Keynes's new economic ideas worked like a tonic. "Employment depends on demand," Alvin Hansen wrote authoritatively in early 1945. "All economists are agreed upon this. Reduce government expenditures by $75 billion and unless other expenditures are substituted, demand will fall and unemployment will rise accordingly."[1]

Starting from the premise that full employment was postwar America's number one goal, President Roosevelt, Vice President Henry Wallace, and many legislators argued between 1943 and 1945 that the only way to sustain a full employment economy of 55–60 million jobs was to increase the production that had doubled GNP to almost $200 billion during the war. Expecting government spending to shrink as war contracts were terminated, the way to maintain high demand for production was to vastly increase consumer demand. But to generate and sustain high levels of consumption required job security and increasing purchasing power for workers through rising wages and low inflation. The war taught that "our postwar problem" would not be production but rather "the maintenance and distribution of purchasing power," as businessman Marshall Field said. The Depression and war also taught that private enterprise alone could not assure these goals. Business and labor must cooperate, and government was needed to prime the economic pump with "compensatory spending" on investment, public works, research, and social security and other income transfers. As early as 1943, FDR said that Americans should expect full employment. During the 1944 campaign, both parties called for full employment, and Republican candidate Governor Thomas Dewey (R-N.Y.) pledged that "full employment shall be a first objective of national policy." If there are not sufficient jobs, he said, "government can and must create job opportunities." Senators James Murray (D-Mont.), Harley Kilgore (D-W.Va.), and Harry Truman (D-Mo.) drafted a postwar economic reconversion bill in 1944 calling for full employment.[2]

Polls found that up to three-fourths of Americans expected a postwar Depression and thought that government should ensure jobs. On V-J Day, a front-page *New York Times* article declared: "Five Million Expected to Lose Arms Jobs." Some economists feared that declining incomes were inevitable, as wartime production ground to a halt, and workers withdrew from the labor force, lost overtime pay, or moved into lower-paying jobs, while Hansen and politicians like Senators Murray and Lewis Schwellenbach (D-Wash.) believed that the U.S. economy had reached a plateau. Labor leaders such as Walter Reuther of the United Auto Workers, citing the success of wartime labor-management cooperation, were emboldened to call for labor to become an equal partner in the U.S. economic system. Between late 1944 and the spring of 1945, major American magazines—from *Fortune, Newsweek,* the *Saturday Evening Post,* and the *New York Times Magazine* to the *New Republic, Harper's,* the *Atlantic,* and the *Nation*—published long articles on full employment and the need for action, and it was a frequent subject for radio shows. A Pabst Brewing Company–sponsored postwar employment essay contest in 1944 drew a remarkable thirty-five thousand entries by economists and others. The second prize went to Leon Keyserling, later Truman's chief economic adviser, whose essay, "The American Economic Goal," called for ambitious goals for production and employment, and an executive and legislative branch body to ensure this and advise the president. Congress clearly agreed with President Truman's declaration, on 6 September 1945, that full employment was a top priority.[3]

Organized labor, at the apogee of its power, echoed such sentiments. The CIO's "People's Program for 1944" called on government to lead in "Planning for Plenty," and the UAW's 1945 "Purchasing Power for Prosperity" argued that high wages were necessary for high consumption and, thus, high production and profits. CIO leader Philip Murray called for a society where "we can abundantly produce." And both AFL leader George Meany and the CIO enthusiastically supported business and government efforts to promote economic growth "so that all Americans would have good incomes" and as "the greatest hope for prosperity."[4]

European, Canadian, and Australian social democrats stood ready to spend their way toward full employment. The bible for the newly elected British Labour government and other leftists, including many Americans, was Sir William Beveridge's influential *Full Employment in a Free Society* (1944) and his 1942 report on social services. The Soviet Union also threatened to become an alternative model of how to provide jobs for all. Businessmen such as Ralph Flanders noted that full employment had been achieved under totalitarian systems, and Senator Murray and others warned that the Soviet Union, unlike the United States, might not have unemployment.[5]

However, this political and academic angst hardly reflected the actual U.S. economy. During the war, employment increased by a staggering 50 percent, as national output doubled and wage compensation more than doubled. Productivity surged, food consumption increased, and new consumer industries such as electronics, television, synthetics, and plastics—born of wartime research—emerged. The federal share of national output swelled from less than 3 percent in 1929 to 44 percent in 1945—never again to fall below 18 percent.[6] By mid-1945, an expanded middle class, with unprecedented savings, was ready and able to buy new homes, cars, and other goods. World War II gave more Americans a taste of greater affluence than ever before.

This prosperity, tempered by fears of a downturn, united Democrats and Republicans, business and labor, in broad support for a full employment bill in late 1944 and early 1945. In January 1945, Senator Murray and Rep. Wright Patman (D-Tex.) introduced the Full Employment Act of 1945, which Patman hailed as "the most constructive single piece of legislation in the history of this nation." The bill assured jobs for all, with the ultimate responsibility resting on the federal government, through planning and spending policies generated by the executive branch and reviewed by a new Joint Congressional Committee on the National Budget. Economists, some serving as staffers to key members, including Leon Keyserling, Gerhard Colm, Alvin Hansen, and Walter Salant, were instrumental in drafting the bill. Presidential historian Clinton Rossiter has rightly said that the "Employment Act articulated the aspirations and fears of the generation."

The legislation—which enjoyed bipartisan support ranging from the Chamber of Commerce and Republican Senate leader Robert Taft to the CIO and the Communist Party—passed the upper chamber on 28 September 1945, by a resounding vote of 71–10. The Senate bill affirmed FDR's declaration that "Americans' most fundamental right is to a remunerative job" and government's "responsibility" to provide "Federal investment and expenditure" to "assure" full employment. It also stipulated that the president submit an annual "production and employment budget" with proposed full employment spending and other policies based on careful economic analysis and planning. The Senate bill called for government forecasting and planning, and for intervention when an economic downturn threatened, with the explicit assumption that laissez-faire free enterprise was fundamentally flawed.

However, the changing political climate in the fall and winter of 1945–46 resulted in significantly different legislation that was finally approved by both Houses in February 1946. The bill President Truman signed on 20 February was not the "economic bill of rights" envisioned by its liberal supporters but "a commitment by the government to the people . . . to take any and all of the measures necessary for a healthy economy," he declared. Progressive ideas that government, labor, and business would be equal partners—as they became in much of postwar Europe—gave way to a very different idea of cooperation in which business clearly played the lead role. Supporters increasingly turned away from arguing that government needed to remedy the ills of capitalism. Instead, Murray added to the bill this opening sentence "It is the policy of the United States to foster free competitive enterprise." Administration, congressional, and other supporters increasingly framed their arguments in terms of the benefits to business. The idea that mass production and mass consumption were interdependent, as were rising profits and American living standards, was captured by AFL president William Green, who argued that selling one suit to 47 million workers was more profitable than selling 3.5 million suits to higher-income Americans. Ira Mosher, the National Association of Manufacturers president, declared: "Here in America, we want and must have more than full employment; we want . . . an ever-increasing standard of living, based on a greater output of goods at more and more attractive selling prices."[7]

The final conference committee bill dropped the "right" to a job and the federal spending pledge, substituted an economic report for the national budget, and changed "full employment" to a "high" employment, production, and purchasing power. Emphasizing that "the way to achieve and maintain high levels of employment is to preserve and encourage the American system of free competitive enterprise," the committee retitled the bill the Employment and Production Act. Nonetheless, it still committed the government to work toward maximum employment and rising living standards, and retained mandates for planning and government action to prevent economic fluctuations. To advise the president and Congress, it also created the Council of Economic Advisers (CEA) and Joint Committee on the Economic Report (which became known as the Joint Economic Committee, or JEC).

By the time thirteen months later that Truman signed the Employment Act of 1946 (with the word *Full* not so subtly dropped from its title), politicians on the left and right, business, labor, and academics alike had begun to reach the broad new consensus about economic growth that would shape American politics, policy, and popular beliefs at least until the 1970s. They began to commit the nation to pursue a perpetually upward spiral of increasing production and purchasing power. Although the bill itself was not "decisive for American prosperity," as its more ardent advocates predicted, it played a key role in the genesis of an ideology of rising abundance framed in the language of economics. Labor's power was still contested for a few years—before public opposition to mass strikes, the 1947 Taft-Hartley Act, and McCarthyism ended its aspirations for power sharing—but its critical role as high-wage, high-spending consumers was already evident during the 1945 debate. Late New Deal ideas about government spending and planning were important ingredients, but it was the wartime boom that led much of the business community to buy in. While debate over the bill progressed in late 1945, a rightward political shift occurred. As the left was weakened by a strike wave, the dawn of the cold war, and Truman's falling popularity, the bill's emphasis changed from achieving full employment to maximizing production and consumption, which were initially seen as tools to achieve full employment.[8] This change—from the more social democratic cadences of FDR's "Four Freedoms" speech or his 1944 State of the Union, when he called for an "economic bill of rights"—resulted in an initially radical bill proposing significant government power to plan production and employment being transformed into a broad commitment to continually increase economic growth. In short, more egalitarian ideas bandied about at the end of the war gave way to a faith that promoting growth would raise living standards for all and create a broad-based abundance.

The Employment Act signaled the emergence of a Keynesian "new orthodoxy." In political terms, the act was a compromise between retreating liberals and conservatives newly convinced that the state could bolster American prosperity. The year of intensive debate and the final bill laid the groundwork for an era when economic growth, mass consumption, and increasing abundance would be central concerns for America. Liberals had retreated since the winter of 1944–45, but Republicans, Southern Democrats, and business also had come a long way from the era of Harding and Coolidge. In the final bill, Republicans and Democrats, business and labor, staked out a broad common ground that guided American economic thinking for at least a quarter century. Conservatives accepted the need for "sound" government economic analysis and planning to forestall economic difficulties, and for federal spending of at least 15 percent of national income—more than five times pre-Depression levels. And liberals were comfortable with increasing productivity to raise living standards. As United Mine Workers president John L. Lewis said: "The enormous quantity of production per man employed will be greatly increased in the postwar years. . . . Less men are going to be able to produce more goods."[9] This consensus cast aside notions that the American economy had reached its peak or that affluence was the province of a small elite. It also did away with the idea that government had only a marginal role in the economy but forestalled more collectivist ideas or labor's hope to be an equal player in the postwar order. Finally, it helped make mass prosperity a defining characteristic of the United States and shifted the terrain for American optimism from philosophical to economic grounds.

For several decades, the Employment Act was seen as a seminal piece of twentieth-century domestic legislation. The CEA and JEC had enormous influence on America's leaders and, directly and indirectly, on Americans' thinking. Edwin Nourse, the CEA's first chairman, said that it paved the way for the triumph of the new Keynesian economics. Leon Keyserling, his successor, called it "perhaps the most significant domestic legislation of this generation," committing the nation to the "principle of constant growth." Henry Wallace called the act the "preamble" to a new "charter" for American capitalism. Economist and Kennedy CEA member James Tobin credited the act with the postwar economy's improved performance. Truman, Eisenhower, and Kennedy all paid obeisance to the act's importance, and on its twentieth anniversary, Patman still called it "one of the most important experiments in economic policy formulation in American history." Arthur Burns, chairman of Eisenhower's CEA and later Federal Reserve chairman, may have said it best. The Employment Act symbolized a consensus commitment to what he called the "management of prosperity." Even more than Lyndon Johnson's Great Society programs, the Employment Act (following close on the heels of the 1944 GI Bill), was the legislative face of both the postwar political consensus on "growth liberalism" and a cultural faith in measuring America by its economic achievements.[10]

For economists, the Employment Act marked their arrival as the nation's most valued public servants. For politicians, it enabled them to claim, with their economic advisers' help, that they could produce economic growth and abundance. And for the American people, it signaled that they would no longer be pawns of a capricious free market but rather the beneficiaries of applied economic wisdom. Historian Clinton Rossiter said that the creation of the CEA established a new and primary role for the presidency as the "manager of prosperity." And as Raymond Saulnier, one of the least activist CEA chairmen, said, the CEA represented "the concrete manifestation of this hope that economists would solve problems."[11] For the president, Congress, and the public, however, the CEA's lengthy Economic Reports of the President represented something dramatically new—not only economic analysis but also public economic education and shifting national discourse into a decidedly new economic key.

The seven-and-a-half-year Truman era witnessed a sea change in America's economic fortunes, mood, and reigning wisdom. The fears of a return to depression were never entirely vanquished until the early to mid-1950s, but change was in the air by the late 1940s. Although the U.S. economy suffered a mild recession and high inflation in 1946 and a milder recession in 1949, the big economic story of the Truman years was that depression did not return, recessions were mild and brief, and economic growth was above 10 percent a year for much of his second term and unemployment and inflation dipped to under 3 percent.[12] It was a time of pent-up wartime consumer demand, a spectacular residential construction boom, and the bringing to market of many civilian spin-offs of World War II–era technologies, ranging from television and computing to plastics and synthetic fibers.

As president, Truman alternated between the populist, Fair Deal rhetoric of 1948 that pleased and placated the New Deal coalition, and, increasingly thereafter, support for a Keynesian capitalism that promised growth for business and workers alike, as Truman dropped FDR's "freedom from fear and want" and replaced them with "freedom of enterprise." Truman stood on the side of the "common man" and believed that social justice and economic growth went hand in hand. However, he more and more came to see the common man's interest inextricably linked with rapid economic growth facilitated by both business and government. While some have argued otherwise, this astute and pragmatic businessman-turned-politician had considerable interest in the American economy and the promise of abundance. Within weeks after the Pacific war had ended, Truman said: "The American people have set high goals for their own future. They have set these goals high because they have seen how great can be the productive capacity of our country." Even in the darker days of early 1946, the president expressed "the conviction that the spirit of our nation is best expressed in the improving standard of American life." And by late 1947 he waxed rhapsodic about how "the rapid growth of our postwar economic activity has exceeded all expectations and has revealed anew the potentialities of our economy." Truman's confident, effusive 1948 State of the Union cited "our amazing economic progress" and called for doubling prewar living standards by 1958 and "stamping out poverty in our generation."[13]

In his 1949 State of the Union, Truman boldly outlined his ideas for extending the New Deal with a "Fair Deal" that would expand the welfare state and ensure "that every American has a chance to obtain his fair share of our increasing abundance." Truman's midcentury State of the Union—which, like many of his economic speeches and CEA Economic Reports of his administration, had considerable input from Keyserling—was breathless about abundance and its promise for America: "We have accomplished what to earlier ages of mankind would have been a miracle. We work shorter hours, we produce more, and we live better. Increasing freedom from poverty and drudgery has given a fuller meaning to American life." Laying out a series of policy and moral preconditions for continued prosperity, Truman confidently predicted that, by the year 2000, American output would quadruple to the then unimaginable figure of $1 trillion, and average income would triple. Foreshadowing ideas that would continue to dominate political and popular thinking into the early Johnson administration, growth would accomplish three objectives that bound liberals and conservatives together in the postwar consensus—ever rising national, personal, and corporate income; the elimination of poverty and the achievement of social justice; and the financial ability to fight the cold war. *Time* reported the death of the "mature economy" theory, and Truman disparaged the "scarcity" mentality, insisting, "the rest of us believe in abundance."[14]

In August 1946, Truman appointed the first members of the new Council of Economic Advisers, with Edwin Nourse, the dour and reclusive sixty-three-year-old head of economic studies at the Brookings Institution, as the CEA's first chairman. The council's two other members were John Clark, a successful, sixty-eight-year-old oil executive-turned-economist who was dean of the University of Nebraska's business school, and thirty-eight-year-old Leon Keyserling, a firebrand and apostle of growth who began climbing the Washington career ladder as an aide to New York senator Robert Wagner and a New Deal official but was widely seen as having an inferiority complex over never completing his Ph.D. in economics. The council—which was required to issue an annual Economic Report of the President, combining a message from the president with data and analysis of the economy—took office in September, and scrambled to release its first report on 8 January 1947. Speaking for the president, and receiving wide media coverage, the report opened with the superlative confidence that was to be a hallmark of subsequent reports and years of presidential messages about the economy: "America has never been so strong or prosperous. Nor have our prospects been brighter." The 1947 and 1948 Economic Reports and presidential messages emphasized the Employment Act's commitment to use government planning to achieve maximum employment. While production targets were stated, employment remained the chief goal, and guarded optimism remained the tone. The 1948 report said that ending poverty was "within our reach," yet this required coordinated government-business action, since universal prosperity "will not come about by accident."[15]

Keyserling, who succeeded Nourse in 1950, said that the goal of government is "the achievement of the highest levels of production and presumably the highest standards of living that are within our reach." Arthur Burns, Eisenhower's first CEA chairman who "fascinated" the president and became one of his most intimate confidants, was not averse to countercyclical fiscal policy, modest economic planning, and public works, believing that it was government's task to arrest recessions and promote growth. Burns, who helped make Keynesianism respectable to Republicans and business, restored the CEA's credibility after Republicans tried to abolish it in 1953 in the wake of Keyserling's activism, and spoke of the "new responsibility for the maintenance of the nation's prosperity [of] the federal government" and the periodic "need [for] contracyclical action on the part of government." Walter Heller—Kennedy's CEA chairman, who was as close to the president as Burns was to Eisenhower—effectively sold JFK and Congress on the idea that economists had the tools to ensure stable, noninflationary growth. This faith continued to a lesser degree under Gardner Ackley and Arthur Okun in the Johnson administration and Herb Stein in the Nixon administration. The breadth of the political support for what Stein and Lekachman called "business Keynesianism" is reflected in Stein's perceptive comment that the "fiscal revolution" was not won against the opposition of business and conservatives but with their broad support. The postwar Keynesians believed that aggregate demand could be adjusted to an appropriate level through government fiscal policy, but then neoclassical market and marginal price mechanisms would come into play, assuring the right level of aggregate supply.[16]

However, the belief by CEA chairmen that economists, guiding government policy, could moderate, if not eliminate, the business cycle and promote economic growth and rising living standards through "fine-tuning" and adept macroeconomic management, went beyond faith in the postwar Keynesian consensus. More significantly for American culture and beliefs, the CEA took it upon themselves to be popular advocates for growth and abundance. While Nourse and Saulnier eschewed the lime-light (and Nourse refused to testify before Congress) and believed that the CEA's job was to impartially and scientifically study the economy and avoid policy recommendations, the somewhat abrasive Keyserling and the charming Burns and Heller became poster boys for the successes of the American economy. Frequently giving speeches and appearing in the press, as well as scripting their presidents, they clearly saw their role as educating the public about the U.S. economy. They were critical figures in spreading the faith in an ever-abundant America, and they had the unique authority to bolster these beliefs among the American people. Newspapers and magazines gave extensive coverage to CEA reports, often reprinting long, major sections, conveying the message that government policy, driven by economists, was key to the nation's future. Nourse recalled that many newspapers described the first Economic Report of the President, hurriedly completed in December 1946, as "must reading."[17]

Although economists in the Treasury, the Budget Bureau, the Federal Reserve, the Commerce, Agriculture, and Labor departments, and elsewhere in government were influential and often drawn into high-level interagency groups such as Eisenhower's Advisory Board on Economic Growth and Kennedy's Cabinet Committee on Economic Growth to manage the nation's prosperity, the CEA was at the pinnacle of economists' influence in Washington. The CEA—never a large organization, despite the hopes of more liberal progenitors—depended on many of the nation's leading economists, who served either as members or staff. The council typically had ten senior academic economists, on leave from university posts, and about ten junior economists. Under Keyserling, Gerhard Colm, Benjamin Kaplan, Walter Salant, and other New Deal veterans, and economist Paul Homan, were key staff members. Truman also turned to economic adviser John Steelman, who recruited the administration's top economists, as well as economists David Bell and Robert Turner. Keyserling initiated "weekly Reports on the Economic Situation" for Truman. John Clark, a businessman-turned-academic economist, and Roy Blough, were also Truman council members.[18]

Nourse's view of the CEA as bringing economics into the "public service" by providing "objective analysis [as] the basis of government policymaking" quickly gave way to the idea that CEA economists were not only technical experts but advocates for growth-oriented policies and public figures who sought to educate the public about the economy. Nourse delivered frequent speeches but refused to testify before Congress, which

would become a routine practice for CEA members after Keyserling became chairman in 1949. Nourse, publicly criticized Truman and did not
campaign for him in 1948—ostensibly, and naively, believing that the CEA
chairman should be nonpolitical and objective, educating the president
and the public. Increasingly, he did not get along with Truman, Keyserling,
or Clark, and was pushed to resign in November 1949.[19] Six months later,
Keyserling was named chairman, and University of Chicago economist
Roy Blough joined the CEA. Under Keyserling, the next four Economic
Reports reflected the belief that economic growth, achieved through a
mixed economy, was the golden road to abundance and should be America's foremost concern.

More liberal and brash than Nourse, Keyserling became the council's
dominant force, winning the president's ear, testifying frequently before
Congress, and tirelessly writing popular articles about the nation's economic potential. Keyserling wrote eight lead articles for the *New York Times
Magazine,* as well as pieces for the *New Republic* and other opinion-shaping
media. In 1949, he wrote that "our unparalleled prosperity has not been
maintained by chance" and that government must "use all its resources to
avoid depression and maintain continuous prosperity." As historian Robert Collins has argued, the 1949 Economic Report, largely authored by
Keyserling, "came close to raising growth from an overriding goal . . . to
a new organizing principle for the United States." Indeed, from the time
that Keyserling succeeded Nourse well into the 1960s, economic growth
supplanted full employment as the nation's chief policy goal. During the
Korean War, Keyserling spoke of "the economy's great non-secret weap-
on—its ability to expand," in an effort to convince Truman that growth
could fund both the military build-up and a liberal social agenda. In his
subsequent Economic Reports, Keyserling hailed America's limitless and
"prodigious" "economic power" and declared that "economic growth is
one of our primary objectives in peacetime [and] has properly been regarded as the main avenue to an increasing abundance more generally
enjoyed," arguing that it was the elixir that would lift tens of millions out
of poverty. He said that the goal of government is "the achievement of
the highest levels of production and presumably the highest standards of
living that are within our reach."[20]

Before the Korean War led the CEA to emphasize growth for military
power in its 1951 and 1952 reports, the 1949 report crowed about "another
year of bountiful prosperity" achieved through government and business
efforts to stimulate growth and continually expand prosperity. Largely au-

thored by Keyserling, it marked the beginning of postwar policymakers' shift from the more labor-oriented emphasis on full employment to an emphasis on expanding output as the nation's chief goal. Similarly, the 1950 report opined about the nation's unprecedented "potentialities," its glorious "high-consumption economy," the possibility of ending poverty in five years, and the fact that "maximum production and maximum employment are not static goals" but mean "more" of both year after year. Flatly rejecting ideas of limits to growth, the report stated five "unifying principles: 1) Our economy can and must continue to grow. 2) The benefits of growth and progress must extend to all groups. 3) This growth will not come automatically, but requires conscious purpose and hard work. 4) The fiscal policy of the Federal Government must be designed to contribute to the growth of the economy. 5) We must deal vigorously with trouble spots which exist in our economy even in times of general prosperity." Keyserling's final report in 1953, with its twenty-seven-page letter from Truman, was not only a testimonial to the outgoing administration but also his most fervent official declaration of the centrality of American abundance: "Whether we shall shrink from or measure up to the challenge of potential abundance is perhaps the supreme issue of the twentieth century," he declared.[21]

Just as the CEA was up and running in late 1946, the Joint Economic Committee took shape after the Republicans' victory in the 1946 congressional elections. Under the leadership of Sen. Robert Taft (R-Oh.), the eight-member committee—which included Vermont businessman-turned-senator Ralph Flanders, an early CED leader—issued its first report on May 10, 1948. Commenting on the first two Economic Reports, the Republican-dominated committee worried about the administration's emphasis on planning, raising the bogeyman of inflation yet joining in optimistic assumptions that continuous growth would yield adequate food, health, social security, and education for all Americans by 1957. The JEC included from five to ten senators and members of the House of Representatives, as well as several staff economists such as Norman Ture and Gerard Brennan to help prepare the committee's responses to the President's Economic Reports and other materials. The committee was particularly influential during its first quarter century and was chaired in the late 1950s and early 1960s by Illinois senator Paul Douglas, a prominent University of Chicago economist before coming to Washington. The committee produced annual reports commenting on the Economic Reports of the President that were typically short compendia of statements by committee members, staff assessments of the economy, and supplementary materials and charts. It also published "study papers" on economic growth and other issues by staff and outside economists such as Robert Lampmann, Joseph Fisher, and John Kendrick, and it held frequent hearings on growth, "measuring the nation's wealth," and promoting economic education, among other topics. Leading economists such as Heller, Friedman, Hansen, and others frequently testified before the committee.[22]

While the Joint Economic Reports of the late 1940s were more cautious about the prospects for continued growth—worrying about World War II debt, whether there was sufficient demand, and the communist threat—the bravado about the U.S. economy, its link to "freedom," and the imperative to keep it growing and "strengthen and expand" free enterprise began to appear in 1950. "The American economy is today the greatest productive unit in the world," the mid-1950 report began, although it cautioned that growth required "hard work" and carefully tailored government policies. "Its strength and balance are the main source of hope for hundreds of millions of people everywhere who cherish freedom. . . . A continuously expanding economy is the sine qua non for national strength and freedom." Senator William Benton (D-Conn.), the former ad executive and CED leader, articulated the idea that abundance defined America: "Our productive power . . . is what distinguishes us from the rest of the world."[23]

The rising influence of economic policymakers also was reflected in the changing role of the Federal Reserve Board in the 1950s. Established in 1913, the Fed only became truly independent of the Treasury in 1951, when Truman pushed for it to lift controls on consumer and real estate credit in the wake of inflationary pressures generated by the Korean War. This "accord" also led Truman to appoint William McChesney Martin as chairman, a position he held for nineteen years, during which he enormously expanded the Fed's role in choreographing the U.S. economy. The elimination of so-called Regulations W and X, to enhance consumer purchasing power, and further efforts during the early Eisenhower administration to ease credit conditions through changes in reserve requirements, explicitly were intended to "sustain economic growth."[24] Thus, more activist Federal Reserve monetary policy dovetailed with efforts by the White House and Congress to make a growing economy and rising living standards a principal raison d'être of government.

Eisenhower and the Bipartisan Faith in America the Bountiful

The Eisenhower era, often thought of in terms of peace and prosperity, was immeasurably more complex. Ike did preside over an era of peace, and made some of the first efforts to ease cold war tensions, yet those tensions still ran high. Domestically, television's sweep of the nation, bigger cars, and fatter paychecks symbolized U.S. prosperity. Yet, as the so-called "growthmanship" debate in the late 1950s signaled, many felt that the U.S. economy was not growing fast enough. Moreover, the U.S. economy experienced mild recessions in 1953, 1958, and 1960, and unemployment began to creep up in the late 1950s. While some nostalgically look back on the Eisenhower years as a conservative period of American innocence before the storms unleashed by the 1960s, in many ways, the former general was a social liberal who solidified the postwar consensus on "growth liberalism." Eisenhower maintained New Deal social programs, expanded Social Security, and extended the minimum wage. As he said in 1956: "If the day ever comes when sound economic policies fail to serve the ends of social justice, our form of society will be in grave jeopardy." Ike, who saw one of government's three purposes as "maintaining a strong and growing economy," increased federal spending to about 20 percent of national output—a level at which it roughly remained until 2009. By 1954, over the objections of a dwindling band of Republicans, Ike accepted Keynesian nostrums of countercyclical deficit spending to stimulate the economy. His administration also initiated two of the largest public-works projects in U.S. history—the Saint Lawrence Seaway (1954) and the interstate highway program (1956). Historian Robert Griffith has argued that Ike presided over a "corporate commonwealth," with government, business, and labor working together harmoniously to create a prosperous, classless society.[25]

Ike looked at the American economy and saw America. By all reports, he was deeply interested in economic matters and raptly followed the economic counsel of advisers such as Arthur Burns and Gabriel Hauge. Eisenhower wrote to his brother Milton on 6 January 1954 that "maintenance of prosperity is one field of governmental concern that interests me mightily," and his two CEA chairmen, Arthur Burns and Raymond Saulnier, respectively, called Ike a "great student of economics" and "extremely interested in economic matters . . . , well-informed about many aspects of the economy, [and] deeply concerned that we promote economic growth." As a deeply patriotic American, Ike linked American greatness with its economic achievements, articulated with a raft of statistics, although he also frequently used the language of freedom and religion to affirm the nation's meaning. In 1956, reflecting the conflicting cultural tugs of religiosity and a focus on quantifiable abundance, Eisenhower attributed American prosperity to "kind Providence . . . whose bounty has been manifold and abundant" and "the great God-given forces which quicken our nation's progress."[26]

Throughout his administration, Eisenhower reveled in how America had become a land of unprecedented abundance. In his 1952 campaign, he spoke the expansive language of the CED, of which he was a trustee, and the Advertising Council, with which he worked closely: "Before us are new frontiers of expanding opportunity, far greater than the geographical frontier of free land." From the beginning of his administration, Ike pledged that "there will be no deviation from the goal of helping every American to achieve constantly rising standards of health, education, and prosperity." He spoke of the U.S. economy as if it were a star athlete, constantly setting new "records" that the American people, as spectators and beneficiaries, could cheer. Ike frequently talked of these "records," using superlatives to say: "Our economy is working at near record level. . . . This year, 1954, is our most prosperous in history." The 1956 Republican platform captured this spirit well: "Good times in America have reached a breadth and depth never before known by any nation . . . with real wages and personal income at record highs."[27]

Like Truman before him, and Kennedy and Johnson after him, Eisenhower saw American abundance and economic might as the genie that could solve the nation's social problems and ensure U.S. global supremacy. In a 1955 message for *Fortune*'s twenty-fifth anniversary ghostwritten by editor Hedley Donovan, Ike declared that "the American standard of living, high as it is, can be raised higher" to provide new highways, schools, hospitals, health care, and old-age security, as well as stamping out the "disgrace" of poverty. Eisenhower's 1956 Republican Convention speech struck the same tone. Citing his commitment to "social justice," Ike listed the benefits of America's unique "prosperity and progress" as the end of "backbreaking toil," reduction of "crippling disease," leisure to allow development of "the life of the spirit, of reflection, of religion, of the arts," and the promise that "the material things that make life interesting and pleasant will be available to everyone." In 1955, Ike affirmed that abundance was the essence of modern America: "Economic well-being sustains our whole national life."[28]

Mainstream Democrats and Republicans certainly spoke with one voice. In both 1954 and 1956, the Democratic-controlled JEC commended Eisenhower's CEA for accepting New Deal and Keynesian precepts and proposing public works and social-welfare measures. Senator Paul Douglas (D-Ill.), the former academic economist who alternated with Rep. Wright Patman as committee chairman from 1955 to 1965, celebrated America's "rate of economic growth, which is the envy of the world." The 1956 presidential campaign also saw the Democratic contender, Adlai Stevenson, speak of a "revolution of rising aspirations," "the most extraordinary growth any nation or civilization has ever experienced," and the advent of a "new America" in which poverty could be eradicated and prosperity could be provided for all. Stevenson, who relied on John Kenneth Galbraith and *Fortune* writer Eric Hodgins as speechwriters and economists Paul Samuelson and Walter Heller as advisers, mixed his optimism about universal American abundance with more critical comments about Americans' prosperity-induced complacency about international and domestic social problems. Throughout the Republican ascendancy of the 1950s, Leon Keyserling—through his Conference on Economic Progress, his leadership of the Democrats' Economic Advisory Committee, and his frequent speeches and articles—continued to be a fervid apostle of economic growth as the solution to all of society's needs. And Walter Reuther, who became president of the UAW in the mid-1950s, was equally enthusiastic about economic growth and the prospects for future abundance. Praising the "genius of the American economy," Reuther predicted that "50 years from now . . . the standard of living will be fantastic."[29]

Two months after riding the coattails of contentment to a resounding reelection victory, Eisenhower triumphantly declared: "We live in a land of plenty. . . . In our Nation, work and wealth abound." Unlike most of his thirty-three predecessors, who chose the solemn ceremony of Inauguration Day to remind America of its highest ideals and noblest aspirations, the president waxed lyrical about the nation's tremendous wealth: "The air rings with the song of our industry—rolling mills and blast furnaces, dynamos, dams, and assembly lines—the chorus of America the bountiful. . . . The American story of material progress has helped excite the longings of all needy peoples."[30]

Eisenhower's CEA became a well-oiled and influential entity under Arthur Burns, although its status at the time of Eisenhower's inauguration was far from certain. Concern that the council had become overly politicized under Keyserling led Congress to suspend its appropriations in

January 1953, and Eisenhower confidant Sherman Adams argued that the administration could do without it. However, Republican Senate leader Robert Taft, together with Eisenhower's economic adviser Gabriel Hauge and Burns, whom Hauge brought in to study the "CEA problem," all urged the new president that the CEA be retained. The fact that Taft and Hauge won the argument, and that Eisenhower quickly became enamored of his CEA and Burns, marks a key symbolic turning-point in which mainstream Republicans came to embrace Keynesianism and the "postwar consensus" on growth.

Burns, a business-cycle theorist and registered Democrat who had headed the National Bureau of Economic Research, was quickly named chair of the council. Amherst College economist Walter Stewart and Neil Jacoby, dean of UCLA's business school, were appointed as well, with Columbia University economist Raymond Saulnier succeeding Jacoby and Stanford University economist Joseph Davis succeeding Stewart when both left the council in 1955. Eisenhower also established an "economic sub-Cabinet" tellingly called the Advisory Board on Economic Growth, which included undersecretaries from the major Cabinet departments and representatives of the Bureau of the Budget and the Federal Reserve. It met every Tuesday in the CEA chairman's office throughout Eisenhower's eight years in office. Burns and Hauge also provided Ike with regular Monday morning briefings on the economy. Eisenhower and Burns frequently met, with meetings regularly running past their allotted time, and they often corresponded through memos and informal notes.[31]

Burns was a masterful politician who became an economic-policy Svengali to Ike. He successfully overcame more conservative administration officials such as Treasury Secretary George Humphrey and Commerce Secretary Sinclair Weeks to convince the president that Keynesian fiscal stimulus and economic growth were more important than the conservatives' preoccupations with balanced budgets and inflation. Shortly after leaving office, in 1957, Burns articulately described the bipartisan economic consensus: "The American People are nowadays broadly united on major goals of economic policy—a high and stable rate of employment in relation to the labor force, expanding production, improvement in living standards, and a reasonably stable consumer price level. The federal government has sought to promote these objectives. . . . Considerable success has attended government efforts in recent years to maintain an environment that favors higher production, expanding employment, and rising living standards."[32]

Although not the ardent public promoter that Keyserling and Walter Heller, under Kennedy, were, Burns nonetheless took seriously the Employment Act's mandate for the CEA to serve a public-education function. In speeches, articles, and press interviews, and in his support for economic education, Burns explained that "economic welfare requires an expanding national income, distributed widely among the people" and that government now had the ability to attenuate the business cycle. He spoke of "the spread of economic opportunity and well-being, which has revolutionized social life in our generation." Playing up the historical uniqueness and exceptionalism of America's new abundance, he said that "the economic growth to which we have been accustomed in our country is a comparatively new factor in the history of mankind."[33]

Burns's three Economic Reports emphasized the goal of government creating the right "environment" for business to generate growth and bring the material and nonmaterial good things of life to every American. While talking repeatedly about economic "records," the reports cautioned that abundance still needed to be brought to all Americans and that, although "a glorious future may be ours, [it] is not vouchsafed us" without vigilant, concerted government and business action. Burns's 1954 Economic Report—a bellwether of the postwar liberal growth consensus—described growth "shared equitably" as an overarching policy goal that would enable both cold war success and an attack on poverty, and lauded the American system as "one of the wonders of the world" because it was "marvelously prosperous by any standard." The next year, he said that "a glorious economic future may be ours," but this required that government play a "highly constructive role." And in 1956, in one of several early Eisenhower reports commended by the Democratic-controlled Joint Economic Committee, Burns spoke of "building for future prosperity," saying that the "underlying goal of America [is] better living."[34]

Even after leaving government, Burns frequently called on government and the people to continue their march toward greater prosperity. In a 1957 book, he wrote: "Our economy has grown rapidly because we had faith in ourselves, because we have developed institutions that encourage enterprise and reward efficiency, and because we have believed in progress sufficiently," a message he repeated in his AEA presidential address two years later. Although often seen as less of a cheerleader for American abundance than Keyserling or Heller, Burns was clearly caught up in the euphoria of his time when he said: "The transformation in the distribution of our national income . . . may already be counted as one of the great social revolutions in history." And in 1962, he linked America's "national purpose" with "producing more consumer goods."[35]

Eisenhower also enlisted other economic advisers, many drawn from the same CED/business press universe of pro-growth "commercial Keynesians." These included Emmet Hughes and C. D. Jackson, two *Fortune* writers who became Eisenhower speechwriters and advisers. In addition, Hauge, chief economist for McGraw-Hill and *Business Week,* served from 1953 to 1958 as the equivalent of Truman's John Steelman and was succeeded by Purdue University economist Don Paarlberg. Ike appointed CED leaders such as Marion Folsom as Under Secretary of the Treasury, Walter Williams as Under Secretary of Commerce, and Meyer Kestnbaum and James Zellerbach as presidential assistants.

When Raymond Saulnier succeeded Burns as CEA chairman at the end of 1956, the voices calling for tight-money policies and balanced budgets to fight looming inflation gained more of an upper hand. Whether as a cause or effect of these changes, the economy slipped in both 1958 and 1960, leading many to criticize the administration for its insufficient emphasis on expanding the pie of abundance. The more conservative and subdued Saulnier focused on controlling inflation rather than promoting growth, igniting the late 1950s "growthmanship" debate among economists, politicians, and the public about whether the United States was growing fast enough. Yet his Economic Reports still celebrated the economy's "remarkable capacity for sustained" growth and "the ability of the American economy to continue raising what has long been the highest living scale in the world."[36]

Saulnier, like Nourse, believed that the CEA should be nonpolitical, but unlike his predecessors and successors, had never been won over to the wonders of Keynesian fiscal policy. Instead, he was more interested in controlling inflation through monetary policy. Saulnier's council at various times included Davis, the University of Michigan's Paul McCracken, Karl Brandt of Stanford University, and Yale University's Henry Wallich. Although he wrote and spoke less than Burns, Keyserling, or Heller, Saulnier too could not avoid talking about the nation's "unparalleled" "economic achievements" and its need to "learn to live with prosperity." Price levels and notions of economic freedom were ostensibly important to Saulnier, yet this mild-mannered former finance professor acknowledged that it was "obvious . . . that the purpose of our economy is . . . to produce more consumer goods." Saulnier's Economic Reports reflected cold war concerns, contrasting the "free" United States with communism and worrying about the dangers of materialism. Nonetheless, they celebrated American growth and high and rising standards of living. The Joint Economic Committee was singing from the same songbook, as the committee's 1957 report opened: "America today is prosperous, with employment, production, and purchasing power at record levels."[37]

Yet the era of good feelings ended with the back-to-back recessions of 1958 and 1960, which saw growth stall and unemployment climb to nearly 7 percent in 1958. The 1957 Sputnik launch shocked many into believing that the Soviet Union was on a path to technologically and economically overtake the United States. This point was driven home by Khrushchev, who grandiosely asserted that the USSR would "bury" the United States economically. Eisenhower's 1958 State of the Union warned of the need to combat "the Soviet economic offensive." Others worried that the United States was being outdone by Western Europe's rapid growth, further catalyzed by the 1957 Treaty of Rome's creation of a European Common Market. The JEC and other congressional committees held a spate of hearings on these perceived growth gaps. Keyserling, Douglas, and other Democrats castigated the Eisenhower administration for squandering "idle resources" and letting the U.S. economy perform at suboptimum levels. Journalists jumped on the story. The JEC also linked economic and geopolitical strength in the cold war. And Republican gadfly and presidential aspirant Nelson Rockefeller sponsored studies to back up his claim that the nation's economy was growing at a pace far below its potential. Eisenhower responded to criticism of his alleged "thrift and drift" in his 1959 State of the Union, in which he laid out a five-to-ten-year plan for economic expansion.[38]

Rockefeller and Keyserling called for 6 percent annual growth, and the Democratic Party campaigned in 1960 to increase growth to 5 percent from the anemic 2.6 percent rate of the late Eisenhower years. Proponents of what Nixon derided as "growthmanship" argued that the U.S. economy was not operating at its "full employment potential" for national income, based on a target of 4 percent unemployment. Rockefeller insisted that U.S. incomes could be 50 percent higher, with a 50 percent expansion of government, and a 15 percent tax cut by 1970, all fueled by higher growth. Keyserling opined that "growing isn't enough if you don't keep up with the potential." And presidential candidate John Kennedy calculated this lost potential in the range of 8 to 9 percent of GNP around 1960. Even Eisenhower's blue-ribbon Eisenhower Commission on National Goals—

prominently featured in the media in late 1960 but delaying its report until after Kennedy's election—urged increased growth.[39]

"Growthmanship," which peaked between about 1958 and 1962, represented an almost caricatured triumph of quantitative, but simple, economic thinking. Numbers about U.S. growth, the country's relative performance in the world, and about a putatively "lost" national income that was weakening America were batted about by politicians, the media, and economists as if these were the principal benchmarks against which to judge the country. Headlines, congressional hearings, scholarly and popular reports, and political rhetoric pounded into Americans the radically new idea that they should be deeply concerned about whether U.S. GNP rose by 3 percent or 5 percent per year. While the growth men were right, at a very basic level, that higher economic growth could yield better lives for Americans, their significance is more cultural than economic. For the first time, the American people were told that they should care about numerical growth targets, with the explicit warning that if they did not, the nation would "lose" quantifiable potential income and the global strength and prestige that accompanied it. Pierre Salinger, who became Kennedy's press secretary, said: "Economic growth has come to resemble the Washington weather—everyone talks about it, no one says precisely what to do about it, and our only satisfaction is that it can't get any worse." Galbraith, in a memo to JFK, added: "The rate of growth is a fetish with economists, and the columnists and politicians they have educated."[40]

Into this political milieu came the 1960 quest to define "the national purpose"—the title of an influential Time Inc. book and the subject of the above-mentioned Eisenhower commission. On the one hand, contributors to *The National Purpose,* such as Archibald MacLeish, Walter Lippmann, Adlai Stevenson, and John Gardner, spoke of America's lost ideals, while others, such as Albert Wohlstetter and James Reston, wrote of the need to increase growth and meet the challenge of Soviet growth. Eisenhower appointed a number of commissions on economic growth at the end of his administration. The Commission on National Goals included economists Samuelson, Stein, Friedman, and Edward Denison. The panel, under the aegis of Eisenhower's nonprofit American Assembly and funded by the Ford and Rockefeller foundations, was sold as a book, *Goals for Americans—Programs for Action in the Sixties.* Calling for increased growth and greater government spending to ensure prosperity, the book was promoted in TV spots by the Advertising Council. Kennedy also formed three task forces on economic issues immediately after his election, including one led by Samuelson, with input from Pechman, Tobin, Heller, and Harvard University's Otto Eckstein. The nation's preoccupation with expanding economic growth was certainly aided and abetted by many economists.[41]

John Kennedy's ideas reflected a particularly deep faith in, and reliance upon, his economic advisers. Kennedy enlisted many of the nation's leading economists in his campaign and administration, prompting one journalist to joke that not quite all of the president's advisers were economists. Kennedy clearly had an affinity for economists and a consuming interest in economics, as Heller, speechwriter Theodore Sorenson, and Deputy Budget Director Charles Schultze, among others, have attested. Kennedy's father had hired John Harriman, an economic journalist for the *Boston Globe,* to be a speechwriter for JFK during his Senate years. JFK also came to know Galbraith when he headed the Democratic Party's domestic policy committee in the late 1950s, and was attracted by both his ideas and his charm. During the 1960 campaign, as Galbraith was seen as a bit too radical, and thus a political liability, Kennedy increasingly turned to MIT luminary Paul Samuelson and Harvard economist Seymour Harris, whom he also had met in Cambridge in the late 1950s. Samuelson and Galbraith frequently met with Kennedy and helped him on many campaign speeches. On Kennedy's Inaugural weekend, the *New York Times Magazine* devoted its cover story to Kennedy's economic advisers.[42]

Both Samuelson and Harris were asked to join Kennedy's CEA, and Samuelson often seemed like a fourth, shadow member of the council, but they recommended University of Minnesota economist Walter Heller to become chair. The poster boy of the Keynesian ascendancy, Heller was, in many ways, a more charming version of Leon Keyserling. Heller represented the economics profession's dream of power and influence. An urbane and witty economist who got along well with JFK, Heller suavely sold the president, Congress, and the American people on what he called "the New Economics," whose central promise was continuous growth, without serious recessions and with broadly shared abundance, achieved through government economic management. Heller wrote constantly to Kennedy, was a darling of Congress, and was frequently on the hustings speaking about the ability of the U.S. economy to grow faster. Like Keyserling and, to a lesser extent, Burns, Heller believed his role was not only to advise the president but to educate the public in speeches and articles about economics and the tremendous potential of the U.S. economy to bring the good life to all Americans. In the first three months of 1962,

Heller delivered twenty-nine public speeches, including five that were televised, in which he called for higher growth, said that America had "banished" the business cycle, and urged an end to racial discrimination to achieve even higher growth. An avid exponent of Keynesian fiscal policy to expand the economy, he called for eliminating the purported Eisenhower-era "gap" between actual and potential output, which Heller estimated at 8 percent of GNP, and said that the U.S. economy could expand by 4.5 percent a year.[43]

Yale economist James Tobin—another Keynesian who believed growth could serve as a "national purpose" that "could inspire, galvanize, and unite the nation"—and Kermit Gordon of the Ford Foundation, both of whom had campaigned for Kennedy, were named as the council's other members. Kennedy pulled together two other pre-inaugural economic task forces—on depressed areas, chaired by Senator Douglas, and tax reform, chaired by lawyer Stanley Surrey, who became an Assistant Treasury Secretary. Heller's CEA was legendary for its influence, its talent, and its success. Heller's star-studded council's nineteen staff economists included Yale's Arthur Okun, MIT's Robert Solow, Stanford's Kenneth Arrow, Wisconsin's Robert Lampmann, and Charles Schultze, who became associate budget director in 1962. After Tobin and Gordon left in 1962, Michigan's Gardner Ackley and development economist John P. Lewis were recruited. Heller formed a Cabinet Committee on Economic Growth, mimicking Eisenhower's Advisory Board for Economic Growth. An ongoing Financial Summit Meeting (the "Troika") brought together the CEA, the Bureau of the Budget, and the Treasury, with the Federal Reserve added later to form the "Quadriad." All of these entities—not to mention Cabinet secretaries such as Douglas Dillon at Treasury, with Seymour Harris as his special assistant, and Arthur Goldberg at Labor—fed Kennedy a torrent of economic advice.[44]

Samuelson—who was Kennedy's first choice for CEA chairman but did not want to move to Washington—and to a lesser extent Seymour Harris at Treasury, Galbraith, and Joseph Pechman at Brookings also provided the president and his council with a steady stream of advice. More than three hundred economic memos were sent to JFK during his thirty-four-month presidency, equal to one every three days. The perception that a disproportionate number of Kennedy's key advisers were economists was reflected in articles shortly after his inauguration such as "Kennedy Economics" in *Life,* and "Kennedy's Economists" in *Harper's.* Hobart Rowen noted that "not the least among Kennedy's achievements has been his ability to attract talented economic advisers who have breathed new life into the CEA, the Budget Bureau, and the Treasury." He also suggested JFK's admiration for the profession, reporting: "When JFK asked Tobin to join the CEA, Tobin said, 'You don't want me in the council. I'm an ivory tower economist.' Kennedy answered, 'That's the best kind. I'm an ivory tower president.'"[45]

Kennedy believed that there were few more important goals than economic expansion. Samuelson headed a blue-ribbon pre-inaugural economic task force that rushed to release its report on January 5, 1961. Within his first month in office, JFK hurried out a series of economic reports and proposals, and had his CEA chairman Walter Heller write his 2 February 1961, speech, "A Program for Economic Recovery and Growth" and prepare his "Program to Restore Momentum to the American Economy." Even when the economy had recovered, increasing growth and expanding abundance were obsessions of the president and his top advisers. Heller told Kennedy that economic growth served three purposes—overcoming poverty and wasted potential, "strengthen[ing] confidence in the free enterprise system throughout the world," and giving hope to developing nations, and in his 1962 Economic Report, Kennedy said: "There are sound reasons for wanting even faster growth in the future—unsatisfied needs at home and threats to freedom abroad, [and] a high rate of economic growth today will enable increasing millions to enjoy better lives tomorrow." "If the performance of our economy is high," JFK declared in 1963, "the aspirations of the American people are higher still—and rightly so." In his 1963 State of the Union Address, he said flatly: "Recovery is not enough. If we are to prevail in the long run, we must expand the long-run strength of our economy. We must move along the path to a higher rate of growth and full employment." Kennedy's stated reasons for focusing on growth were complex. Faster growth was needed to meet the Communist challenge, fight poverty, provide the famous "rising tide that lifts all boats," and enhance national pride. As Heller so memorably put it, economic growth was "the pot of gold and the rainbow."[46]

Kennedy ushered in a more activist Keynesianism and asked Americans to meet the challenges of a "New Frontier," calling for more flexible monetary and fiscal policies to increase growth and spending on education, health, old-age security, worker training, housing, and antipoverty measures. Speaking on the hundredth anniversary of the Emancipation Proclamation, JFK justified his support for civil rights by speaking of the "economic waste of discrimination." Kennedy's CEA prepared a 1962 report,

The Economic Costs of Racial Discrimination, which claimed that eliminating racism would raise GNP by 3.2 percent, as America was "wasting about one-third of the potential contribution of nonwhite workers." Like Truman and Eisenhower, he expressed the optimistic postwar faith that "man holds in his hand the power to abolish all forms of human poverty."[47]

In the annals of American political economy, few speeches were more influential than JFK's 11 June 1962 commencement address at Yale University—a sophisticated, explicit embrace of Keynesian fiscal policy. JFK sought to focus on "myth and reality in our national economy," saying that much economic rhetoric is "out of date." Expressing, par excellence, the postwar era's faith in economic management, he said that "the national interest lies in high employment and steady expansion of output"—goals that could be achieved by finding "technical answers," not "political answers." Deficits were not necessarily evil, and could stimulate the economy, whether through new spending or cutting taxes. The Yale speech reiterated the message of a May 1962 White House Economic Conference and launched the campaign to win passage of the first tax cut explicitly designed to promote economic growth.[48]

The link between economic strength and national strength and pride was a recurring theme in Kennedy's speeches. Some was cold war bluster, but much was emblematic of the economic machismo that characterized the postwar idealization of economic growth. "I stress the strength of our economy because it is essential to the strength of our nation," JFK told Congress in 1961. In a 1962 TV address, he said: "The economy and economic statistics are really the story of all of us as a country" and ensure that America's "strength shall forever be second to none." A few months later, he told business journalists that America's "prosperous and growing economy" was essential to the "maintenance of our position of world leadership." And in an address to the Economic Club of New York, JFK said: "America's rise to world leadership . . . has reflected more than anything else our unprecedented economic growth."[49]

As growth was taking hold by 1962, Kennedy was more unambivalently ready to celebrate the triumphs of the American economy, in keeping both with JFK's vigorous personal style and with the growing faith that the U.S. economy truly was the measure of America. In his 1962 State of the Union Address, he mockingly declared: "The economy which Mr. Khrushchev called a 'stumbling horse' was racing to new records in consumer spending, labor income and industrial production." Seven months later, he used charts to reinforce his message to TV viewers that "you and

I may have confidence in the long-run strength of our economy because it is solidly built on the largest output, on the highest wages and profits and most bountiful standard of living that any people have ever known." And, in a 1963 speech to the American Bankers Association, Kennedy said that economic growth has provided "an unprecedented standard of living" and an "unparalleled position" in world history for the United States.[50]

Like Truman, Keyserling, Eisenhower, Burns, and Kennedy, Heller's council believed that economic growth was America's paramount goal and would enable the country to solve all problems. And it worked. Between 1961 and 1966, real GNP grew by more than 5 percent per year, unemployment fell below 4 percent, job growth averaged 2.5 percent per year, inflation stayed below 2 percent, and the U.S. poverty rate fell from 22.4 percent to 14.7 percent—a level from which it would barely change in the succeeding forty-five years. The Kennedy tax cut, enacted in 1964, was more evidence that Keynesian ideas, translated into policy, would further increase American growth and prosperity. The encomiums came fast and furious. Samuelson declared in 1968 that the New Economics "really does work," and Milton Friedman and Richard Nixon famously concurred with *Time* magazine's 1965 judgment that we are all Keynesians now" (a phrase first used by Robert Lekachman in 1956) and its assessment that postwar prosperity was a function of "living in the Keynesian era."[51]

The outpouring of grief after Kennedy's assassination, Lyndon Johnson's legislative skills, his 1964 landslide victory, and the rapid economic growth that continued until 1968 brought many of the ideas of the postwar consensus to the apogee of their influence. In his 1964 State of the Union Address, delivered barely six weeks after Kennedy's death, and his subsequent Economic Report, Johnson gushed over the statistics of economic success: "The $100 billion rise in output in 2 3/4 years knows no parallel in our peacetime economic annals. The advance of $51 billion in labor income is also unparalleled. Average real income of nonfarm workers has risen by $345 a year, a gain not exceeded in any previous comparable period." Until the growing civil-rights crisis and the Vietnam War increasingly turned his attention elsewhere, Johnson was at least as enraptured by the vision of America as a supremely abundant society as his three predecessors. Opening the 1964–65 New York World's Fair, he boasted that "the abundance and the might represented here is far beyond the vision of those early settlers." And in a fall campaign speech, LBJ said: "We no longer struggle among ourselves for a larger share of limited abundance. We labor, instead, to increase the total abundance of

us all." The 1964 Democratic Party platform reinforced the message of
America as the economic wonder of the ages: "The free enterprise system is one of the great achievements of the human mind and spirit. . . .
It is now the productive marvel of mankind. . . . We have achieved the
longest and strongest peacetime prosperity in modern history. . . . It is the
national purpose, and our commitment [is] to continue this expansion of
the American economy toward its potential" so that all citizens can share
in this prosperity.[52]

But it was LBJ's vision of the "Great Society" that carried the postwar era's teleology of a march toward economic perfection to its logi-
cal conclusion. On 22 May 1964, at the University of Michigan, Johnson
proclaimed: "We have the opportunity to move not only toward the rich
society and the powerful society, but upward to the Great Society. . . . The
Great Society rests on abundance and liberty for all." Emboldened by his
1964 electoral mandate, Johnson, in his 1965 State of the Union Address,
spoke of "the greatest upsurge of economic well-being in the history
of any nation," saying that America now stood on the threshold of the
"Great Society."[53]

In many ways, 1965 was the high-water mark for conflating America's
economic success with its identity as a great nation. LBJ hailed America's
achievement of "the greatest abundance in history," and Keynes, long
dead, was named *Time* magazine's Man of the Year.[54]

Yet if there was a political coda to this generation-long story of the
romance between political leaders and economists, it may well have been
the Joint Economic Committee's February 1966 hearings marking the
twentieth anniversary of the Employment Act. Like a "golden oldies"
program, the hearings brought together everyone from Leon Keyserling,
Arthur Burns, and Wright Patman to Raymond Saulnier, Walter Heller,
and Gardner Ackley. While Patman, Burns, and Heller were upbeat about
progress toward achieving abundance for all, Keyserling remained cranky
about insufficient growth and Saulnier self-justifying about his role during
the low point of the postwar economy. However, it was Patman, who was
there at the creation in 1946, who summed up the optimistic faith that
"proper coordination of government and private policies could . . . produce a more stable, prosperous, [and] more rapidly growing America."[55]

The very idea that America could have it all—finance its geopolitical
might, build a Great Society for all its people, provide rising incomes
and consumption for all and healthy profits for business and investors—
represented the stunning self-confidence of policymakers and economists.

Riding high, most of the economics profession convinced itself, political leaders, and the public that they had solved the problem of providing abundance for all. This was both modern Americans' birthright and the great achievement of U.S. history. The profession's crowning glory came in 1968, when the Swedish Academy decided to establish a Nobel Prize in Economics. Although always controversial, it was the first and only prize in the social sciences.

As Alan Wolfe has written, by the Kennedy administration, "economists would try to succeed where capitalists in the past had failed; they were going to make the system work. Armed equally with mathematical models and exuberant self-confidence, economists dared the state: allow us to work for you, and we will stabilize the economy so that the future of American prosperity will be assured."[56]

And, for a time, they did and succeeded.

3

Business's New Paradigm, "People's Capitalism"

Of all the great industrial nations, the one that clings most tenaciously to private capitalism has come closest to the socialist goal of providing abundance for all in a classless society.

Twentieth Century Fund, 1947

After spending the Depression in the doghouse, American business roared back into public esteem in the 1940s thanks to its dazzling record of World War II production. Business sought to consolidate its good graces after the war, but it took the confluence of several developments for the business community to find a cluster of messages that resonated with the American people.

From the late New Deal into the 1960s, business associations and major corporations sought to convey much more than that business was a beneficial presence in the community and country. Instead, business leaders worked hard to spin out elaborate philosophies not only of the centrality of a "free enterprise system" to the American way of life and the American creed but also of a distinctive new ideology that measured the meaning of life and citizenship in the United States in economic terms. Hardly created of whole cloth, it was an amalgam of ideas—warmed-over free-market economics; quasi-Jeffersonian individualism; early-twentieth-century ideas about the primacy of "scientific" business management; watered-down New Deal and Keynesian ideas about mass purchasing power, full employment, and the need for some sort of welfare state; a half-Fordist, half-Keynesian belief that high production could only be sustained through high consumption predicated on high wages; a kind of economic Wilsonian belief in America's exalted role in the world; and a somewhat reactive and sanitized redefinition of "capitalism" as a system in which all could participate as home-, stock-, and other property owners.

These messages coalesced into a new version of American exceptionalism shared by other opinion-shaping elites, founded on the nation's purportedly unique capacity to provide broad-based, quantifiable abundance.

Emblematic of these business public-communications efforts was the widely expressed idea that America had developed a "new," or "people's capitalism." Business leaders often favored the term *free enterprise,* and New Deal Democrats tended to speak of a mixed economy, with people's capitalism, an attempt to split the difference. Many also recognized that in the international war of ideas the United States needed to develop an explicit ideology.[1] Under this new system, the exploitation and inequality of early capitalism had given way, only in America, to a classless workers' and consumers' paradise in which living standards were equalizing and rising, and everyone had an economic stake in society. Moreover, business messages, by the 1950s and early 1960s, expressed a new belief that never-ending economic growth was possible. With only a touch of hubris, business leaders argued that they could orchestrate such growth, with assistance from government and labor, and provide both a private utopia for the American masses and the economic underpinnings for almost everything on the nation's domestic and foreign policy agendas.

The National Association of Manufacturers (NAM), the Committee for Economic Development (CED), the U.S. Chamber of Commerce, the Advertising Council, and other business groups and individual companies embarked on massive efforts to sell the American people on this new paradigm of America as an economy whose achievements could be quantified in terms of abundance. Upward of $100 million a year was spent by business organizations and companies on public relations, employee relations, and advertising these messages, selling workers/consumers a new set of reasons to be proud of their country. In a remarkable October 1946 memo of the NAM's National Industrial Information Council, "The Public Relations Program of NAM," the organization unabashedly presented its PR task: "Business is faced with the greatest selling job it has ever faced—the job of selling the solid benefits of the American Way to the American people against the competition of the glittering promises of the Collectivist way." Although other business organizations such as the CED and Advertising Council—and even the NAM a decade or so later—took a more nuanced view that the task was more about selling the wonders of American abundance than relentlessly bashing any hint of communism or New Deal/Fair Deal "collectivism," this statement reflected an important aspect of the postwar business efforts to influence American public opinion. Similarly, the chamber launched a "Program for American Opportunity through Advertising" in 1947, working with the Advertising Council's two constituent organizations to burnish business's image, and declaring:

"Business cannot make friends . . . without making its own approach to the public mind."[2]

Although business messages were part and parcel of broader cultural influences—including political, media, education, and economic scholarship—it is hard to overestimate the power and influence of business communications. Millions upon millions of pamphlets and booklets were published and disseminated between the late 1940s and early 1960s. Extensive and sophisticated advertising campaigns were launched on radio and television, in magazines and newspapers, on billboards, and elsewhere. Classes, replete with printed materials, were held in factories and offices throughout the United States. Business groups made a major effort to review and reshape K–12 history, economics, and civics curricula, playing an enormous role in defining what America's children learned about their country. So-called public service campaigns coordinated by the Advertising Council only occasionally devoted themselves to tame subjects such as fire safety, leaving the industry's greatest creative talents to sell new ideas linking economic abundance and Americanism. Associations such as the CED, the Ad Council, the chamber, and the NAM led many of these campaigns, and scores of companies used their advertising muscle not just to sell cars, plastics, or machine tools but a coherent vision of an American way of life. The NAM, DuPont, and others exploited the new medium of television to relentlessly present shows and advertisements on the wonders of America's new capitalism. While foreign trade shows received considerable cold war–influenced attention, domestic displays of America's capacity to provide "better things for better living," in DuPont's parlance, or "carefree luxury," as Alcoa put it, were prominently on view in settings such as Disneyland, which opened in 1955, the 1962 Seattle World's Fair, and the 1964–65 New York World's Fair.

Business leaders in the 1940s and after hardly spoke with one voice, and ideas propounded by some influential individuals and groups were anathema to others. Schematically, business was divided between old-line, heavy-industrial manufacturers and distributors of consumer goods—the beneficiaries of massive new government military, technology and infrastructure spending—and small businesses. For example, the NAM took far-right, anti–New Deal, anti-union, anti-Keynesian positions, while the chamber was only somewhat more moderate during the 1940s. By contrast, the politically savvy and intellectually sophisticated CED, with its roots in the Commerce Department's Business Advisory Council, attained enormous influence thanks to its openness to Keynesian economics, partnership with government and labor, and ability to work well with Democrats and Republicans. The Ad Council became a mouthpiece for CED-like ideas, as did magazines such as Henry Luce's *Fortune* and the *Saturday Review.* Old-line manufacturing industries tended to be more conservative, denouncing government, whereas the newer technology, entertainment, and retail industries were more open to the notion of a mixed economy.

The Chamber of Commerce was less strident than the NAM, and even the NAM by the mid-1950s came to join the growth consensus, singing hymns to classless American abundance. By the late Eisenhower and Kennedy years, with a few right-wing exceptions, American business was largely singing from the same song book. The sharp political differences of the mid-1940s had dulled considerably by the late 1950s. While the NAM and chamber still stood to the right of the CED on many issues, by Eisenhower's second term they agreed that what made America distinctive was its mass, measurable abundance; that economic puissance was the measure of American greatness; and that—at least in their happy, public ideology—business working in partnership with government and labor was the font of that abundance.

Business Communications before 1940

Business has had a central, albeit often rocky relationship with the American people and role in U.S. history from Colonial times and Alexander Hamilton's early republic to the present. Until the late nineteenth century, with the exceptions of the railroads and Southern agricultural interests, most American production and distribution were decentralized and relatively small-scale. Early mass-marketers such as Sears and late-nineteenth-century department stores, and savvy distributors such as Procter & Gamble developed the rudiments of brand loyalty by the turn of the twentieth century. Yet the growth of the oil, steel, and other "trusts" in the decades before World War I evoked widespread animus toward big business. Unions grew in the late nineteenth and early twentieth centuries, and strikes were frequent and often violent. Muckraking journalism and Progressive politics led to food-and-drug and worker-safety laws and regulations, antitrust action, and stirrings of discontent about unsubstantiated advertising claims.

By 1912, when four presidential candidates vied for how actively they could bash business, it seemed that business's public esteem was at its

nadir. But over the next fifteen years that all changed. The National Civic
Federation argued during the 1910s that business, together with government and social science, could help Americans attain better living standards. During World War I, business and the state joined hands to win the
war under Bernard Baruch's War Industries Board. This cooperation—a
harbinger of what was to come a quarter century later—was rewarded
with a relaxation of Progressive strictures on business and a new respect
for America's captains of industry. Advertising leaders such as Edward
Bernays and Paul Nystrom presented consumer choice and America's
"pluralism of commodities" in the 1920s as new characteristics of American democracy.[3]

The 1920s were no golden age of prosperity—as recessions hit in both
1923–24 and 1926–27; agriculture suffered a severe slump; and, for most
Americans, incomes did not rise and much consumer buying was on credit. Nonetheless, the 1920s were a predawn of the consumer age. Visionary
business leaders such as Henry Ford, Edward Filene, GE executives Gerard Swope and Owen Young, Massachusetts paper manufacturer Henry
Dennison, Kodak's Marion Folsom, and Ernest Draper of Hills Brothers
argued that production meant nothing if people could not consume what
was produced. They also asserted that workers needed guaranteed employment and unemployment insurance to maintain financial security
and purchasing power. Swope argued that increased productivity could
not only bring higher profits and living standards but help solve society's
problems.[4] With the stock market climbing to new heights by 1929 and
business enjoying widespread prestige in the late 1920s, Commerce Secretary Herbert Hoover cultivated business-government links through trade
associations and harnessed early economic data to help strengthen the
economy.

Filene, Ford, Hoover, and a few others began heralding the advent of
a new American economy in which all would prosper in a rising tide of
mass production and consumption, but the prophecies proved short-lived.
The October 1929 stock market crash and a deepening depression left few
Americans ready to swallow the bromides of a discredited business community. Hoover and, initially, Franklin Roosevelt, sought to enlist business
in recovery schemes such as FDR's National Recovery Administration. A
few businessmen such as Swope and Dennison were early converts to the
belief that government and business needed to collaborate to restore the
nation's economic health. Even the chamber and the NAM flirted with
such ideas during the waning days of the Hoover administration, before

launching vicious attacks on government and labor. The early forbearance of the NAM and chamber to the New Deal's National Industrial Recovery Act and the Department of Commerce's Business Advisory Council ended by 1934, as more right-wing leaders such as Alfred P. Sloan Jr., Pierre S. DuPont, and John Jacob Raskob established the Liberty League, whose express purpose was to thwart FDR at every turn.

The NAM, originally created in 1895 to develop a recovery program for the Depression of the 1890s, fell on hard times after 1929. However, conservative leaders such as Charles Hook, Ernest T. Weir of National Steel, and Tom Girdler, the virulently anti-union boss of Republic Steel, worked to reinvigorate it during the Depression, and again made it an organization of big manufacturers, muscling out smaller businesses. In 1934, it convened a Congress of American Industry and established both a National Industrial Information Council (NIIC) and a Public Relations Advisory Committee to get its message out. For thirteen years, the NIIC churned out a steady diet of leaflets, speeches, films, school materials, and outdoor advertising. The NAM launched a radio show, *American Family Robinson,* and a newspaper feature called "The Voice of Business" that reached 4.5 million daily readers and appealed to Hollywood to produce pro–free enterprise films. In 1937 alone, NAM movie shorts were seen by about 6 million Americans.[5]

The Chamber of Commerce likewise was hardly shy about publicizing its distaste for the New Deal. Chamber president Henry I. Harriman vilified "the economic and fiscal policies of the administration" in September 1934, and followed with a torrent of tracts suggesting that the nation was on the road to "Collectivism and Dictatorship." The chamber's thirty-six-page *American Economic System* (1936) highlighted "the enduring character of private enterprise," the importance of "economic freedom" in America, and the nation's unique success in achieving a "standard of well-being unsurpassed in the history of other nations." Yet these themes were at least a half dozen years ahead of their time.[6]

Individual businesses also got into the act. DuPont in 1935 launched the long-running radio show *Cavalcade of America.* J. Walter Thompson published *A Primer of Capitalism* in 1937. Westinghouse presented *The Middleton Family at the World's Fair* in 1939 to offer a picture of middle-class normalcy. And Monsanto launched a "spirit of enterprise" campaign. Perhaps the most involved corporate effort to sell a rebranded capitalism was the General Motors "Futurama" exhibit for the 1939–40 World's Fair, designed by Norman Bel Geddes—still one of the most compelling examples of a glittering vision of life based on mass consumption, technology, and unfettered free enterprise.

But the suffering of millions of Americans as well as the rhetoric of Huey Long, Sinclair Lewis, Congress of Industrial Organizations (CIO) organizers such as John L. Lewis, and even homegrown communists made the mid-1930s pronouncements of the NAM and the chamber seem ludicrous at best. By the time that FDR lurched to the left in the mid-1930s with his attacks on "economic royalists," even *Fortune* magazine concluded that the NAM "was debating economic principles while breadlines formed."[7] NAM propaganda may have been churlish and insensitive during the 1930s, but the chamber's output was not much better. Yet, both organizations were laying the groundwork for a change in attitudes about American business that would bear fruit by the 1940s. An important part of this process was their beginning to link the idea of an "American Way" with economically measurable successes.

Anticipating an Economy of Abundance: The Early 1940s

If the NAM and chamber appeals mostly fell on deaf ears during the 1930s, that all began to change rapidly with World War II. The war inaugurated a social, economic, and cultural revolution that enabled new, business-promulgated ideas about America's mission, economy, and society to win droves of converts. Of course, the nation's wartime production record—a collaboration between business and government—was unprecedented: national income shot up by more than 50 percent in four years, idle factory capacity was a thing of the past, and the crippling unemployment of 1938 had by 1943 turned into a labor shortage. Once-ignored academics such as Stuart Chase who had talked of an "economy of abundance" were now echoed by Vice President Henry Wallace, and a newly confident FDR pledged a postwar "economic bill of rights" in which all Americans would have jobs, social security, and freedom from want.

Many business leaders recognized that the successful business-government collaboration of the war could be spun into a grand narrative of a new American capitalism and mission. Business was not monolithically opposed to the New Deal but rather divided between Republican isolationist industries and a "new bloc" of capital-intensive, internationalist ones such as GE, the Rockefellers, and the non-Morgan banks that also supported new management and industrial relations ideas. New Deal policies such as free trade, deficit spending, social welfare legislation, and the Wagner Act were supported by this sector of business.

Business also realized, as a 1941 Chamber memo suggests, that they needed to make their case to the American people. Jesse Jones, the powerful Texan who led the Commerce Department, and his associate Daniel C. Roper gathered many business leaders under the agency's Business Advisory Council (BAC). Gerard Swope was named the BAC's first chairman in 1933, and many corporate liberals who had emerged in the late 1920s and were to have such influence in the 1940s were early leaders of the council, including Dennison, Filene, W. Averell Harriman, Walter C. Teagle of Standard Oil of New Jersey, and Morris Leeds of Leeds and Northrup. BAC leaders, in books such as *Toward Full Employment* (1938), offered an early vision of business and government working and planning together to strengthen the national economy.[8]

Henry Luce's influential 1941 *Life* magazine editorial on the "American Century" gave a popular, quasi-intellectual patina to these new ideas. The far-sighted University of Chicago economist-turned-treasurer of Macy's, Beardsley Ruml; the Swedish social scientist Gunnar Myrdal; and business mavericks such as Kodak's Folsom, Paul Hoffman of Studebaker, chamber president and later Motion Picture Association of America leader Eric Johnston, ad executive William Benton, shipbuilder Henry J. Kaiser, machine tool executive and later Vermont senator Ralph Flanders, Philip Reed of GE, entertainment executives such as Jesse Lasky and Eugene Meyer, department store magnate Marshall Field, Harry Bullis of General Mills, and financiers like John Hay Whitney all began to articulate a new story about America, a new perspective on public policy, and a compelling, new conception of the nation and its future.

The story line varied and changed during the quarter century between the early 1940s and mid-1960s—and was contested by both the far left and the far right—but the key message was that a new, socially responsible capitalism could produce and rely on economic growth rather than a redistribution of income or social power to bring prosperity to all and meet society's needs. In exchange for steadily rising wages, or "purchasing power," and government-provided income security and Keynesian fiscal policies to boost demand, business would obtain steadily rising revenues and profits. Conflict—between labor and capital, government and business, or consumers and business—would be minimized. Instead, all groups would have a stake in advancing the shared cause of economic progress. The metrics of American success would be economic.

The Committee for Economic Development

While the NAM, the chamber, and individual businesses did jump on the bandwagon by the mid-1950s, the seminal years were the 1940s, and the key players were a remarkable group of American businessmen who co-alesced less than a year after Pearl Harbor and gave themselves the po-litically palatable name, the Committee for Economic Development. As Marion Folsom recalled, the very fact of close business-government col-laboration during World War II and even the early days of the BAC led many business leaders to gain new respect for the difficulties of running a nation and managing an economy. The CED was pivotal in planning a postwar economy and conceptualizing a postwar America. In addition to political leaders such as FDR, Henry Wallace, New York senator Robert Wagner, and others who began talking about a "postwar America" just months after millions of U.S. troops were mobilized for duty in Europe, Asia, and elsewhere, a number of economists and FDR "Brain Trusters" in the early 1940s began pondering the possibilities of an "economy of abundance."[9]

The brainchild of Commerce Secretary Jesse Jones, Paul Hoffman, Wil-liam Benton, and Beardsley Ruml, dating to 1939, the CED was incorpo-rated in 1942 to "enlist the services of the best brains from our universities and business" to solve "the problems of how high productive employment could be attained and maintained in a free society." Hoffman, the presi-dent of Studebaker, was an enormously influential figure in shaping post-war beliefs about the United States and its economy. In addition to being a driving force behind the CED, Hoffman was a leader of the Advertising Council and later president of the Ford Foundation, one of several major foundations that led the propagation of these ideas. Hoffman also was the domestic administrator of the Marshall Plan, a policy initiative that the CED played a major role in selling to the U.S. business community. Benton not only was a co-founder of the prominent advertising agency Benton & Bowles but also was a vice president of the University of Chicago, a Tru-man administration appointee, publisher of the *Encyclopedia Britannica*, a delegate to several United Nations agencies, and a Democratic senator from Connecticut from 1949 to 1953. Ruml, while still a dean at the Uni-versity of Chicago in the late 1930s, organized the American Economic Council, which, among other things, produced a radio show called *The University of Chicago Roundtable*. The CED's early trustees included many media and publishing executives such as Benton, Walter Fuller, Raymond

Rubicam, Philip Graham, Gardner Cowles, Leon Shimkin, Frank Stanton, Roy Larsen, and Johnston.[10]

Hoffman, Benton, and their associates felt strongly that business and academia had been separate, if not antagonistic, for too long, and that each sector could benefit from the other's wisdom. Even more important, early CED organizers had a strong sense of public purpose—a belief that American society, economics, and politics could be made better by conducting careful, objective research into social and economic problems, resulting in "findings and recommendations for business and public policy which will contribute to the strengthening of our free society, and to the maintenance of high employment, increasing productivity and living standards, greater economic stability, and greater opportunity for all people." More liberal than the NAM or chamber, the CED embraced "careful Democrats and open-minded Republicans," as later CED president Robert Holland put it. In many ways the core of the postwar liberal consensus, the CED inverted the oft-misquoted "What's good for General Motors is good for America" philosophy to argue, in the words of another CED president, Sol Hurwitz, that what is good for America is good for business.. The CED saw postwar planning as its paramount objective, and even intended to disband when the war was over. The organization—which drew heavily on manufacturing, retail, and media companies—established nearly three thousand local CED committees throughout the United States, enlisting sixty thousand business leaders between 1942 and 1945. This field division drew all stripes of businesspeople who shared the goals of economic expansion and full employment.[11]

Complementing the field division was a research division established by Flanders, Ruml, Hoffman, Benton, Harry Scherman of the Book-of-the-Month Club, and seven noted economists, including Sumner Slichter and longtime CED research director Theodore O. Yntema. It is hard to underestimate the CED's influence in shaping postwar America's economic policy. Ruml's 1942 pay-as-you-go tax plan was largely adopted in the 1942 Revenue Act, which brought most Americans into the tax system for the first time in 1943. The committee's 1944 booklet, *A Postwar Federal Tax Plan for High Employment,* espoused the conventional wisdom of a balanced budget but also called for new spending on social security to boost purchasing power. Ruml and Herbert Stein, later CED's research director, developed the concept of a "full employment budget" in which budgets were to be balanced "over the cycle" but could be in deficit when the economy needed to be stimulated. Perhaps equally radical for a business group was Benton's and Yntema's 1944 *Economics of a Free Society,* reprinted from *Fortune,* which was a far-reaching manifesto for a mixed economy. Public and private enterprise both had their roles to play. Labor unions were a positive social force. The government was responsible for preventing depressions though fiscal and monetary policy, and it ultimately was government's responsibility to ensure that all Americans could find jobs. With all players doing their part, there would be no limits to America's potential abundance. This seventeen-page document, CED's first "supplementary paper," emphasized that an economy is designed to serve "the good of all," that wealth is a prerequisite to other freedoms, and concluded that "America stands at the gate of an age of plenty."[12]

The CED issued a flurry of book-length research reports and shorter statements on national policy from 1944 to 1947 and beyond, repeatedly emphasizing government's role in ensuring full employment and high production. Although the committee urged a reduction of wartime taxes, it frequently recognized the need for additional spending and a "large shelf of public works," and introduced the idea that government tax-and-spending policy could serve as "automatic stabilizers" that would cushion fluctuations in the economy. It also took the remarkable position that "taxes should reduce inequalities in wealth, income, and power [which] are abhorrent to democracy." By the 1950s, CED booklets hammered home the message that America's preeminent goal was to increase production, productivity, and wages, and to avoid recessions. The CED's support for a mixed economy and its embrace of Keynesian economics—still anathema to the NAM and chamber in the mid-1940s—also led it to provide significant support for the Employment Act of 1946. In *Jobs and the Market* (January 1946), CED writers such as Gardiner Means, Stein, and Yntema called for a "committee of high officials"—a draft version of the Council of Economic Advisers—to advise the president on how to best plan high levels of investment and employment. Indeed, the CED played a crucial role not only in institutionalizing the role of economists and other social scientists as leading policy advisers but also in educating the public about economic issues so that they could be informed policy-influencing citizens.[13]

The CED's commitment to an economically informed citizenry took many forms. It distributed hundreds of thousands of copies of the several dozen booklets that it produced each year. It placed editorials in hundreds of newspapers and got its research quoted in thousands of articles. CED trustees included publishers and executives of the *Washington Post, Newsweek,* Time Inc., the *Des Moines Register,* the *Louisville Courier-Journal,* and NBC. Later, from 1959 to 1973, the CED collaborated each year with the *Saturday Review* to publish extensive, multi-article annual issues on the U.S. economy, which brought it a host of influential readers. By the late 1950s, the CED each year distributed 1.1 to 1.3 million publications, placed twelve hundred to fourteen hundred editorials, and saw its work cited in sixteen thousand to seventeen thousand news stories. By 1947, the CED established research centers at fourteen universities as a way of formalizing business-academic collaboration. The universities of Wisconsin, Colorado, North Carolina, Michigan, and Minnesota, and Emory, Brown, and Northwestern universities were among the most prominent centers. These "College-Community Centers" sought to bring together scholars, business leaders, and the public to address local economic development issues. In addition to a bevy of economists, the CED's trustees in the late 1940s included presidents of Dartmouth, the University of California, Washington University, Vassar, and Colgate, and the dean of the Harvard Business School. In 1947 and 1948, the CED collaborated with NYU educator G. Derwood Baker and others to cofound the Joint Council on Economic Education and provided significant seed money to help develop and disseminate curriculum materials to millions of schoolchildren to shape their ideas about the U.S. economy.[14]

The CED influenced both Democratic and Republican administrations. As president of Columbia University, Dwight Eisenhower was an early CED trustee, and as U.S. president, he appointed CED leaders such as Marion Folsom; Walter Williams; Meyer Kestnbaum of Hart, Schaffner & Marx; and James Zellerbach to high government positions. Unlike the NAM or chamber, whose politics were predictably conservative Republican, the CED appealed to many Democrats and Republicans from the Truman to the Nixon years. John Kennedy was even more enamored of the CED, naming CED economic adviser Walter Heller as his CEA chairman and praising the organization in a speech on its twentieth anniversary for having "helped bring about a fundamental change in the economic understanding of the nation in general."[15]

By the 1950s and 1960s—arguably the CED's peak years—the committee included about 250 members and twenty-six hundred corporate supporters. In 1956, economist Herb Stein became the CED's research director; he would stay with the organization for twenty-two years, making a name for himself as a leading public-policy scholar. By the second Eisenhower administration, under the powerful influence of Chicago economist Theodore Schultz, the CED had begun to focus on social issues such as slum clearance, urban decay, municipal services, and traffic congestion, as well as the U.S. economic competition with the Soviet Union. Beginning with the Korean War, but especially in the late 1950s, the CED frequently worried about "rapid Soviet gains" yet noted the general backwardness and regimentation of the Soviet economy. On its fifteenth anniversary, the CED rightly celebrated its "international prestige" and its role at "every major watershed" in changing U.S. "economic thinking, policies, and practices."[16]

In the late 1950s, as it became clear that the CED's longtime predictions about the emergence of a new U.S. economy of abundance were panning out, the organization stepped back to produce major economic policy pronouncements. In *Economic Growth in the United States: Past and Future* (1958), the CED surveyed the achievements and predict the future successes of the American economy. Aimed at the educated lay and business reader, the book used uniformly rising charts and glittering prose to describe America's "high, rising, and broadly diffused income" for the common man. Forecasting the "inspiring prospect" of unprecedented wealth by 1980, the authors concluded that "it lies within our power to lead the world into a material utopia which in the past has been a mere dream." Two other star-studded, book-length publications were its *Problems of U.S. Economic Development: Papers by 49 Free-World Leaders* (1958) and *Problems of U.S. Economic Development: The 50 Winning Papers in the CED's Free World-Wide Competition on the Most Important Economic Problems to be Faced in the United States in the Next 20 Years* (1958). The first book was a compendium of two-thousand-word essays by some of the era's leading economic lights—Moses Abramovitz, Kenneth Boulding, Henry Steele Commager, Peter Drucker, Milton Friedman, John Kenneth Galbraith, Alvin Hansen, Roy Harrod, Friedrich von Hayek, Simon Kuznets, Jean Monnet, Hans Morgenthau, Reinhold Niebuhr, David Riesman, Paul Samuelson, and Sumner Slichter. Many writers called for increased public provision of goods and services, eliminating poverty and redistributing income, taming inflation, increased economic growth to meet defense needs, expanded aid to less developed countries, and establishing targets for economic growth.

However, an undercurrent of worry was present. Some writers focused on the idea that, with abundance achieved, what significant goals could possibly remain for America? As Riesman wrote: "We are a generation prepared for Paradise Lost who do not know what to do with Paradise Found." Similarly, Walter Lippmann wondered whether "the highest purpose of the American social order [might be] simply the production of more and more consumer goods so that Americans will enjoy ever higher standards of material well-being."[17]

The Advertising Council

The Advertising Council reinforced CED-like ideas among the broader U.S. population in a series of sophisticated and massive "public service" ad campaigns in the late 1940s and 1950s. Like the CED, the council had its genesis in the early days of World War II. In November 1941, five hundred ad executives led by industry pioneer James Webb Young gathered at a joint meeting of the American Association of Advertising Agencies and the Association of National Advertisers with the twin goals of promoting American business and diminishing public concerns that advertising threatened Americans' freedom of thought. The following year, a newly formed War Advertising Council was established to work with the Office of War Information, under Theodore S. Repplier, to help develop and propagate a compelling message about America's society and economy.[18]

After V-J Day, the group rechristened itself the Advertising Council, with the goal of demonstrating business' social conscience and concern with the larger issues of American life. Repplier became its first president, serving from 1946 to 1965. The council worked closely with the Truman and Eisenhower administrations to develop domestic and foreign information campaigns and serve as a private advisory arm to the government. The council's signature "public service" campaigns ranged from benign appeals such as Smokey the Bear and fire safety and promoting increased religious faith to selling American foreign-policy goals and more philosophical, big-picture campaigns to educate Americans about the nature and benefits of their economic system. Its program "American Opportunity through Advertising," launched in 1947, sought to "correct the misinformation about profits, dividends, management salaries, etc.," and drew on market researchers and pollsters such as Everett Smith of Macfadden Wage Earners' Forum, Ernest Dichter, and George Gallup.[19] For Repplier, serving the national interest was as important as buttressing advertising's public image.

Also like the CED, with whom it shared a number of leaders, the Ad Council took a relatively enlightened view of the new capitalist partnership among business, government, and labor. State control and planning of the economy were taboo, but government was seen as a positive tool for promoting economic growth. The council drew together figures such as Paul Hoffman; Twentieth Century Fund president Evans Clark, who chaired the council's Public Policy Committee in the late 1940s; Time Inc. president Roy Larsen; Brown University president Henry Wriston; and labor leaders such as the AFL's William Green and the CIO's Philip Murray. The council held roundtable discussions in the early 1950s explicitly to "distill the American way of life into a formula that could be diffused" through domestic and overseas communications. Advertisers played an essential role in subtly redefining freedom from civil and political liberties to freedom to find satisfaction in one's choice of goods to buy.[20] The evolution of the council's ideas on how to frame what America was all about is evident in late 1940s and 1950s campaigns such as "American Heritage" "Our American Free Enterprise System," "Future of America," and "People's Capitalism."

The council's "American Heritage" campaign of 1947–48 was initially called "United America" and conceived as a gentle attack on prejudice, reacting to Soviet propaganda on American racism. However, prejudice became too hot a topic for many council supporters. It was repositioned to emphasize American freedoms and attack state control of the economy, although it also turned into something of an apologetic for loyalty oaths, Jim Crow, and the Taft-Hartley Act. Nonetheless, the council—working with the American Heritage Foundation—sent a "Freedom Train" on a tour of 322 cities, distributing 1.5 million booklets. It was so popular that most visitors were turned away.[21]

Perhaps the council's largest postwar campaign, "Our American Free Enterprise System," was rolled out in November 1948 and was active into the early 1950s. It was designed to show "why, in spite of its shortcomings, the American economic system has given us the highest standard of living and the greatest freedom in the world." Developed by three ad agencies and the Twentieth Century Fund, the campaign promoted free enterprise, business-government cooperation, and labor's right to organize. Magazines and newspapers were deluged with ads, radio spots were broadcast, several hundred thousand bus and trolley cards were distributed, and four thousand billboards proclaiming "The Better We Produce, the Better We Live" lined America's highways. MGM produced a 1949 cartoon, *Meet King Joe,* that made the same points. Fact sheets distributed to radio announcers provided talking points, buttressed by statistics. The message: "It is a simple historical fact that the American Economic System has brought greater material means for happiness to more people than any other the world has known. We have been able to out-produce every other nation—to turn out more goods and services for every hour we work—to enjoy a steadily rising standard of living."[22]

A harbinger of ad campaigns, political rhetoric, and journalism to come, the council distributed more than 1.1 million copies of a free booklet, *The Miracle of America,* which was reprinted in *Look,* in a half million copies of *Scholastic* in March 1950, and 6 million times in scores of company magazines. Its corporate supporters also disseminated nearly seventy-five thousand copies to most of the nation's principals, school superintendents, and other school officials, six hundred ads were placed in newspapers and magazines, six thousand billboards were posted, and three hundred thousand transport cards were disseminated. Emphasizing the benefits of free enterprise and business-labor-government cooperation, *The Miracle of America* argued that a joint effort to increase productivity would allow American incomes to rise and working hours to fall, while enabling the nation to preserve its liberties in the battle against communism. Filled with charts demonstrating the unparalleled gains of American production during the twentieth century, the booklet concluded that "through our free, competitive American system," the United States outproduced Western Europe by more than two to one and the Soviet Union by seven to one. The publication's ten-point Platform for Americans, ringed by photos of twenty luminaries supposedly representing a cross section of American interests included four points emphasizing economic freedom and one calling for "expanding productivity as a national necessity." To secure labor buy-in, and demonstrating how far business had come to embrace the postwar consensus, collective bargaining was supported. Government was to be a partner with the private sector in minimizing the hazards of life and supporting "socially desirable projects."[23]

The 1954–55 "Future of America" and "Confidence in a Growing America" campaigns returned to, and elaborated on, themes of measurable abundance. Led by Hoffman and Repplier, they included upbeat pamphlets, radio and TV spots, a filmstrip, and a half-hour TV show narrated by Hoffman that aired on all four networks on 2 January 1955. Aimed to counter lingering fears of depression, one "Future of America" booklet proclaimed: "This dynamic country of yours has been in a period of tremendous growth. This has meant more jobs, more money, more security, more homes, and more opportunities for everyone"[24] The 1960 "Promise of America" campaign also sought to increase confidence in a "growing" nation.

One of the council's most successful efforts to shape public attitudes about the nation and its economy was its mid-1950s effort to rebrand the American economic system as "people's capitalism." Widely embraced by politicians, journalists, and propagandists in the new U.S. Information Agency (USIA), people's capitalism was at once an attempt to articulate a coherent description and philosophy of the new, postwar America and a conscious rebuttal of Soviet efforts to co-opt the phrase "people's" in vilifying capitalism. People's capitalism was a spin-off from the idea of "democratic capitalism," which emerged in the late 1940s, and figures as varied as John Foster Dulles, Ludwig von Mises, Robert Heilbroner, Reinhold Niebuhr, and Henry Hazlitt used it from the mid-1950s until the early 1960s. The phrase recognized that merely talking about "free enterprise" or an "American way of life" left Americans and foreigners alike with little understanding of what was truly unique and admirable about postwar America.[25]

The basic idea, repeated in a variety of media, was that all Americans are capitalists because they own homes and stocks, that America is a consumer's and worker's paradise where luxuries are necessities, and people are equal and prosperous as never before. Far from being the exploitative, selfish system of 1900 or that portrayed in Soviet propaganda, the new "people's capitalism" was distinctive because of "the very wide participation in a high standard of living." The success of the new system, also described as "democratic capitalism" or the "new America," was predicated on the nation's commitment to limited government, freedom of initiative, adaptability to change, and equality of opportunity. Business leaders were quick to highlight the differences not only between this new and an older capitalism but also the differences between the enlightened, consumer-oriented, technologically driven, and competitive new capitalism of the United States and a paler, less appealing version still practiced in Europe and elsewhere. As historian Lizabeth Cohen has argued, Americans were told that they enjoyed "equality" because they were relatively equal in the standard package of goods that they could consume, and "freedom" because they had abundant free choice in what they could consume. An emblematic, often-used quote in the campaign, drawn from the Twentieth Century Fund, which published short, popularized versions of its 1947 and 1955 reports on the U.S. economy, proclaimed: "This momentous development (the wide distribution of the gains in material progress through a steadily rising standard of living) has been taking place not in communist Russia but in capitalist America. Of all the great industrial nations, the one that clings most tenaciously to private capitalism has come closest to the socialist goal of providing abundance for all in a classless society."[26]

The National Association of Manufacturers

While the CED and Advertising Council were developing and selling their visions of an abundant new America, older business groups and companies also were active in influencing American public opinion. The NAM and chamber had enormous influence, with NAM members claiming to employ 75 percent of America's industrial workers in the late 1940s, and the chamber claiming to represent 1.5 million business people in 1952 and 3 million in 1962.[27] Calling itself the "Voice of Industry," the NAM sought to restore confidence in business, curtail labor's power, and influence the broadest possible public—from schoolchildren and workers to policymakers and all Americans. Theirs was a vision of America's meaning and purpose that linked free enterprise, abundance, freedom, and American exceptionalism.

The NAM's public stance evolved from a more shrill defense of "free enterprise" during the first decade after the war into a celebration of measurable abundance by the late 1950s that echoed the ideas of the CED, Henry Luce, the Advertising Council, Dwight Eisenhower, and Democratic "growth men" such as Leon Keyserling and John Kennedy. Well into the McCarthy era, NAM booklets, radio and TV programs, newspaper and magazine ads, and supplementary school materials remained a fairly ham-handed rhetorical conflation of free enterprise and American freedom. Like the postwar films noirs, the NAM's pronouncements had more than a whiff of paranoiac threat to them: Communism was on the march, and American freedoms were at risk—none more so than the vaunted "freedom of enterprise."

The NAM was generally ebullient about the nation's postwar economic prospects, but this was tempered during the early Truman years by fears that free enterprise stood at the verge of collapse. Patriotic Americans needed to support the NAM's efforts to battle "collectivism," "totalitarianism," and a "master plan to remake America" led by liberal planners and CIO labor radicals. The organization remained largely in thrall to ultraconservatives such as J. Howard Pew, the Sun Oil Company chairman who headed the NAM's NIIC, DuPont vice president Jasper Crane, and intellectual hangers-on such as longtime *Newsweek* columnist Henry

Hazlitt, who supported a more virulently right-wing side venture called *The Freeman,* published from 1950 to 1957. Styling itself as a voice of the libertarian right, it featured Hazlitt and equally prickly *Newsweek* columnist John Chamberlain in addition to the work of conservatives such as Ludwig von Mises; Lawrence Fertig; Leo Wolman; Florence Norton of Regnery Publishing; Leonard Read of the ultraconservative Foundation for Economic Education in Irvington-on-Hudson, New York; and Robert LeFevre, who launched an academy of "economic freedom" in Colorado Springs in 1956. Its influence was marginal and it was never financially successful, largely bankrolled by businessmen Jasper Crane of DuPont and Howard Pew of Sun Oil.[28] The NAM continued to rail against the power of organized labor and growing government, and the "purchasing power fallacy," and was hardly subtle in juxtaposing American "free enterprise" with communism and even British "socialism."

While many criticized the NAM during the 1940s for taking this tack, including *Fortune,* which derided the NAM's "shocking lack of faith in the American people and, in some cases, downright contempt," the organization embarked on a crusade to sell a set of ideas about America and its economy. In 1948 alone, the NAM produced five short films seen by 2.5 million high school students and workers, distributed 2.5 million pamphlets such as "Free Enterprise" and "Our Material Progress," issued 1,275 press releases, published forty-five articles in magazines and newspapers, aired twenty-six quarter-hour episodes of *It's Your Business* on ABC Radio, and placed countless ads in mass-circulation magazines such as *Life* and the *Saturday Evening Post.* Free enterprise" or "economic freedom" became part of a "tripod of freedom" that included democracy and free expression. Speakers' kits declared that "private enterprise is our way of life, . . . the very heart of the Constitution, . . . the soul of our liberties, [and] . . . the great American idea."[29]

The NAM hired conservative Columbia University professor and *Newsweek* writer Ralph Robey to abstract six hundred school textbooks to make sure that educators only would use those explicitly favorable to free enterprise. The NAM became extremely active in the 1950s economic education movement, distributing an annual catalog of its "Educational Aids for High Schools" and producing a multimedia curriculum unit called "How Our Business System Operates," used by 3.5 million students during the early 1950s, as well as a "You and Industry" film-and-workbook series emphasizing industry's contributions to social progress and higher living standards. The NAM also produced a college-level textbook, *The*

American Individual Enterprise System, published in 1946. During the late 1940s it sent a monthly magazine filled with suggestions of how to teach about the economy and business to forty-eight thousand educators. The NAM had an Industry Leaders Training Program that, at its peak, held fifteen hundred meetings a year to train employers how to communicate the benefits of the American system to employees. The organization even had a program for "Church and Industry Cooperation" to dissuade clergymen from the "scriptural injunction to share and be generous with worldly goods" and to encourage support for "continually advancing our living standards."[30]

NAM pamphlets of the early 1940s predicted a postwar world of untold abundance, urging soldiers and production workers to fight for this vision of a land of plenty. American freedom, according to the NAM's "Program of Plenty," is fundamentally about the "right" of the housewife to buy bacon, workers to change jobs, and investors to risk capital. A twenty-two-minute 1944 film produced with Paramount, *Three to Be Served,* described the U.S. economy as a "triangle of plenty" based on capital, management, and labor. The organization argued against the initially more leftist Full Employment Bill in the twelve-thousand-word *Program for Permanent Prosperity* in September 1945. NAM president Ira Mosher said that the legislation was not ambitious enough about increasing production and national income "in excess of any previously attained" to provide truly full employment and rising living standards.[31]

The NAM mellowed by 1954, conceding that cooperation among business, labor, and government would allow Americans to "march arm-in-arm down the familiar American road which leads to greater abundance." The similarly optimistic *Platform for Prosperity and Progress* (1956) opined that Americans "have before us the possibility of the greatest surge of material growth and progress in all our history." The same year, an elaborate thirty-two-page Sunday newspaper supplement, "The NAM's Goal: New Dimension for the American Dream," celebrated America's "unequalled record" due to its conception of free enterprise.[32]

Perhaps the most ambitious NAM public-relations effort of the 1950s was its weekly television show, *Industry on Parade,* co-produced with NBC from 1950 to 1960. Broadcast on 270 stations by 1957, shown in schools, and distributed by the USIA in thirty-three countries, the series had a breathless tone featuring the wonders of American industry, the cornucopia of new products always becoming available to Americans, the wizardry of scientists and technicians in facilitating rising abundance, and the good citizenship of the American corporation. By 1952, it was television's second-highest-rated show. Produced by Johnny Johnstone, NAM's radio and TV director, and NBC producer Arthur Lodge, each thirteen-and-a-half-minute show typically included four vignettes, although late-1950s shows tended to focus on a single theme. With an authoritative male narrator and bouncy music, every episode opened with the line that viewers were being presented "a brand new look at our America." Segments were interspersed with forty-second "messages from industry" in which a NAM announcer summarized the meaning of the show's disparate tales of how business was making life better for Americans. As one declared:

> History shows that we Americans have attained the highest standard of living in the world. The competitive American system based on freedom for the individual has encouraged us to develop the use of new and better raw materials, and to improve our buildings, equipment and tools. As a result, we now produce three or four more times per hour than we did in 1900, and we have twice as much leisure time. We can have an even higher standard of living in the future by increasing our productivity, which will mean more and better products for all.[33]

The hundreds of episodes of *Industry on Parade,* played and replayed on TV and elsewhere, were one of the best examples of business reaching out to a mass audience to convey the wonders of an abundant new American economy. A 1959 episode about overseas, cold war trade fairs opined about the "pattern of advantages never before enjoyed in all world history by so many." Rhetorically asking what these "advantages" were, the show surveyed American homes, clothing, highways, foods, and leisure, and concluded: "First, comes to mind the material—the tangible things. . . . Abundance is the best description—a word easier said than demonstrated to the people of other nations." Factories were shown as miraculous, mighty creators of the good things of American life. Images of white-coated scientists devising the latest technologies were juxtaposed with those of housewives taking dinners out of gleaming new ovens and children playing in spacious backyards. Economic statistics were liberally but creatively sprinkled onto images of homes, highways, clothing, food, and other consumer goods—all of which were accessible and affordable to virtually every American. The march of consumer progress, and economic progress, was framed as the steady transformation of yesterday's "luxuries" into today's "necessities." The NAM continued its use of TV in the early 1960s with a series on National Educational Television called *The American Business System.* The ten half-hour episodes, aired in 1963 and subsequently distributed widely to schools, emphasized "how abundantly the needs and wants of the American people are met through a business system of free choice." The show made it clear that America's economy is "one of the most significant achievements of the American people" and "the envy of the world."[34]

Although the NAM still viewed free enterprise as the linchpin of the American system and tilted at an endless array of presumably "socialistic" windmills, its booklets and educational materials of the mid to late 1950s—not to mention *Industry on Parade*—were much closer to messages being conveyed by the CED and Advertising Council than its earlier more histrionic messages of the 1930s and early 1940s. Just as Ad Council leaders recognized that "free enterprise" was a vague and not especially compelling way to describe America or instill patriotism and pride, the NAM's public-relations apparatus also realized that emphasizing America's abundant economy was a much more successful strategy than simply pitching "free enterprise." While the NAM declined in power and became less interested in public advocacy, it is worth noting that by the mid-1960s it too had come to accept the mixed economy. As NAM leader Werner Gullender said: "We no longer curse the government but try to work with it."[35]

The U.S. Chamber of Commerce

If the NAM initially occupied the right flank of business politics during the postwar era and the CED took up a center-left flank, the venerable U.S. Chamber of Commerce came from a center-right position. Like the NAM, it recognized by the mid-1950s that touting America as a land of plenty rather than a bastion of anti-communist "free enterprise" went over much better with the American people. It also came to accept the mixed economy earlier than the NAM, essentially supporting an Eisenhower-like vision of business-government cooperation for economic expansion that would strengthen America's position in the world.

Organized in 1912 at a "National Commercial Conference" called by President Taft to promote business cooperation, the chamber during its first two decades mostly produced materials to assist manufacturers, distributors, and merchants. The Depression politicized the chamber, which spent the New Deal–era warning of the "plague of locusts" of incipient "collectivism." Yet it also became an active participant in the public debate about how to organize a postwar economy that would assure jobs and prosperity. It published a series of 1943 "bulletins" on "Postwar

Readjustments," and its Committee on Economic Policy, led by economist Emerson P. Schmidt, issued a raft of publications on how to achieve
"full employment." While these pamphlets rightly noted that few either
could oppose this goal or define what it meant, the chamber's stock answer was that "greatly expanded production" was the key to America's
future and the essence of "the American tradition." Like the NAM, the
chamber opposed the initial version of the Full Employment Bill, playing
a major role in reshaping it to become an official endorsement of the free-
enterprise system. The chamber damned Truman and the Democrats for
taking a "backroad to socialism," but in 1943 and 1944 booklets such as
The Possibility of Postwar Prosperity, The Adventure of Tomorrow, and *America
Unlimited,* chamber leaders Eric Johnston and Ralph Robey wrote of a
dawning world in which nothing would be economically impossible for
the United States.[36]

Unlike its 1920s publications, which had been dryly written for businessmen, or its stridently political pamphlets of the 1930s, the chamber's
1940s booklets took a more conversational tone, addressing the common
man's hopes and fears for the postwar world. The chamber hardly eschewed its ideological message in *Freedom and the Free Market Inseparable,*
its warnings of communist "infiltration" of government and unions, and
its attacks on the Truman administration, yet it more prudently—and se-
ductively—began to promise, "If in the future we continue to work together to increase productivity still further, we can indefinitely raise our
living standards." Working with the Ad Council, the chamber developed
the "Program for American Opportunity" campaign in the late 1940s to
explain the "American enterprise system" and ensure that Americans believed in its principles, because "our standard of living and freedom are
the envy of the world." It organized workplace meetings and publications
to win over employees and produced booklets, radio spots, films, and
"economic discussion workbooks" to "organize and conduct a successful program for developing spokesmen for the American Free Enterprise
System."[37]

By the mid to late 1950s, the chamber's magazine, *Nation's Business,*
with a circulation of 750,000, and its endless pamphlets and films depicted
an America that was rich and getting richer, and whose bounty was dependent on free markets and wise businessmen. Linking free enterprise,
Americanism, and abundance, chamber publications and films argued
that "free markets make free men," and that the American system enabled
"today's employee [to] earn more in fewer hours than his ancestors did."

Other booklets predicted the end of poverty through greater productivity, a doubling of wages, and one of the chamber's many films opined that "practically everybody is a capitalist" in America. The chamber also jumped on the "people's capitalism" bandwagon, as the organization's president and publisher of *Parade* magazine Arthur Motley contrasted its "revolutionary" success with the failed revolutions in Russia, Cuba, and elsewhere. The chamber also joined the CED, the NAM, and others in producing "economic understanding projects" and organizing "business-education days" for teachers to help educate America's children in the right principles of political economy and patriotism. During the Eisenhower years, the chamber had become more accepting of government's role in attenuating slumps and providing needed public investments, and had endorsed the Employment Act. It also supported the Keynesian rationale for Kennedy's tax cuts, and by 1968, chamber president Winton Blount hailed business-government cooperation as essential to address America's social and economic needs.[38]

The Conference Board

The Conference Board played a more behind-the-scenes role in influencing public attitudes. Founded in 1916 as a research and education organization that studied business and economic issues, the National Industrial Conference Board produced several dozen reports, "chart books," and books each year for distribution to business and congressional leaders, journalists, and universities, as well as weekly "Road Maps of Industry" that were sent by the millions to America's schools beginning in the mid-1950s. The majority were specialized reports on subjects such as farm prices, Latin American trade, and department store sales, yet many ventured into the broad terrain of "business conditions," where authors expounded on the scope and meaning of postwar economic and social changes.[39]

The Conference Board prided itself on its objectivity and never sought to directly shape mass opinion, yet many of its postwar publications treated America's prosperity and growth alternately as a "miracle" and as a carefully tended flower requiring the right mix of business, government, and labor activities. Drawing on economists such as Solomon Fabricant of NBER and Jules Backman of New York University, Conference Board writers joined the chorus praising rising productivity as the socioeconomic equivalent of "miracle drugs" that could raise American living standards, enable the nation to exercise global leadership, and solve domestic social problems. The group's chart books, released at the board's annual May meetings, were glossy thirty- to forty-page booklets with attractively packaged economic statistics and glowing prose explaining the unique success of the American system and the nation's consequent preeminence in the global race for abundance. As early as 1943, the Conference Board argued that America's productive power was the nation's key to freedom. By the heady mid-1950s and early 1960s, it spoke of "future economic growth taken almost for granted," marveled that "our prosperity is so widely shared," and joined the popular parlor game of projecting doubled American living standards by the year 2000.[40]

Corporate Ads and Public Exhibitions

"Economic education" programs about the virtues of the American economic system were common in hundreds of large enterprises, and were often seen as a way of countering unions' communications to their members. These included newsletters, pamphlets, films, and classes. General Motors' Personnel and Employee Relations department published scores of pamphlets between 1948 and 1973 as part of its Information Rack Service. In *Design for Prosperity* (1950), GM predicted that, if radical ideas about "redividing the country's wealth" could be staved off, "there is every reason to believe that ways of life in our country will be improved far beyond our fancies and wishes." Booklets emphasized that rising productivity would lead to increased wages and lower prices, further raising living standards. The company eagerly argued that postwar America was a revolutionary new kind of capitalist democracy, the result of "one of the greatest social revolutions in history." Similarly, General Electric's employee magazine highlighted the responsibility that came with stock ownership. As the *Harvard Business Review* reported in 1952: "Practically every prominent leader of business in the U.S. today is talking about teaching economics to employees. Many of the largest corporations have launched economic education programs. . . . Hundreds of courses, pamphlets, articles, and advertisements have been written and printed. There has been a flood of movies, sound-slide presentations, films, lecture series, and discussion programs."[41]

Many companies' advertising slogans during the 1950s sold the idea of economic abundance as a social value at least as much as particular product lines. DuPont's tagline was "Better things for better living." General Electric told consumers, "Progress is our most important product," and

Alcoa promised that its products would ensure "carefree luxury." IBM ads proclaimed that the company was "helping science and industry produce more good things for more people." AT&T advanced the idea of people's capitalism by announcing in 1951 that "for the first time in the history of the U.S., a company is owned by a million people," updating this by 1959 to note that the company had 1.65 million stockholders. The link between national identity, patriotism, and measurable economic progress was explicit in the regular ads that Warner & Swasey, an Ohio machine-tools company, ran in major news magazines. Precursors of later "adver-torials," ads by companies from Chrysler to Texaco emphasized that only the U.S. economy could produce such abundance to satisfy all needs and create mass wealth "beyond anything the world has seen." Moreover, the cornucopia of plenty shown in TV ads, beginning in the 1950s, hardly could fail to convince Americans that a new America was here.

After World War II, American business also created exhibitions-as-messages that resonated with most Americans' image of themselves and their country, and their aspirations for both. Inspired in part by a 1948 Chicago Railroad Fair displaying a futuristic "X" train that would whisk Americans across the country at 150 miles per hour, Walt Disney began to embark on a secret project that would be nothing short of revolution-ary in shaping and mirroring postwar American culture—"Disneylandia." When the park opened in 1955 amid California orange groves and the hoopla of a live TV broadcast hosted by Ronald Reagan and a pantheon of Hollywood celebrities, it quickly became one of America's most iconic symbols. Disneyland—loved, hated, and analyzed to death—is certainly a complex cultural creation. On the one hand, as many scholars and visi-tors have noted, it hearkens back to a premodern vision of a small-town, frontier, quasi-Jeffersonian America. Yet part of the Magic Kingdom's cultural magic is that Main Street USA conflates a mythic American past with postwar beliefs to depict the United States as middle class, prosper-ous, and homogeneously so. As Karal Ann Marling has written, it "cel-ebrates the real-life pleasures of exuberant postwar consumerism." While many have focused on the nostalgic, mythic "history" of Main Street USA and Frontierland, Disneyland not only reinforced postwar self-images of America on Main Street but also as one turned right into Tomorrowland. This, as Marling said, was "a technological wonderland available for pur-chase on easy credit terms" and the "consumerist vision of the world to come." In Tomorrowland, and even more so at the later EPCOT Center in Disney World, Disney echoed and gave three-dimensional form to the

CED–Twentieth Century Fund–Keyserling–*Fortune* vision that economic abundance, married to technology, could cleanse America of any residual problems it might have.[42]

Cars raced on the Autopia freeway, much like those at GM's Futurama. Rockets carried visitors to the moon and Mars, just as Pan American Airlines later was to promise passengers. However, Disney's most remarkable exhibit was Monsanto's House of the Future, which made its debut in 1957 and survived, with eerie symbolism, until the eve of America's troubled year of 1968. Promoted as "featuring futuristic things you'll be able to buy in the future," and constructed entirely of synthetic materials, it presented a host of high-tech consumer goods seen as central to what all Americans could expect in their ever-advancing economy. Dishwashers cleaned with high-frequency radio waves, closed-circuit TV cameras introduced visitors, giant-screen TVs hung from the walls, "microwave" ovens cooked meals in seconds, remote controls manipulated appliances, and lights could be turned on and off with a clap of the hands. Perched on an above-ground pedestal and designed by MIT's Department of Architecture, the House of the Future was a taste of what middle-class Americans could look forward to, thanks to the virtuous cycle of a growing national income, undergirded by technology, and facilitated by—and facilitating—ever greater consumption.

World's fairs in the postwar era followed in the cultural footsteps of the 1930s fairs in Chicago and New York but included a greater emphasis on business messages about the wonders created by a growth-producing people's capitalism and a cold war internationalism in which America's way of life, measurable in dollars-and-cents consumption, income, and production, was superior to anything else on the planet. Much like Disneyland and overseas trade fairs and Expo '58 in Brussels, world's fairs such as those in Seattle in 1962 and New York in 1964–65 conveyed a similar set of American self-images and aspirations to tens of millions of visitors. The 1962 "Century 21" Exposition in Seattle offered a vision of a techno-consumer utopia filled with TV telephones, personal "gyrocopters" for transportation, hypersonic air travel, push-button kitchens, and personal computers. But abundance was not only calibrated in technological terms. The fair's souvenir program confidently predicted other economic advances ranging from twenty-four-hour work weeks to indoor swimming pools in every home. As in Tomorrowland, Seattle projected a technology-driven economic growth trajectory into the distant future of the twenty-first century.

The 1964–65 New York World's Fair—criticized for recycling the "corporate futurism" of the 1939 fair—also used technology to depict a new American "frontier" of science-driven consumer abundance. As author Roland Marchand noted of the 1939 fair, exhibitors shifted the message from "tour of factory" to "share our vision" of American life. Unlike Soviet displays of the era, images of production were mostly avoided in favor of ones of consumption. The Space Age, the Atomic Age, the Information Age of computers and communications, and the Consumer Age were all central themes of a fair that billed itself as a "Millennium of Progress." A remarkably creative array of gadgets—many that never made their way to consumers—were displayed in GM's Futurama II, GE's Progressland and Carousel of Progress, the Gallery of Kitchens, the Festival of Gas, DuPont's Wonderful World of Chemistry, the Kodak Pavilion, Johnson's Wax Pavilion, the Electric Light and Power Pavilion, and other pavilions, demonstrating to Americans that—thanks to their technology and economic system—theirs was the best of all possible worlds.

Futurama II portrayed a "near future" in which Americans would work, live, and vacation on the moon, under the seas, under the Antarctic ice shelf, in the jungle, and a futuristic city of "midtown airports, high-speed bus-trains, super-skyscrapers, moving sidewalks, and underwater conveyor belts for freight," with solar energy providing power—"all solidly based on fact." General Electric's dome-shaped Progressland depicted "progress" in similar terms—from the simplicity of a late-nineteenth-century home where "its inhabitants struggle" to today's "kitchen that all but runs itself" to the purported "first demonstration of controlled thermonuclear fusion." Not far away, the Better Living pavilion presented early 1960s America's "leisure life" and the "house with the most." The futuristic National Cash Register building and IBM's egg-shaped pavilion designed by Eero Saarinen displayed a tomorrow of miniaturized computing that could contain a Bible on a chip and retrieve news stories since 1851. Sure of America's future, Westinghouse offered a time capsule to "say 'hello' to the 70th century." And the abundant amenities of America's continually more prosperous homeowners, as at Disneyland and trade fairs, were a popular theme in exhibits such as Westinghouse's "Dream House," the American Interiors pavilion, Formica's "World's Fair House," and the "House of Good Taste and Better Living." In these, the fair's 51 million visitors were tantalized, thanks to their munificent economy, into seeing themselves living in four-story homes with "no fewer than three pools" and even an indoor barbecue pit.[43]

Between the 1940s and early 1960s business devoted unprecedented efforts, resources, and intellectual energy to communications about the nature of America and its economy. Never before was advertising used to convey an overarching political and philosophical message on such a large scale, and often these campaigns had the approval of the nation's political leaders. While partly motivated by a desire to restore business' good graces, perhaps, the threats of fascism and communism and the perceived antibusiness sentiments of the New Deal led corporate leaders to seek to reconceptualize in a clear, appealing way what America was all about. Rebutting Soviet propaganda may have played a role, but well before the cold war many believed that America needed an easily understood, coherent, and attractive way to describe itself to its own people and the world. As Theodore Repplier wrote in 1955: "Throughout much of the world, 'capitalism' has an unpleasant odor." The flurry of activity beginning in the mid-1940s by the CED, the Ad Council, the NAM, and the chamber was clear evidence that this was a high priority among business and political leaders. Vague talk about "free enterprise" and even an "American way of life," which had been tried with limited success, was no match for selling America as an earthly paradise of measurable material abundance. Business leaders came to believe that the task of expanding economic growth and providing broad-based abundance was central to what made the United States distinctive. Perhaps, reacting to ideas about the closing of the American frontier and economists' claims that America was a "mature," stagnant economy in the 1930s led many to assert that growth and expansion were not only possible but eminently American. The spectacular economic success of World War II undoubtedly emboldened business leaders to envision continued rapid growth. As traditional American ideals may have seemed frayed, and communism may have seemed a more cohesive ideology, in a postwar world of both rising aspirations and the need for a new idealism—in the United States and globally—a better, upbeat image of America's virtues was clearly necessary.[44]

The very fact that every major business association and many individual businesses got in on the act, spending what were then huge sums of money, speaks volumes, as does the fact that politicians of both parties, the media, and educators also eagerly reinforced these campaigns. While it was all well and good to talk of the Declaration of Independence and Constitution, or to pay homage to Washington, Lincoln, and Jefferson, the United States needed to be "rebranded" for a new era. The nation was a land of liberty, but it also was an economy of rising abundance. Key to the new image of America that business worked so hard to convey was the idea that no other country came so close to providing steadily rising incomes, assuring everyone of an economic stake in society, and providing a truly classless society. America could be judged—and judged a resounding success—by its material accomplishments and promise. Abundance, statistically demonstrable, was an easy sell. But the torrent of messages simply reinforced what the vast majority of Americans could see and feel in their daily lives. They had rising incomes. They had new homes. They had new cars. They had gadgets galore. Working hours were shorter, providing ample opportunity for leisure activities. The Advertising Council's "Miracle of America" and "People's Capitalism" or the CED's erudite pronouncements on the economy hardly seemed disingenuous or phony. This was the real America.

4
The Big Postwar Story

Of what stuff is the new nation made? It is made of wealth and the things that wealth has brought.

Newsweek, 12 December 1955

About everybody in America today is well-off.

U.S. News & World Report, 26 October 1956

Journalists recognized that one of the biggest stories of the postwar decades was America's dramatic economic growth and mass prosperity, and the changes that these were bringing about in American society, politics, and culture. Longtime *Fortune* editor Hedley Donovan recalled in his 1989 memoir: "It is hard to remember, now that we have had so much of it for decades, what a big story prosperity was. . . . We analyzed and celebrated the American boom—in prose, photography, paintings even, and of course in tables and diagrams and charts."[1]

The postwar era was a watershed in U.S. financial journalism. Financial reporting, which dated to late-nineteenth-century American industrialization, changed from a dry recitation of stock quotes and company earnings and puff pieces on businessmen and companies to broader stories about the national economy and what economic trends meant for average Americans. Readership of business publications expanded enormously during the twenty years after World War II, and economic reporting gained a more prominent place in major newspapers and magazines. What once had been intended for a small, well-heeled cognoscenti of mostly Northeastern businessmen was now geared to the burgeoning postwar middle classes, who were keenly interested in the changes transforming their lives and their nation. *Fortune's Changing American Market* (1954), for example, described itself as being "not solely for the businessman, the market research analyst or the professional economist. Rather [it is] . . . an exciting new kind of travelogue of the contemporary U.S.A."[2] Indeed, this "travelogue" was of an America painted in economic brushstrokes. Economic ideas and knowledge were much more integrated into financial journalism, as increasingly well-known economists wrote for, and were quoted.

Business journalists gave prominent play to economic concepts and new statistics such as the GNP, as well as the new role of government in the economy.

Postwar economic print journalism focused on a cluster of overarching themes, elaborated with a number of related subthemes. The big story—at once economic, sociological, and ideological—was that the United States was rapidly growing into a land of ever-rising abundance, thanks to a new, and uniquely American, economic system, in which almost everyone was a member of a prosperous middle class. The new prosperity, marked by measurably rising incomes and consumption, was a central preoccupation. Writing about America's emergent prosperity evolved from fearful amazement between roughly 1946 and 1948 to wondrous superlatives between 1953 and 1957. Liberally larded with economic statistics, articles regularly heralded new "records" being set, as if America's economic progress were the national sport to be tracked by elaborate box scores. CEA chairman Walter Heller, writing in *Life* in March 1961 likened the economy to a steady .300 hitter.[3] But the statistics were just scaffolding for writing that celebrated the growth of a newly affluent middle class, one that enjoyed "everyday elegance" and democratized "luxury." Everyone was getting richer, incomes were becoming more evenly distributed, and poverty was soon to be banished.

Commentators spoke of a "new era" of "people's capitalism," or a "changed America" that had conquered the business cycle, where "everybody's rich." The idea that a new chapter in the history of America and capitalism had dawned was a frequent subject, particularly after the Korean War, as *Life* even produced a wide-screen Cinerama movie called *The New America*.[4] Echoing many economists, business publicists, and government officials, journalists became enamored of the story line that postwar America, because of its economy, was a qualitatively new world, measurable by its economic achievements. Reportage had an almost utopian exuberance. The "new era" story typically highlighted several related ideas. For one, capitalism was no longer the exploitative, ruthless tyranny depicted by Karl Marx, Charles Dickens, or Lincoln Steffens but instead a new "people's capitalism" in which workers, responsible businesspeople, government, and assorted experts cooperated to improve living standards for all, and in which home-owning, stock-owning average citizens now owned the means of production. Mass production and, even more important, mass consumption were the linchpins of this new economy, facilitated by technology-driven productivity gains and a Keynesian calibration of aggregate demand. Thanks to government and the expertise of economists, the economy was no longer subject to severe depressions or the instability of uncontrollable boom-and-bust cycles. A hallmark of the new era was the advent of a "mixed economy" in which business and government worked together to ensure growth and prosperity, making government economic policy a central journalistic concern.

These themes led journalists to place increased emphasis on the U.S. "system" of "free enterprise." This newly ideological component of postwar economic journalism reflected contemporaneous business and government messages and the cold war. Stories highlighted the "freedom" of free enterprise, compared with the Soviet system, and America's comparative abundance and classlessness, especially in the late 1950s and early 1960s. The Advertising Council/U.S. Information Agency concoction of "people's capitalism" reflected the oft-reported quest for an explicit American ideology to counter communism in the struggle for the world's hearts and minds.

The Major Media

The *Wall Street Journal,* which had languished as an elite businessman's publication since its founding in 1889, expanded its coverage and increased its circulation sixteenfold between 1945 and 1961 under editor Barney Kilgore, from barely 50,000 to nearly 800,000. *Fortune,* cerebral and lavishly produced, expanded its circulation from 130,000 in 1939 to 325,000 by 1959, despite its high cover price and three-hundred-page issues. *Business Week* expanded rapidly, and *Forbes* more than tripled its readership between 1954 and 1964 to 410,000.[5] The rise in readership tells only part of the story of economic journalism's growth. Mass-circulation, general-interest publications such as the three major news magazines, *Life,* and *Reader's Digest* recognized that the in-depth stories appearing in *Fortune* and the *Wall Street Journal* could be successfully packaged and told to a vast middle-class audience. So too did newspapers such as the *New York Times.* This, in turn, reflected the increasingly prevalent belief that economics was no longer an arcane, technical subject but rather something about which every educated American should know and care. Thus, tens of millions of Americans were treated to at least digested versions of stories about the wonders of the U.S. economy. Magazines frequently supplemented the articles with colorful graphs and charts showing an upward trajectory of U.S. economic growth. Photos included tableaux of happy families as consumers and mighty mass-production factories. And articles generally quoted a wise economic expert or two.

Economic stories had appeared in opinion magazines such as the *New Republic* and the *Atlantic* during the Progressive era and the Depression, but they tended to reflect an older tradition of political economy. The first major business magazines—*Business Week* and *Fortune*—were founded in 1929 and 1930, hardly an auspicious time to report glowingly on the U.S. economy. Financial reporting was all but limited to generally flattering articles on companies and businessmen and short-horizon perspectives on business conditions that included only rudimentary data. The *New York Times* published an "Annual Financial Review" in the 1930s, but these were geared to the "business man, investor, banker and broker" and focused on stock and bond prices and U.S. and European finance[6]—quite unlike the "Annual Economic Reviews" that it published in the 1950s and early 1960s, which treated the economy in sociological terms and was more geared to its general readership.

Articles about "the economy" as a seemingly autonomous entity or about the social consequences of economic change began to appear in the late 1920s and 1930s, and stories about government economic policy surfaced during the New Deal. However, macro-level stories rich in economic data and overlaid with a philosophical bent only came into their own after the war. Many were written by economists, such as John Kenneth Galbraith, Leon Keyserling, and Sumner Slichter, who, for the first time, courted an educated lay audience. As a result, the number and caliber of those writing about the economy and business rose significantly. Many economists became staff writers, researchers, and columnists for major publications. Other journalists—from Washington political columnists to soft feature writers for *Ladies Home Journal, House Beautiful,* and similar publications—added significant economic dimensions to their stories. And several business journalists became top presidential aides or speechwriters—notably Gabriel Hauge of *Business Week,* Emmet Hughes of *Fortune,* and C. D. Jackson, of *Fortune* and *Time,* all of whom worked in the Eisenhower administration.[7]

Henry Luce's *Fortune* was by far the flashiest business magazine. Luce conceived the magazine in the late 1920s to remedy what he saw as journalism's failure to explain capitalism's success—a project he was unable to launch in earnest until after World War II. Under editor Hedley Donovan, *Fortune*'s mission "was exploring the American economy"—not just business—and "the interplay between the American economy and the society and the political order around it." As Galbraith, a staff writer for *Fortune* from 1943 to 1948, put it in his first *Fortune* article, in January 1944, business reporting needed to break new ground with "good coverage of the tightly fused relationship of one development to another."[8]

As we have seen, Luce began to introduce Keynes's ideas to Americans during World War II. *Fortune* supplements in November 1941 and October and December 1942—based on the secret work of Luce's "Q Department" on how to organize the postwar world and economy—were a foretaste. The seventeen-page 1941 supplement, "Roundtable on Demobilizing the War Economy," was based on a conference convened by *Fortune* in the Berkshires that drew together New Deal opponents, labor leaders, economists such as Galbraith and Slichter, and liberal businessmen such as Ralph Flanders. Articles by Galbraith, John Davenport, and CED cochair William Benton promoted Keynesian economics to hitherto skeptical business leaders and suggested that the postwar economy would be much different, and more dynamic and abundant than the U.S. economy of 1939. Galbraith's 1944 "Transition to Peace: Business in 194Q," with its reference to the Q Department, affirmed that Americans should be "expecting prosperity after the war." Comparing the British economist to Madison and Hamilton, Davenport's long profile of Keynes praised his "brilliance and stamina" in working to prevent future depressions.[9]

Reorganizing *Fortune* in 1948, Luce "defined its mission as not just the reporting of private enterprise but its active defense and articulation." The goal was to defend free enterprise, focus on big ideas, concentrate on political economy as much as business, and add new features such as the Business Roundup. The magazine, which had a staff of fifty-seven in 1954, established an in-house economics department in 1950 with economists such as Sanford S. Parker, Davenport, Charles Silberman, and Todd May publishing original economic analysis in the Roundup section and supporting six- to eight-thousand-word middle-of-the-book articles. Staff writers such as Galbraith, Daniel Bell (the labor columnist from 1948 to 1958), William H. Whyte Jr. (whose *Fortune* series became *The Organization Man*), and Eric Hodgins (author of *Mr. Blandings Builds His Dream House*) were given up to three months to write these features, with reporting assistance from the economics department and a researcher. *Fortune*—and in particular "Holly" Whyte—pioneered the new genre of "business sociology," which explored the effects of the new economy on the lives of managers and other white-collar Americans. It is noteworthy that three *Fortune* veterans wrote some of the most incisive critiques of a newly rich

America in Galbraith's *The Affluent Society,* Bell's *Work and Its Discontents*
and *The Cultural Contradictions of Capitalism,* and Whyte's *The Organization Man.* Yet *Fortune* epitomized the era's celebration of a "new era" and
a "new capitalism." As Daniel Bell said, the Luce magazines preached the
gospel of a productive new capitalism to business and the middle class,
while *Reader's Digest* played a similar role for small-town, lower-middle-
class America.[10]

Intended to be America's "most beautiful magazine," *Fortune* featured
art by the likes of Jacob Lawrence, Ben Shahn, and Saul Steinberg and
photographs by Margaret Bourke-White and Walker Evans. It was an early leader in public-opinion polling, hiring Elmo Roper in 1935. As a further
bow to quantitative economic reportage, it introduced its annual list of
the largest U.S. companies, the Fortune 500, in 1955. And thanks to Luce's
interest in big-picture stories *Fortune* became adept at covering and analyzing the economy's impact on public behavior and attitudes. The magazine
published four widely read multi-issue special reports conceptualized by
Donovan and Parker, each including a number of lengthy articles, that
were quickly turned into books: *USA: The Permanent Revolution* (1951),[11]
The Changing American Market (1954), *The Fabulous Future* (1956), and *Markets of the Sixties* (1960). The 1951 book updated a 1940 special issue, which
was a prelude to Luce's 1941 proclamation of the "American Century."
Fortune's February 1952 issue devoted one hundred thousand words to the
U.S. government, and its 1955 twenty-fifth-anniversary issue, with articles
such as "The American Breakthrough," "The New Economy," and "The
"Fabulous Future," mixed economics and sociology to speculate about
U.S. life in 1980.[11]

Equally revolutionary was the postwar transformation of the *Wall
Street Journal.* Managing editor Barney Kilgore greatly expanded the paper's reporting and emphasized writing style and comprehensibility for
mass audiences. He recognized that the dramatic American economic expansion that helped win World War II represented the leading edge of a
great and ongoing economic story that the *Journal* was uniquely placed to
cover. Under Kilgore, the paper's sixteen to thirty-two slightly oversized
pages featured six columns of lively writing and macro-level trend and
analysis stories about the economy as well as in-depth, more conventional business and financial coverage. Despite its editorial antipathy to big
government, the *Journal* recognized the new importance of federal economic policy, devoting a daily front-page column to government policy
and Monday, Wednesday, and Friday front-page columns ("The Outlook,"

"Tax Report," and "Washington Wire") to national affairs through an economic lens. Convinced that business reporting could appeal to more than executives and bankers, Kilgore also introduced a daily front-page column known for its quirkiness and stylish writing.[12]

While Kilgore broadened the paper's coverage, business manager Joseph Ackell developed a printing system that allowed the *Journal* to become the first truly national paper. With simultaneous printing at five plants around the United States by 1955, it could distribute copies to readers in every state. Circulation, which reached 145,000 in 1949, climbed to 295,000 in 1954, 570,000 in 1958, and 784,000 in 1961. Ad linage increased from 2 million in 1942 to 20 million in 1958. Throughout this period, the *Journal* tirelessly promoted itself with pitches such as "The men who get ahead read the *Wall Street Journal*." *Journal* executive Robert M. Feemster declared: "People who read the *Wall Street Journal* are not the ordinary kind. Each one is a person with ambition . . . [who] constantly strives to find a better way to work and live"—a goal that he equated with the "American way of life" itself. The *Journal* was so successful at attaching cachet to itself that in 1959 *Harper's* noted that readers liked to boast that it was their "favorite breakfast reading."[13]

While the paper's news coverage broadened significantly, the *Journal*'s editorials mixed ringing rhetoric about U.S. capitalism with partisan right-wing politics. Pulitzer Prize–winning editorial page editor Vermont C. Royster—who, with Kilgore, reshaped the paper in the postwar era—succinctly proclaimed the *Journal*'s philosophy in 1952: "Business, free enterprise, is the economic manifestation of the free society, the principal reason for America's pre-eminence." The *Journal*'s editorial policy was predictably pro–free market, pro-Republican, and anti-Keynesian. Truman was considered a neo-socialist; Eisenhower's policies were generally praised, but his administration's spending increases were criticized; and liberal Republican governor Nelson Rockefeller's 1959 plan to boost growth through expanded government spending was vigorously denounced. The paper's leave-business-alone philosophy was expressed well in a 1959 Christmas Eve editorial declaring that America's "abundance [is] due to our own efforts, not to a tax-stuffed Santa Claus."[14] The Santa editorial is illustrative of a liveliness that made the *Journal* quite different from the dry, little-read paper of pre–World War II days.

McGraw-Hill's *Business Week*, a drab, slender, publication of 32 to 40 pages during the 1930s, expanded to about 120 pages by the late 1940s and more than 300 by 1956. It had a large staff of domestic and foreign cor respondents, editors, and stringers, and its own economics department, long headed by Dexter M. Keezer and including Leonard Silk after 1957. Not as lavish as *Fortune,* this weekly included at least thirty major articles in twelve "departments" per issue in the mid-1950s, some running ten to fifteen pages, as well as eight regular brief features. *Business Week* articles explored the sociological ramifications of economics, liberally employed statistics and graphics, and were imbued with wonder about the new American economy. Like the *Journal,* its reportage tended to equate the economy with the nation, and like the *Journal* and *Fortune,* its stories and features suggested that the economy was a weighty, consequential subject, that government and its policies were essential to economic well-being, and that economic statistics—the more the better—were the way to keep score.

By contrast, *Forbes* remained a largely conservative mouthpiece for its flamboyant owner, Malcolm Forbes, and continued to focus on companies, executives, and investors more than big-picture economic stories. Pitching itself as the magazine that "speaks the language of business," *Forbes* expanded its staff in the early 1950s and published somewhat fewer vanity pieces on smiling, successful executives after Robert K. Heimann became managing editor.[15] The fifty- to sixty-page biweekly also increased its circulation fivefold between 1945 and 1960. By the late 1950s, *Fortune, Forbes,* and *Business Week* each had a circulation of approximately three hundred thousand.

The *New York Times*—a bellwether for other dailies' financial reporting—gave extensive and increasing coverage to the economy's growth and prospects, and used its Sunday magazine as a platform for many leading economists and popular economic writers. Government and academic sources were common in *Times* stories. The paper, like other major dailies and business and news magazines of the 1950s, devotedly covered the CEA's Economic Reports of the President with such gravity as to suggest the reports were wisdom coming from Mount Olympus. On 17 January 1952, for example, the *Times* reprinted the entire report in eleven pages of dense type, and most papers played it as a prominent front-page story.[16] Commerce Department and United Nations reports on the new subject of national income also received lavish attention.

However, nowhere was the *Times*'s newfound fascination with economics more apparent than in its annual economic surveys published in early January during the 1950s and early 1960s, a format copied by a number of magazines in the 1950s. This "National Financial and Business Review" section, about 45 pages long in the early 1950s, grew to become a 126-page "National Economic Review" in the 11 January 1960, edition. During the mid to late 1950s, these huge U.S. surveys were followed with lengthy surveys of the "world economy" and the economy of the "Americas." These massive, eight-column, advertising-rich sections included scores of articles, covering the past year's performance and outlook for every imaginable sector of the economy, including many arguably obscure sectors. The labor force, equities, banking, and consumption were treated exhaustively, with articles about such specialized subjects as hot dog consumption and telephone call volume; it is never quite clear whether the rationale for inclusion was sober comprehensiveness or human interest and humor.

Luce's *Time* and *Life* provided a distilled version of *Fortune's* reportage. *Time,* which aimed to cover every subject, albeit superficially, glanced off business and economic stories until about 1954, when it too came to realize that the booming, changed economy was the era's big story. Economic stories moved from the back of the magazine to the lead, National Affairs section. CEA reports warranted two-column stories, lengthy annual reports on the economy also had a healthy dollop of statistics to provide gravitas, and lead features beginning in the mid 1950s solemnly declaimed about the historic transformation of America. Although *Time* had no signed columns or articles during this era, a particularly influential figure in *Time/Life* economic coverage was John K. Jessup, the magazine's longtime business editor, *Fortune's* first editorial writer, *Life's* chief editorial writer until 1969, and the head of Luce's Postwar Q Department. Proposals for the postwar economy generated by this group—which also included Charles Stillman, Raymond Buell, and Galbraith—were first published before Pearl Harbor as a twenty-thousand-word supplement and reprinted as a pamphlet. These ideas were presented in *Time, Life,* and *Fortune* articles between 1943 and 1945.[17]

Luce's—and Jessup's—efforts to develop a postwar philosophy for America, and journalistic venues in which to convey them, continued from the mid-1940s through a prominent 1950 Luce editorial, "The American Business Economy," and well beyond 1960, when the Jessup/*Life* book *The National Purpose* was published. In his 1950 editorial, Luce said that "the American Business Economy, in a tacit deal with its government, has licked the most serious problem of the economic cycle, namely real want in the midst of plenty." The 1960 book, which included articles by Jessup, Adlai Stevenson, Archibald MacLeish, David Sarnoff, Billy Graham, John

W. Gardner, Clinton Rossiter, Albert Wohlstetter, James Reston, and Walter Lippmann, grew out of a 1960 *Life* series simultaneously published in the *New York Times* and thirty other newspapers and promoted by a like number of national organizations. *Life* followed with articles by presidential candidates Nixon and Kennedy. As a principal architect of the Time Inc. perspective on economics, Jessup helped bring Eisenhower Republicans and Kennedy Democrats under one big tent, believing that the American "system," with some fine-tuning, could bring the nation to the promised land of abundance. As Jessup wrote in 1962: "The American economy is the most marvelous machine for producing and distributing wealth, goods, and services in human history." *Life,* with its massive reach into the middle class, further popularized the great postwar economic story—as well as the language and outlook of economics—in upbeat articles such as "The American and His Economy," "Higher Income and More Luxuries in the Best Year of Their Lives," and "The Good Life."[18]

U.S. News, founded in 1933, combined with *World Report* in 1948, and expanded rapidly from about 50 to 160 pages during the early 1950s. It devoted up to one-third of each issue to economic and business topics. Although its back-of-the-book business section was a jumble of regular mini-features ("Trend of Business," "Plus and Minus: Indicators of Business Activity," "News-Lines for Business," "Finance Week," "Labor Week," etc.), the magazine frequently produced longer special reports on the U.S. economy and society. Strikingly, *U.S. News & World Report* printed many chapters of the President's Economic Report in their entirety, as well as lengthy excerpts of speeches and academic reports on the economy. The 13 January 1950, issue, for example, included a remarkable forty-two-page reprint of the CEA's report in tiny, ten-point font. The magazine also had a five-person Economic Unit, long headed by A. S. McLeod, and was liberally laden with statistics and charts, although less attractively packaged than *Fortune. U.S. News* leaned fairly hard to the right with weekly editorials by David Lawrence denouncing communism and federal spending, often in one breath, and conservative economist Ludwig von Mises was given twenty dense pages of one 1956 issue to vitriolically attack socialism. Yet, like other conservative, mainstream magazines, *U.S. News* began around 1953 to accept the Keynesian consensus and the idea that the U.S. economy could manage permanent prosperity.[19]

Newsweek's economic coverage followed *Time's* lead. During the first two decades after it was founded in 1933, *Newsweek* had a modest, six- to seven-page business section at the back of the book with dreary briefs on companies and new products. Between 1952 and 1954, big-picture economic stories began appearing in the National Affairs section at the front of the magazine, the business section expanded with more stories on the economy, a regular feature called Periscope began statistically charting economic trends, and a yellow-striped banner featuring an economic "special report" began to appear on the cover almost every other week. These reports in the late 1950s and early 1960s trumpeted the achievements of the new economy.

Conservative columnist Henry Hazlitt long wrote a *Newsweek* "Business Tides" column. Hazlitt, who had worked for the *Wall Street Journal,* the *New York Post,* and the *New York Times,* not only wrote for *Newsweek* from 1946 to 1966 but his 1946 book, *Economics in One Lesson,* sold seven hundred thousand copies and his syndicated columns reached millions more. Hazlitt played a significant role in introducing the work of conservative free-market economists Ludwig von Mises and Friedrich Hayek to an American audience. His 1959 book, *The Failure of the "New" Economics: An Analysis of the Keynesian Fallacies,* devoted 450 pages to deriding Keynesian economics almost point by point, emphasizing Keynes's alleged lack of originality, saying that he failed to refute Say's Law of Markets and overplayed the role of consumption, and that fiscal policy could not be relied upon to create full employment and growth.

Other mass-circulation magazines—*Look,* the *Saturday Evening Post, Reader's Digest,* and *Ladies' Home Journal*—took a similar tack. Even more than business or news magazines, these magazines domesticated the economy. They transformed concepts such as GNP growth, productivity, and government policies and business objectives into housewife-friendly topics ("The Fabulous Fifties: America Enters an Age of Everyday Elegance") and instructive tales ("If Our Pay Envelopes Are Fatter Now, It's Because Workers Produce More"). *Reader's Digest,* which billed itself as a "pocket university," reprinted many *Life, Time,* and other stories touting the new capitalism and the dawn of classless abundance. In articles such as "Wanted: A New Name for Capitalism," "America's Vast New Leisure Class," "Fresh View of Capitalism," "Revolution in the U.S.," "Second U.S. Revolution That Shook All Mankind," "Our Gadgets Set Us Free," and "What Marxism Promises, U.S. Capitalism Delivers," tens of millions of readers learned that a revolutionary new era had arrived.[20]

As mass-circulation, general-interest publications celebrated the new economy and trotted out statistics, many opinion magazines differed mostly in the sophistication of the message, only occasionally raising a critical voice. The *Atlantic*, the *Saturday Review*, and the *New York Times Magazine* tended to feature writers discussing the economy through the lens of mainstream New Deal/Keynesian liberalism. *Harper's*, the *New Republic*, and *Commonweal* were somewhat to the left, and only the *Nation* offered a more critical, leftist take on the new economy and society.

Prominent Harvard economist Sumner Slichter was a regular contributor to the *Atlantic* and the *New York Times Magazine* from the late 1930s to the late 1950s, singing a moderate Keynesian hymn to the mixed economy. Truman's liberal, fiery CEA chief, Leon Keyserling, also frequently wrote articles and letters published in the *Times Magazine*, the *New Republic*, *Harper's*, the *Washington Post*, the *Nation*, the *New Republic*, and elsewhere, and appeared on early TV news programs, sounding the clarion call for higher economic growth and increased public spending. Both Slichter's and Keyserling's articles were typically cover stories. Keyserling published twenty-three major articles in the popular press between 1947 and 1965, and Slichter contributed forty-seven articles between 1945 and 1959. Liberal businessman Paul Hoffman, who first wrote for the *Times* in 1929, continued to publish articles until 1971 (as well as for *Look, Life,* and even *Senior Scholastic*), and economist Alvin Hansen published thirteen articles. Galbraith, who had left *Fortune* for Harvard and Democratic politics, also frequently wrote for these more highbrow magazines. He was easily the most prolific between the mid-1950s and 1960s, publishing two dozen articles in the popular press in 1953 alone. Frederick Lewis Allen, chief editor of *Harper's* from 1941 to 1953, helped popularize the idea of a "big change" in postwar America. In articles such as "This Time and Last Time: Postwar Eras I and II," "Unsystematic American System," and "What Have We Got Here?" as well as his best-selling 1952 book, *The Big Change: America Transforms Itself, 1900–1950,* Allen was especially influential in arguing that a new America had emerged.[21]

As noted, in 1959 the *Saturday Review* began a distinctive fourteen-year collaboration with the Committee for Economic Development to produce elaborate annual special issues on the macro-level economic issues of the day. Each of these themed issues, released during the second or third week of January, included about a dozen articles by business and academic leaders. The series included the thirty-page "The American Economy 1959: A New Concept in Economic Reporting" and, in 1965, "The Challenge of Prosperity." The 1959 issue featured a dozen or so dense articles by CED leaders such as Marion Folsom, Paul Hoffman, Donald David, and Theodore Yntema, other businessmen, and Chicago economists Theodore W.

Schultz and W. Allen Wallis. They celebrated America's "solution" to the problems of mass unemployment and stagnation, the benefits of government economic intervention, and the economy's unlimited potential. While many issues focused on specific topics such as the Soviet economy, collective bargaining, and "education in the ghetto," both the 1959 and 1965 issues took broad-brush looks at the U.S. economy—its triumphs, its potential, and its problems. The inaugural *Saturday Review*/CED issue took an expansive view of the role of government, with Folsom calling for more spending on research, health, education, the arts, and improved human relations, and three articles calling for more "U.S. investment in a needy world." A recurring theme was the idea that the U.S. economy has had a historic, transformative effect on the world, bringing material wonders beyond the comprehension of anyone who had lived a mere twenty years earlier. As W. Allen Wallis, dean of the University of Chicago Business School, said: "We take it for granted that our economy is capable of infinite prodigies."[22]

Liberal economists such as Galbraith and Robert Lekachman offered more critical perspectives on America's "wasteful" "opulence" and "economic hypochondria" in *Harper's*. Other writers in the *New Republic* gently questioned the preoccupation with growth, and echoed Galbraith's call for greater spending on public needs. In general, however, the *New Republic,* under editors Michael Straight and Gilbert Harrison, were pro-growth, pro-Keynesian, pro-planning, and only mildly critical of the failures of an economy that left 6 percent unemployed in the late 1950s. The magazine became a platform for the out-of-office Keyserling to pontificate about the need to accelerate growth and criticize the Eisenhower administration for slow growth. The magazine devoted several issues to reports on the U.S. economy, with a remarkable 1962 issue featuring thirty-four dense pages of articles by eighteen leading economists such as Simon Kuznets, Walter Heller, Alvin Hansen, Gerhard Colm, Robert Solow, Kenneth Boulding, and Moses Abramovitz. This issue, headlined "Time for a Keynes," simultaneously praised the Kennedy administration for its "neo-Keynesian" emphasis on government activism to spur growth, graphically showed Americans' rising purchasing power, mildly endorsed the wealth-equalizing tendencies of "people's capitalism," and hailed growth as a panacea for poverty.[23]

The *Nation,* with its tiny liberal readership, was almost alone in taking a more jaundiced view of the idea that a beneficent new capitalism would bring a paradise of ever-rising wealth for all. *Nation* writers questioned the Keynesian "mythology of all-powerful fiscal policy." The magazine sardonically referred to Americans "so incomparably and beyond human experience filthy with money." It criticized the "cult" of ever-rising consumption as immoral, and prophesied that the bubble would inevitably burst. The *Nation* frequently argued for greater "community planning" to attenuate unemployment and economic insecurity.[24]

Will the Good Times Last? 1946–1953

Although the Luce magazines echoed some political and business leaders that an "economy of abundance" was possible after the war, most reportage in the mid-1940s reflected the earlier conventional wisdom that the United States was, in Alvin Hansen's words, a "mature economy" that had boomed because of World War II but was destined to slide back into depression as wartime production ended and millions of GI's streamed back into the labor market. Luce's 1941 essay "The American Century" was a notable exception. Many articles worried about whether "full employment" could be sustained. The efforts of the National Resources Planning Board, the CED, and other government and business groups to plan for a postwar era received widespread coverage between 1943 and 1945. The recurrent theme was that government and business needed to act wisely and decisively to create high purchasing power, which would maintain high employment and output.[25]

Thus, as the economy kept booming, there was widespread nervousness that it was only a matter of time before it would falter. After the war, many journalists clearly were apprehensive and puzzled about the U.S. economy. Since almost everyone expected a crash, or at least a deep recession, journalists had difficulty reckoning with month after month of continued economic expansion. *Fortune,* for example, asked in its December 1946 lead story, "The Boom: A Second Look": "What's happening to [the economy]? Something, but no one knows precisely what." *Time, Newsweek, U.S. News,* and the *New York Times* were equally tentative, with headlines like "Full Speed Ahead?" and "Boom: It's Started, but—." As Hedley Donovan recalled, although "the *Fortune* table of contents generally reflected a sense that the late 1940s were good years for America," there was "a precarious-seeming novelty" to the era's prosperity.[26]

The years between 1946 and 1953 offered many tantalizing, and reported-on, hints that a new economy was emerging. The uncertainty gave way to guarded optimism by May 1947, when the Twentieth Century

Fund released a much reported-on 840-page study, *America's Needs and Resources*. In it, twenty experts projected what America's economic capacity would be in 1950 and 1960. The report generated a nine-page spread in *Fortune*, filled with colorful graphs showing income, productivity, and consumption rising and the work week declining—although its forecasts for GNP growth turned out to be very low. News accounts were optimistic but hardly so effusive as commentary would become in the mid-1950s. "The U.S., without redistributing incomes, can produce enough to supply nearly everyone—but not quite—with a minimum standard of living," *Fortune* wrote. The *New York Times* devoted two articles to the report's predictions of the coming "boom," plus a review by Galbraith. In *Life*, the Fund's modestly optimistic conclusions were given a gloss in "Good Times a-Comin': Twentieth Century Fund Experts Forecast a Rosy U.S. Future." Luce's influential triad of magazines gave *America's Needs and Resources* considerably greater play than *Newsweek* or other publications. *Time* noted that the report countered the "mature economy" theorists, and presciently concluded that, "in light of current production, the report seemed conservative."[27]

Continued expansion and blue-ribbon forecasts of better times ahead, in sharp contrast to what Americans had been led to expect just a few years earlier, brought some journalists to conclude that they were onto a bigger story by the late 1940s. *Business Week* captured this nascent thinking in a 4 October 1947, article, "Our Postwar Economy—Bigger or Different?": "Everyone has been proceeding, in effect, on the theory that, while our postwar economy is bigger than it was before the war, it is not fundamentally different. We may be having a boom, to be sure—so that thesis goes—but it's bound to be followed soon by the inevitable bust. Only the bust hasn't come. Can it be that our postwar economy isn't just bigger, but also different? In a multitude of respects, the answer is a resounding yes."[28]

The contours of this new economy began to emerge for some journalists in the late 1940s. It would be one characterized by growth (albeit modest), not economic "maturity." More jobs would be created, as commentators eagerly watched to see when the 60-million-job mark would be passed. Productivity would rise. And the biggest sociological wild card—for a society that had lived with shortages during the Depression and war—was that consumption would rise for the first time since the mid-1920s. With its characteristic ideological patina, *Fortune* proclaimed in January 1948, at the beginning of the cold war: "Who's Utopian Now?

Democratic Capitalism Has Made Good on Most of the Socialist Promises." Business leaders Paul Hoffman and Eric Johnston penned articles for
the *New York Times* in the late 1940s advocating that a "democratic capitalism" must bring benefits to all.[29]

A brief downturn and the Korean War brought a lull to reporting about
America's new economy and prosperity between 1949 and 1952. Yet in
more than a half dozen stories in 1949 and 1950, Slichter offered a rosy
forecast for the U.S. economy. Keyserling wrote of planning for a $300 bil-
lion economy" in the *Times Magazine*,[30] and a 1951 *Fortune*'s series became
the book *U.S.A.: The Permanent Revolution*.

Reporting on the "New America" and "People's Capitalism," 1953–1965

Whereas stories of American abundance predated 1953, and the country experienced strong growth during the Truman years, it was only after
the Korean War that public consciousness began to accept that economic
growth and prosperity were here to stay. The liberal belief that the economy had changed in fundamental ways after the war—initially doubted
by conservatives—was reflected in a 1953 ad taken out in the *Nation* by
U.S. News, headlined "Seven Reasons Why the Bottom Won't Drop Out,"
which read like an epistle to the Keynesian, consumption-driven, mixed
economy. For the remainder of the 1950s, American readers were treated
to a cascade of stories about a new economy bringing unprecedented
prosperity and greater wonders ahead. Most articles were remarkably upbeat—from Frederick Lewis Allen's 1953 *Life* essay "Where Do We Go
from Here?" to *Look*'s "I Predict We'll Have Greater Prosperity." After
worries in the late 1950s generated by Sputnik, the 1958 recession, and
books critical of the consumer society, confident articles that the nation
had solved (or was close to solving) all economic problems again became
common during the Kennedy and early Johnson years. Articles gloried in
"the good life" and "the Soaring Sixties," and wondered about "the choices ahead for new prosperity" and "the challenges of prosperity."[31]

It is hard to exaggerate the sense of wonder about America's new, rising
abundance and how much in thrall journalists were to economic reports.
Time, in a splashy story on the CEA's 1955 report declared that "the story
between the lines of the Economic Report [is] as exciting a story as modern man has ever read." Describing the 1957 CEA report, *U.S. News &
World Report* sounded like a Hollywood publicist: "Since 1946, this coun-

try has had an explosion of growth. . . . An amazing story is told for the first time in a report by the President's Council of Economic Advisers." Similarly, a *Newsweek* publisher's note described its twenty-two-page cover story, "The Big Surge: The New America," as "the biggest story . . . we have ever attempted," telling for the first time of "a prosperity that had to be seen to be believed."[32]

Such articles clearly both shaped and reflected public attitudes. With its characteristic penchant for sweeping, synthetic statements and its desire to instruct the American people, *Life* provided a good synopsis of the "new America" story: "During the past dozen years or so we have been watching, in the U.S., something close to a miracle. . . . [The United States] has become—incredibly—a nation with full employment, sensationally booming production and the widest distribution of plenty ever known anywhere. . . . The once sick American economy has become the wonder of the world."[33]

Throughout the first Eisenhower administration, virtually every major magazine published lengthy articles, "special reports," and series surveying America's economic growth and describing the dimensions of American prosperity. Utilizing a host of statistics, quoting leading economists and government officials, and employing colorful graphs, journalists reveled in telling how U.S. output, productivity, consumption, and living standards had risen since World War II. *Fortune*'s yearlong 1953 series became the book *The Changing American Market,* and a nearly forty-article 1955 series became *The Fabulous Future.* With writers and editors seeming to love the sound of big numbers, articles provided a remarkable array of economic statistics to lend authority to the story line that America was rich and getting richer. As a 1953 *U.S. News* series, "Trillion-Dollar Country," began: "The United States is an immensely rich and rapidly growing country." Three years later, describing the 150 percent income increase since 1941 and its meaning for consuming every imaginable commodity, the magazine declared: "In 15 prosperous years, this nation has advanced far toward a cherished goal of New Deal days—'abundance for all.'"[34]

Going beyond reporting on mere week-to-week, or even year-to-year change, stories took up the mantle of history. As *Fortune* declared: "All history can show no more portentous economic phenomenon than today's American market. It is colossal." Or, as *Life* said in 1954: "Never before, so much for so many." *Look,* six years later, added: "No people in history ever had it as easy, or so good." The *Wall Street Journal* also proclaimed that "Americans are working under better conditions, are making more money, live in better homes, and have a higher living standard generally than their counterparts in any previous period of history."[35]

As in business and political rhetoric of the time, a recurrent trope in these articles was that the American economy was forever setting records. Publications developed a cottage industry in economic tracking and forecasting. They used newly developed government statistics, their own in-house economics and research departments, and business and academic studies by key economists, foundations, and research units such as the University of Michigan's new Institute for Social Research. Todd May, an economist who spent thirty-one years with *Fortune* and was hired instead of Alan Greenspan by Hedley Donovan in 1952, said: "Macroeconomic statistics, which were new in the 1940s, were very important to us. We became very close with technicians who did them in Commerce, Treasury, and the CEA." In addition to long annual economic roundups and forecasts in the *New York Times, U.S. News,* and the *Saturday Review,* many magazines began regular sections devoted to economic statistics. Regularly appearing statistical compendia included *Fortune*'s "Business Roundup," which billed itself as "a monthly report on the economic outlook," and *Business Week*'s "Figures of the Week" and "Charts of the Week." In addition, *U.S. News* offered "Plus and Minus" and *Forbes* the "Forbes Index," which tracked production, employment, hours worked, durable-goods orders, spending and saving, construction, and the money supply. This pairing of economic statistics with upbeat stories that translated macroeconomics into a tale of ever-rising personal living standards whetted the public appetite for ever more such reporting.

New York Times headlines such as "Robust Economy of the U.S. Smashes Many Records" and "U.S. Economy Enjoys Its Second-Best Year" sounded the same celebratory tone of the Luce magazines and other publications. *U.S. News*'s annual economic outlook sections in the first issue of each year also featured regular headlines such as "New Year to Set Some Records" and "Headed for a New Record in '57." A breathless *Fortune* series began in October 1956 with a long, graph-laden article called simply "What a Country!" Writing with a greater eye to history and sociology, and greater flair than other magazines, *Fortune* captured the emergent abundant society: "Never has a whole people spent so much money on so many expensive things, and in such an easy way, as Americans are doing today. Their appetite, as Hamlet put it, grows by what they feed on. In the exhilarating process of exchanging cash (or a signature) for goods and services, they even seem to be laying to rest the twin specters of 'saturation' and 'oversaving.'"[36] For a culture long accustomed to seeing "progress" in its midst—and which may have been less likely to see it in geopolitical or moral spheres during the cold war—economic statistics became the new, and most reliable, barometer of national progress.

Forecasting economic progress was as popular as reporting on records just broken. Whereas attempts at economic forecasting before the 1940s had been largely discredited by the Depression and wartime boom, the new knowledge, methods, and hubris of the economics profession made forecasting seem trustworthy by the 1950s. The prestige of CEA and other government forecasts, and weighty studies by the Twentieth Century Fund, the Rockefeller Brothers Fund, and other foundations, business and academic institutions imbued economic forecasting with an official seal of approval, and journalists eagerly reported on them. End- or beginning-of-the-year issues, as well as issues at the start of the 1950s and 1960s, were common venues for forecasts.

In 1955, *Fortune* published an article each month on the world twenty-five years hence by Adlai Stevenson, George Meany, David Sarnoff, and others. "There is no element of material progress we know today that will not seem from the vantage point of 1980 a fumbling prelude," Sarnoff wrote. The magazine developed and published its own economic forecasts every six months. *Newsweek* devoted almost its entire December 14, 1959, issue to forecasts for the 1960s, with economic predictions of 4 percent annual growth and 37 ½-hour work weeks as prominent as the technological predictions of automatic highways and self-operating lawnmowers. Writing about the "house of tomorrow" with its panoply of "labor-saving" appliances dated to the 1930s but became a staple not only of home magazines such as *House Beautiful* but general-interest magazines in the 1950s, as in *Life*'s Modern Living department. The intermingling of economic and consumer-oriented technological forecasts was common, as *Look* paired forecasts by five government leaders for "greater prosperity" with predictions of easier-flowing ketchup bottles. In an era enamored of science fiction, this style of techno-economic forecasting often took on a somewhat fantastic quality, as *Time* predicted that a 1953 newborn's family would be twice as wealthy before her high school graduation and that a worker a hundred years hence would produce in seven hours what was now produced in forty. The prevailing economic optimism was well expressed in *Look*, which predicted in 1960 that Americans would enjoy their "plentiful existence right through the sixties and maybe forever."[37]

Central to the story of America's postwar prosperity was the tale of the country's newly "affluent" middle class. The basic theme—told over and over in narrative, charts, and photographs—was that the accoutrements of the good life, once reserved for wealthy executives and professionals, were now available to almost all Americans. Not only was virtually everyone earning and buying more, but differences in income and, especially, consumption were diminishing. Americans were the "leisured masses," a homogeneous "new moneyed class," the "rich middle class," and the "high-income masses." *House Beautiful* wrote: "The luxury item of yesterday, owned by the richest few . . . is the necessity of today, owned by the many." On the eve of Eisenhower's reelection, Sumner Slichter wrote in the *Atlantic:* "The economic and social structure of the country has undergone a near revolution. . . . [Most wage-earners have the] same standard of consumption as professional and technical workers and many administrators. . . . The narrowing of the differences in incomes during recent years has been almost sensational," noting that the bottom fifth of the population had seen its incomes rise by 78 percent between 1935 and 1950, while the top 5 percent had experienced income gains of just 17 percent." *Life* perhaps put it most pithily, saying: "There seems to be a new trend toward people getting more and more on a level with each other in what they earn." Stories hailed these developments as the apotheosis of the American dream.[38]

Charts and stories purported to show that poverty and extreme wealth were now rare in the United States, as more or less everyone was "middle class," part of one vast "mass market." *U.S. News* remarkably opined that yachts and big estates were disappearing and that "about everybody in America today is well-off," while *Business Week,* in a four-part-series, wrote that "incomes are more nearly equalized." The realities of continuing differences in wealth and power, and sizable islands of poverty and lack of opportunity, were all but ignored until the late 1950s. The reduction of hardship for countless Americans since the Depression was often taken to mean that poverty had been vanquished thanks to the mighty tide of advancing abundance. *Fortune* and *Time* declared that the "elimination" of poverty was just around the corner in the mid-1950s, and *U.S. News* scooped its competitors by announcing in 1957 that "poverty was all but eliminated." The best evidence was not so much income statistics as consumption data. Nearly every American household now owned cars, telephones, household appliances, and other "gadgets," and enjoyed vacations—the luxuries of the prewar era. Journalists often reported on the "upgrading" of most Americans' tastes and wants. Elegant fashion, home design, and food were now available and enjoyed by all. *Business Week* announced that "the mass market has become a lot more massive and the class market has virtually disappeared." In an economic variant on the old "man bites dog" story, *Fortune* gleefully reported the presence of a Sears buyer at a Paris fashion show: "What it amounted to was an announcement to the world that the U.S. had achieved a living standard so high and a prosperity so widely distributed that the nation's largest purveyor to the average man had found itself obliged to keep abreast of the latest in haute couture."[39]

Many journalists, like academics and politicians, concluded that the nation had undergone nothing short of a revolution. This idea was first systematically presented by Peter Drucker in his 1950 book, *The New Society,* which opened: "The world revolution of our time is 'made in the U.S.A.'" This revolution was just as significant as that of the 1770s and, ultimately, would be far more important in world history than the Russian Revolution. The sense of wonder was palpable, as *Business Week* heralded "a new and mysterious society, an economy that no one really understands." *Newsweek* gushed: "What has happened in the past 10 years is that a new America has been created. . . . Of what stuff is the new nation made? It is made of wealth and the things that wealth has brought." Longtime *Fortune* reporter Dan Seligman recalled, "We certainly had a sense of being in a new era, and 1954 was the critical year."[40]

Many popular magazines produced lengthy reports or devoted entire issues to describing this "new America." It was a land measured by ineluctably increasing abundance, bringing luxuries and good living to everyone. Work would continue to become less onerous, as leisure would increase apace. As *Life* reported in 1964: "Americans now face a glut of leisure. The task ahead: how to take life easy." Writers loved to describe this new land in material terms with economic statistics and as a cornucopia of ever-more goods and services. Many argued that abundance would allow Americans to devote more energies to matters of the mind and spirit. In the parlance of John Reed's famous line about the early Soviet Union, reporters of the 1950s seemed to conclude: "I've seen the future, and it works." Only the "future" was none other than the present-day United States.[41]

Journalists, like politicians, business publicists, and academics, clearly grasped that the "new America" needed catchy yet ideologically potent descriptors if the nation had truly changed so much. Unlike the exploitative capitalism of yore, journalists explained, the new capitalism was a cooperative, egalitarian affair. Business, government, and labor collaborated to increase production and living standards, and both shared in the benefits. Labor was seen as an equal partner in the American pageant of abundance, although many business leaders and Americans worried about the inordinate power of "big labor." Classes—or, at least, the old-style "working class"—had given way to a single all-American middle class that shared the same objectives and putatively consumed the same things. The *New York Times* expressed the common view that other peoples simply did not understand that modern U.S. free enterprise was as different from nineteenth-century capitalism as night and day. As the *Wall Street Journal* declared in 1960: "We represent the nearest approach to a classless society." And *Business Week*, reporting on a 1959 Department of Labor report, said: "The separate identity of the 'working class' in this country is fading away."[42]

Workers, journalists reported, had attained most of their traditional demands, including higher pay, shorter hours, fringe benefits, and employment and income security. In the new America, all Americans' interests were the same—to produce more in order to consume more. In fact, Americans should no longer be described as "workers," a meaningless term that embraced thousands of disparate occupations. Instead, their true identity in the new America was as "consumers," homeowners, and stock owners. Journalists as early as the late 1930s and early 1940s began reporting the ascendant Keynesian argument that "demand," or consumption, was key to the new economy. However, the belief that increasing purchasing power was necessary to increase consumption only became a mainstream article of faith after the late 1940s. Almost anything that could increase consumption—technological innovation to boost productivity, government fiscal policy, even civil rights—was presented as a worthwhile goal. As *Newsweek*, quoting RCA president Frank Folsom, reported: "'Equal job opportunities for Negroes and other minority groups will increase the income of this part of our population and hence widen the market for many products.'"[43]

This message was conveyed by *Ebony*, the African American *Life*, since its inception in the late 1940s. The magazine, founded by John Johnson, put forth an image of an emerging, or future, black middle class that measured its successful march toward equal Americanness by metrics of income and consumption. *Ebony*'s frequently updated five-hundred-page *Negro Handbook* was like an African American version of the book-length *Fortune* or Twentieth Century Fund extravaganzas. Writing with similar superlatives, and similarly adorned with statistics, the 1966 *Handbook,* for example, spoke of "the past 10 years [as] the most significant in the history of Negro business," the "sizable," 53 percent increase in black income during the 1950s, and a parallel expansion of black consumption, with African Americans increasingly seeking a "luxury atmosphere and a degree of glamour."[44]

Like business and political leaders, journalists increasingly spoke of "consumers" as a synonym for "Americans." If brawny, Stakhanovite workers were the heroes of the Soviet Union, wealthy, free-spending consumers, typically women, were the heroes of postwar America. In the triumvirate of the abundant "new economy," business (or "free enterprise") may have been the dynamo driving production and innovation, and government may have served as the great "stabilizer," but consumers were the new embodiment of the American demos. By 1953, *Business Week* was ready "to crown the consumer as king of the American market." Similarly, *Fortune* approvingly quoted Eisenhower's CEA chairman Arthur Burns's declaration that the economy depends on the consumer. And *Time,* following Keynesian logic, credited the consumer as the nexus of a virtuous cycle that created more production, which in turn created more wealth, and went on to generate more spending. Consumption was not only a patriotic responsibility to boost the economy; it was also the fulfillment of the American dream. In the eyes of journalists and others by the 1950s, what else could Jefferson have meant when he spoke of "the pursuit of happiness"?[45]

As we have seen, this classless, cooperative, consumer-oriented "paradise" was the essence of what journalists, as well as politicians, business leaders, and cold war propagandists called the new, "people's capitalism." In 1956 alone, the phrase was used in thirty-two *New York Times* stories. Two articles, in *Fortune* in 1951 and in *House Beautiful* a half decade later, illustrate the media's enthusiasm. "Nothing demonstrates the strength of the American way of life and the adaptability of the American system better than the transformation of American capitalism. Fifty years ago American capitalism seemed to be what Marx predicted it would be and what all the muckrakers said it was—the inhuman offspring of greed and irresponsibility," *Fortune* reported. *House Beautiful* declared in 1956: "[This story of] how the American people benefit tangibly from their own labors is the story of American capitalism, the people's capitalism. The people's capitalism is, in short . . . the glory of America."[46]

Journalists who wrote about the "new America" or "people's capitalism" explicitly compared the U.S. system not only to the Soviets' but also to European capitalism and Gilded Age U.S. capitalism. Indeed, the glorying in America's economic abundance in these articles often veered into a shrill cold war juxtaposition of the United States with communist regimentation and penury. By the mid to late 1950s, journalists found a related story in U.S.-Soviet economic competition, with many wondering if the United States could always stay ahead. Comparisons concluded that the "U.S. economy far surpasses that of the Soviet Union." Yet, reporting on congressional hearings and blue-ribbon panels on the Soviet economy, many articles worried that faster Soviet growth might enable the USSR to overtake the United States, as Khrushchev predicted, unless U.S. growth accelerated.[47]

Beyond the high-consumption, cooperative, non-exploitative, home-owning, stock-owning qualities of the new American capitalism, journalists also highlighted the fact that America was no longer a laissez-faire economy (if it ever had been) but instead a "mixed economy" or a form of "welfare capitalism"—recycling the 1920s term—in which government social policies and Keynesian fiscal policies ensured full employment and income security and smoothed out the business cycle. When Eisenhower joined the bandwagon, supporting a "mild" welfare state, journalists were quick to report that most Americans had similar views. As *Time* proclaimed, Americans had "at last stopped thinking in terms of boom and bust" and were instead "thinking in terms of graph lines going upward." What a mixed economy should look like was contested, as some businessmen resisted government intervention and labor power, and some liberals and labor leaders pushed for more planning and social spending. Nonetheless, an increasingly broad swath of the political spectrum embraced the idea that government was a necessary and beneficial helpmate in realizing the new, abundant America. Twenty years after World War II had ended, and nine years after Robert Lekachman had proclaimed that Democrats and Republicans were all Keynesians, when *Time* put Keynes on its cover and quoted Milton Friedman as saying, "We are all Keynesians now," there were few dissenters.[48]

Government "Growthmen" as Midwives to Prosperity

On the one hand, business, "free enterprise," and the American people were variously credited with achieving the nation's prodigious output. On the other, journalists—with a few exceptions such as the *Wall Street Journal*'s editorial page and columnist Henry Hazlitt—described "government" and economic policymakers as "skillfully" eliminating the threat of depression and promoting prosperity. Conservative and middle-of-the-road publications felt no compunctions about praising, often effusively, the role of government. *Time* cheered "government's role in the twentieth-century breakthrough of American capitalism." *Business Week* confidently declared that, having "discovered basic techniques for reversing recessions, any present or future Administration would use those weapons," adding that "the longest business upswing on record is changing economic ideas that have been held for more than 100 years." Hedley Donovan, *Fortune*'s editor, recalled the prevailing view that America's "marvelously proficient" economy "had been strengthened by many government 'interventions' of the previous 25 years."[49] Again, a high-water mark in journalists'—and Americans'—faith in the mixed economy was the famous 1965 *Time* tribute to Keynes:

> In Washington, the men who formulate the nation's economic policies have used Keynesian principles not only to avoid the violent cycles of prewar days but to produce a phenomenal economic growth and to achieve remarkably stable prices. . . . In 1965 they skillfully applied Keynes' idea—together with a number of their own invention—to lift the nation through the fifth and best consecutive year of the most sizable, prolonged and widely distributed prosperity in history. . . . Washington's economic managers scaled these heights by adherence to Keynes's central theme: The modern capitalist economy does not automatically work at top efficiency, but can be raised to that level by the intervention and influence of the government."[50]

If government policymakers, Keynesian demand management, and fiscal policy were generally admired in America's media, the individual heroes were often economists. Although most academic economists toiled in obscurity, as did most economists in the bowels of federal agencies and big business, journalists lionized top presidential economic advisers as the architects of America's mass prosperity. As noted, a handful of other, celebrity economists frequently were featured in major magazines as authors or experts. Long before the 1960s counterculture and Reagan Republicans dealt their body blows to social-science expertise and the faith in wise public servants, these economists were treated as the best and brightest of the nation's leadership elite. The media lavished coverage on economic advisers such as the new CEA and its Economic Reports of the President. More than one newspaper described the first Economic Report, at the end of 1946, as "must reading." The *New York Times Magazine,* which featured lengthy interviews with Kennedy's incoming council members just days before JFK's inauguration, wrote: "The great influence of government policy on the nation's economy has made the CEA one of the key groups in Washington." A *Business Week* reporter wrote, tongue in cheek, that not all of Kennedy's advisers were economists.[51]

The general story line of the United States as a mighty economy hardly went away after the mid-1960s, yet the twenty-year postwar era clearly was the golden age for journalists to celebrate American abundance. This was a big, new story. It filled countless columns of type. It generated countless headlines. It attracted a huge audience, and it commanded their rapt attention.

A more critical culture and journalism after the late 1960s—not to mention economic difficulties since the 1970s—certainly dampened enthusiasm for the glowing economic stories that were such a staple of the 1950s and early 1960s. For many reasons—television being just one—articles became shorter, so the in-depth attempt to explain America became less feasible and fashionable. Only a foolish policy journal—not a mass-circulation magazine—would publish endless pages of a CEA or foundation report, as had been done in the late 1940s and 1950s. Moreover, financial reporting increasingly came to emphasize personal finance over national economics, as individual financial success came to loom larger for those with investment resources in a more economically stratified and narcissistic culture. Economics was as prominent as ever in U.S. media after the 1970s, but fawning macroeconomic stories increasingly were replaced by advice on how to catch the rising wave of securities or property markets. This, arguably, reflected U.S. culture's broader turn away from a we're-all-in-it-together mentality of abundance for all to what Vice President Joseph Biden's economic adviser Jared Bernstein has called a "you're on your own," or "YOYO," economy, in which the one with the most toys, or assets, wins.[52]

Nonetheless, the story of economics as the measure of America or Americans had legs. It was durable and powerful.

Financial journalism in the postwar era both evolved with and shaped the times. The intense interest of reporters, editors, and their growing readership in the big-picture story of American abundance was self-reinforcing. In tune with the messages of business, political, academic, and other leaders of the time, economic journalists reported and repeated the story of quantitative American prosperity and the qualitatively new society that it was creating. This was a big, heroic, confident story in an era when Auschwitz, Hiroshima, and Stalin evoked fear and pessimism about the human condition. It was a story that could be told with gusto—with the paraphernalia of weighty statistics, august expert reports, and dramatic photos. And it was a story that touched the average American, with the country's success made tangible in the paychecks, consumption, and lifestyles of millions.

However, it also was a complex story. It was nominally economic, which was why it was typically covered by the business press. Yet it went far beyond a dollars-and-cents account of output, growth, and sales. While Whyte's, and Luce's, "business sociology" captures some of its flavor, it also went beyond sociology. The reportage attempted to capture what America and American identity were becoming, which was why it found a major place in general-interest newspapers and magazines.

Yet journalism tells a story in more than one way. It recounts and relates facts as reporters and editors see them. But it also tells stories in the more normative sense of implicitly exhorting audiences to see the world in ways that media and other elites see fit. This is not to suggest that media function as a culture-industry cabal indoctrinating readers or listeners. By and large, journalists are neither stooges of media corporations, or business more generally, nor are they the reflexively liberal, critical elite that some have seen. Yet they are enmeshed or "embedded" in the culture in which they live. This is a culture writ small and large. It is the culture of influential intellectual, political, and business elites who formulate and refashion ideas to explain and guide the nation. It is also the culture of millions of Americans, worried about current issues, generally patriotic, and pleased or at least complacent about, the blessings of life that America has brought most of its people. While American newspaper and magazine readers were learning the new economic metrics to assess their country, their children also had a new lesson plan to teach them about the salient facts of U.S. identity, and cold war adversaries were given a varnished version of America's mighty economy. In these ways the postwar story of an abundant new America both reflected and influenced U.S. culture during the decades after World War II.

5
Defining the New America for the World

America's 44 million families own a total of 56 million cars, 50 million television sets, and 143 million radio sets. And they buy an average of nine dresses and suits and 14 pairs of shoes per family each year. . . . They hold their heads high as they proudly enjoy the highest standard of living of any people in the world's history.

RICHARD NIXON, Moscow, 24 July 1959

Indeed, the nation's leaders, with their economic and cold war advisers, recognized by the 1950s that the set of ideas about "what distinguishes us from the rest of the world" could be used to project this new image of America around the globe. While the U.S. government felt compelled to explain its policies and what it stood for to foreign audiences during both world wars, it was only during the Truman and Eisenhower years that the United States developed a large-scale, permanent capacity for "public diplomacy," or propaganda. The new programs were to curb the spread of communism and win economic and military allies by disseminating messages in a variety of media to discredit communism and extol the virtues of the United States. However, the messages sent, and the American virtues highlighted, shifted from the liberal idealism of the late 1940s to messages centering on American economic prowess, and what came to be called "people's capitalism," in the mid to late 1950s—messages consonant with those conveyed domestically.

This change in how U.S. leaders presented America to the world can be seen in U.S. propaganda magazines such as *Amerika,* a Russian-language monthly published for Soviet audiences between 1945 and 1952, when vigorous Soviet efforts to obstruct distribution led the United States to stop publication; *Free World,* a magazine sent to East Asia that began publishing in English and various Asian languages in 1952; and *America Illustrated,* a Russian-language monthly published for three and a half decades beginning in 1956, as well as many pamphlets, comic books, and other printed material for overseas audiences. During this period, while political and philosophical ideals of liberty, democracy, and freedom continued to be widely touted, print propaganda focused increasingly on more materialistic "virtues," such as the country's high and rising standard of living and its economic dynamism and growth. For example, in the early 1950s, U.S. overseas propaganda articles and booklets often emphasized America's time-honored "quest for freedom of mind and spirit," and belief that "all men are created equal in the sight of God." By the revised edition of the late 1950s, workers were still enjoying these pre-consumerist beliefs as well as "the fruits of people's capitalism." However, there was no more discussion about the "quest for freedom," "freedom of mind and spirit," or about all Americans being "created equal."[1]

The United States was a reluctant latecomer to the international propaganda business, although, after the Second World War, the Truman administration successfully argued that sharing information among nations promoted peace and a permanent information service was necessary. Intense domestic disputes continued into the early 1950s over the propriety, goals, and content of U.S. propaganda—with opinion ranging from George Marshall arguing that "people believe implicitly what we say," to U.S. ambassador to the Soviet Union Averell Harriman saying that America should tout its virtues, to his successor, Walter Bedell Smith, calling for head-on attacks on communism and the Soviet Union. Truman, Eisenhower, Kennedy, and the propaganda agency heads and advisers they appointed believed in the efficacy of U.S. propaganda in recalibrating attitudes about the United States behind the Iron Curtain and globally. Scholars and propagandists themselves have questioned how to gauge the effectiveness of a publication, a broadcast, or other propaganda. Many scholars believe that exposure and the familiarity created by propaganda generally lead to more positive views in target audiences, and that messages that appeal to the aspirations of an audience or deeper values tend to be most effective. Nonetheless, a 1946 joint congressional committee, describing the extent of anti-Americanism, "notably in the economic area," recommended that the government should assume a larger propaganda role. Congress passed the Smith-Mundt Act in January 1948 to "promote better understanding of the United States," bringing the Voice of America under the State Department's new Office of International Information and Educational Exchange, and a considerably expanded budget and staff to disseminate information about the United States through publications, print and broadcast media, motion pictures, and information centers.[2]

When Eisenhower created the USIA under the authority of the Smith-Mundt Act, all information programs except educational exchanges were brought under the aegis of the new agency and separated from the State Department. He also established an interagency Operations Coordinating Board, which swallowed Truman's Psychological Strategy Board and brought together the CIA, the NSC, the USIA, State, and other representatives. A long-suppressed 1953 study of the objectives of U.S. propaganda found deep divisions about whether to counter Soviet propaganda strongly or "tell the truth" about the United States, whether to fight communism or make people more friendly toward the United States, whether to serve as a "mirror" or "show window" for the United States, and—if a show window—which themes to portray. Only with the eclipse of McCarthyism in the mid-1950s did the USIA begin to grow. Under director Theodore Streibert, the agency inaugurated a campaign to deluge communist countries with magazines, pamphlets, exhibits and trade fairs, radio and TV shows, and traveling sports teams and other delegations. By the late 1950s, the USIA had twelve hundred overseas information officers and libraries in 162 foreign cities and was distributing millions of pamphlets and magazines (including *Free World* to Asia and *America Illustrated* to the Soviet Union), showing educational films to millions of non-Americans, and had mounted dozens of large-scale trade fairs.[3]

From Liberal Idealism to "People's Capitalism"

During the late 1940s, idealism about American identity was fueled and reinforced by a number of factors. The country had successfully led a world war to destroy fascism and bring the blessings of freedom and democracy to Europe and Asia. It had led efforts to create in its own image a United Nations as the linchpin of a rational, democratic world order. It was the benevolent benefactor helping to rebuild a destroyed Europe and Japan. In the early stages of the cold war, the Truman Doctrine posed the struggle as one between communist "terror" and "oppression" and a U.S. "way of life based on the will of the majority, distinguished by free institutions, representative government, free elections, guarantees of individual freedom, freedom of speech and religion and from political oppression."[4] Moreover, despite political setbacks for the more liberal wing of the New Deal coalition, many Americans looked fondly on Roosevelt's idealistic vision of a polity girded by his "Four Freedoms." It can be argued that the liberal, or more idealistic, view of the cold war did not really succumb to a more hard-edged Realpolitik until after the consolidation of Soviet rule in Eastern Europe in the late 1940s, the 1949 Berlin airlift, the 1949 "fall" of China, the outbreak of the Korean War in 1950, and the simultaneous beginning of McCarthyism.

Amerika, the glossy Russian-language monthly magazine, published fifty-five issues for Soviet distribution by the State Department's Office of International Information and Cultural Affairs (USIA's precursor) from late 1945 to 1952. The generally seventy-two-page, eleven-by-fourteen magazine featured varying combinations of stories about American political institutions, leaders and history, American arts and culture, a profile of a state or region, and Americana, with a smattering of other subjects. A content analysis of 157 articles in fourteen representative issues reveals that 43 percent were devoted to upbeat, *Reader's Digest*–style stories about American life, ranging from fashion, sports, and hobbies to motherhood, games, and holidays. A striking 26 percent were devoted to the arts, pointedly asserting that the United States had a vibrant cultural life. About 12 percent focused on America's democratic traditions and ideals. Another 14 percent addressed science and technology topics, ranging from advances in medicine to atomic energy. Just 6 percent were devoted to economic topics, and, with two or three exceptions that partially took a bigger-picture look at the nation's economy, these tended to focus on particular industries.[5]

It is striking the emphasis given to American political ideals and principles. A 1951 article described how "in a democracy, ideas compete, and democratic society constantly absorbs and digests the best ideas, responding with the necessary changes to meet economic, social and political needs." America's great political leaders and their beliefs were another common feature. Freedom of the press, freedom of worship, free scientific inquiry, and civil rights were subjects of six articles between 1946 and 1951. America's global role in promoting democracy and freedom also was frequently emphasized. A seven-part, seventy-three-page series called "A Brief Survey of American History," in 1948 and 1949, highlighted the country's abiding principles of "individual liberty, dignity, and self-government."[6]

This emphasis was mirrored in some of the pamphlets and booklets such as *The March of Freedom* (1952), which described the Declaration of Independence and the UN Declaration of Human Rights as the culmination of a "march of freedom" that began with Hammurabi's code." A *Primer for Americans* (1952) listed forty-one rights and principles gleaned by ad agency Young & Rubicam from America's founding documents, the golden rule, and common sense. At the same time that many pamphlets and articles extolled America's democratic virtues in the early 1950s, many also directly and scathingly attacked communism as the antithesis of American freedom. The most hard-hitting attacks on communism and the Soviet Union for foreign consumption coincided with the period when the most virulent attacks on communism were taking place domestically. During the heyday of McCarthyism from 1950 to 1953, U.S. readers were treated to more articles demonizing the Soviet Union and communism in *Reader's Digest* than during any other period in the magazine's long history.[7]

In some of the few economic articles during this period, one spoke of the government's responsibility for individual "security" and economic "stability."[8] More intriguing are three articles that appeared in 1950 and 1951, which began to tout America's "high standard of living" and a variant of capitalism that was creating an allegedly "classless society." A 1950 essay by economist Robert Heilbroner stands out in emphasizing the emergence of "the greatest economic well-being America has ever known . . . more widely and evenly shared than ever before: there are fewer rich, fewer poor, and more people in the middle."[9]

The shift to propaganda messages more focused on America's greatness lying in its economic strength and abundance began to get under way early in the Eisenhower Administration, in 1953 and 1954, after the Korean War and the worst of McCarythism had ended, and as propagandists at the newly formed USIA started to pull back from the strident anticommunism characteristic of 1950 to 1954. *Amerika* stopped publishing after 1952 due to Soviet efforts to stop circulation, and its successor magazine for the Soviet Union, *America Illustrated,* only began publishing four years later, when the political climate improved after Stalin's death and Khrushchev's liberalization. *Free World,* USIA's forty-six-page magazine for "the free nations of Asia" that began publishing in 1952, focused on East Asian subjects, but each issue also included at least two features about the United States.[10]

Discussions of American liberties still appeared along with articles about American prosperity, and discussions of abundance often were couched in terms of its underpinnings in American political freedoms. "America 1900–1950: Fifty Years Brings New Concept of Good Living for Everyone" described the country's transformation during the preceding fifty years in terms of "the goal of American democracy" being a "better life and equal

opportunity for all." Articles emphasizing American freedoms predomi-
nated, but, just as Heilbroner's *Amerika* article foreshadowed a change of
tone, a 1954 article by CED leader and Studebaker chairman Paul Hoffman, titled "Mutual Capitalism—An American System," suggested a new
way of defining America to the world. Picking up a theme that had been
gaining currency among opinion leaders in the early to mid-1950s, Hoffman wrote: "One of the deep sources of America's strength and prosperity that is too little understood both at home and abroad is the unique
character of our economic system. . . . It is a new kind of capitalism that
benefits everybody, not just the capitalists." He went on to claim: "In our
mutual capitalism, decisions are made by the many, rather than the few
. . . There are few have-nots in America . . . [and] most of us are property
owners."[11]

Hoffman, who also headed the Economic Cooperation Administration
that oversaw the Marshall Plan, argued in a 1951 book for a more aggres-
sive propaganda effort based on a "crystallized" "free world doctrine."
Although he began by rooting this doctrine in Christ's Sermon on the
Mount and the Declaration of Independence, he quickly turned to the
key selling point—"the new, socially conscious capitalism which, in the
United States, has been developed to an extent which the world as a whole
little understands; a system based on widespread ownership, diffusion of
initiative, decision and enterprise and an ever-widening distribution of its
benefits."[12]

The New America of People's Capitalism

Hoffman's and others' ideas that America embodied a "new" capitalism
began to take root in U.S. propaganda by the mid-1950s. Pamphlets such
as *Meet Some Americans at Work, Consumer Capitalism in Action* (1953), and
The Structure of the American Economy (1955)—of which millions of copies were distributed—reflect this change. The latter proclaimed: "A new
economy is evolving in the U.S. which has no parallel anywhere in the
world" both in "magnitude" and "structure." The ideas had gelled by
1955, but those selling the new America needed a catchy name for this
new order. Although some opinion leaders like Hoffman and New York
Stock Exchange President Keith Funston had been batting around the
term in the early 1950s, in 1955, T. S. Repplier, who headed the Advertising Council from 1942 to 1966 and maintained close relations with the
White House, and provided USIA director Streibert with the outlines of

a "people's capitalism" campaign that would include print, broadcast, and trade fairs. Repplier had spent much of 1955 evaluating U.S. propaganda efforts, concluding that they were too fair and balanced, too vague, and too focused on Soviet negatives. "Our propaganda "needs to sharpen its ideas," and counter the "unpleasant odor" that the term "capitalism" has in much of the world, Repplier wrote to Eisenhower. "There still exists an urgent need to make clear that a new economic system has been born—a system which gives more benefits to more people than any yet devised—a system I should like to call 'People's Capitalism.'" The name played off the communist use of "people's" and was intended to counter Soviet attacks on "Wall Street capitalism." In "People's Capitalism: Man's Newest Way of Life," which he wrote to accompany a trial propaganda exhibition at Washington's Union Station in February 1956, Repplier said that the United States had accomplished what the communists only promised—equal comforts and benefits for workers and bosses.[13]

"People's capitalism" had many enthusiasts in high places—from President Eisenhower and Henry Luce to Defense Secretary Charles Wilson, Treasury Secretary George Humphrey, and Commerce Secretary Sinclair Weeks, as well as prominent journalists. Between 1956 and 1960, pamphlets, articles, and trade fairs extolling American "people's capitalism" inundated every corner of the world within the USIA's reach. This became the dominant message of U.S. propaganda, and a good overview of these ideas can be seen in a three-part series in *Free World* in 1956 and 1957 that was linked to the USIA's worldwide "people's capitalism" exhibitions. "A New Name—'People's Capitalism' in America" began with the bold assertion: "'People's capitalism' is a term which accurately describes the economic system under which 166 million Americans enjoy the highest standard of living in the world today—a system that has been fabulously successful in benefiting not the few, but the many." Gushing with superlatives, this was a far cry from more cautious, late-1940s depictions of the U.S. economy providing "security" and "stability." Instead, the article—like many others to come—combined three principal features to make its case: an almost Soviet-like recitation of economic statistics, the story of an "average American," and florid, Panglossian language that all but suggested that America was on the verge of becoming the promised land. Average American "Ed Barnes" was shown playing with his three children in his five-room house, while his wife shops, above a caption saying that they "use only 29 percent of their income on the vast array of foods found in the markets." The article went on to explain that "Mr. Barnes is a capitalist because it is his invested capital, and that of millions like him, that industry uses." Stories about "people's capitalism" were widely published in the United States, although a few, like David Riesman, poked fun at the idea of America culturally winning the cold war by bombing the Soviet Union with consumer goods.[14]

Another article hammered home that people's capitalism was producing both a consumer's and a worker's paradise: "Competition [has] provided dream homes and powerful automobiles and labor-saving machines that are in the price range of the majority . . . [and is also producing] better working conditions, higher wages, and shorter hours." In "Classless Capitalism," the series' third installment, the author asserted that the new capitalism has brought "a time in history when men are equal as never before." Not only are they equal, but they are prosperous as never before, as "items formerly considered luxuries leap overnight into the category of necessities."[15]

A 1957 pocket-sized brochure, *People's Capitalism*—also a supplement to *Free World* and reprinted in a number of languages—captured the new ideology: "Capitalism in America is something new under the sun. . . . People's capitalism—far from creating progressive poverty—has spread wealth ever more widely among Americans." Noting the decline in the work week from seventy hours in 1900 to forty in 1956, it went on to say that the work week "may become still shorter in the not distant future. Meanwhile, an hour's work produces more and at a higher rate than ever before. . . . People's capitalism, by reducing the number of very rich and very poor, has produced a very large, growing middle class; the so-called 'class struggle' has lost its meaning in the United States. . . . The prosperity of the United States has all but removed want as a major social problem and leisure time increases steadily. . . ."[16]

It is striking how *Free World*'s formulaic Asian visitor stories also shifted from emphasizing U.S. freedoms to U.S. prosperity, as in a 1959 article by an Indian man. In "The Common Man in America," he wrote that Americans are "brought up on a religion of work, output and productivity. . . . [They] exert themselves to the utmost to make money and live well, [yet] curiously enough, they do not believe in amassing great wealth."[17]

Nowhere are these themes more evident than in *America Illustrated*, launched in 1956 as a result of a U.S.–Soviet accord, which was an expensive, full-color, *Life*-magazine-style monthly described by one former USIA officer as making "*Vogue* look cheap." A sixty-two-page magazine printed on large, heavy color stock paper, it cost taxpayers $2.92 per copy

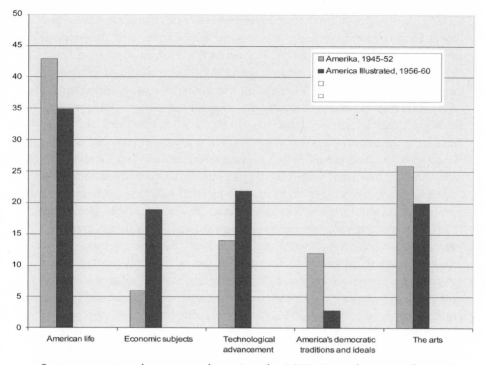

Content comparison between articles in *Amerika,* 1952–56, and *America Illustrated,* 1956–60

in the late 1950s, and about fifty thousand copies were sent to the Soviet Union each month. Describing itself as being about how Americans "live, work, and play," *America Illustrated* reprinted many articles from popular U.S. magazines such as *Collier's, Life, Look, Reader's Digest,* and the *Saturday Evening Post.*[18] What most differentiated its overall content mix from that of *Amerika* in the late 1940s and early 1950s was the new and frequent appearance of articles on Americans' high and rising living standards and the reduced number of stories on U.S. political beliefs and institutions. A content analysis of 106 articles in eight issues between 1956 and 1960 reveals that while 35 percent were still devoted to stories about American life, ranging from a boy and his cat to the traditions of Thanksgiving, 19 percent were about economic subjects and 22 percent focused on how technology facilitated American economic strength. The arts still accounted for 20 percent of articles, but stories on American political and philosophical ideals now made up just 3 percent of the total.

Many articles took up the message about America's new capitalism and remarkable growth, reveling in statistical superlatives and descriptions marveling about the fruits of the U.S. economy. Profiles of well-off "average Americans" and stories about the many consequences of prosperity were especially common. The lead article in the first issue, "America Today," reflected this changed emphasis: "The fabulous march of twentieth century technology and science has led to the most abundant and stable economy the country has ever known. It has wrought deep social changes in community and family living, in increased freedom and increased responsibility so far-reaching it is only beginning to be understood." The same issue included three other articles on high U.S. living standards—a profile of an oil worker whose family lives "in a comfortable house that Lou built himself," a story on American farmers' "production miracle," and a feature, "Vacation Time," describing how "most people take a trip." Average Americans included "Joe Giacoletto, a certified mechanic and shop steward," whose progress "Up the Labor Ladder" was evidence of the "system of job advancement worked out by management and labor at many American plants to give ambitious young workers an opportunity to get ahead." One story looked at three San Francisco workers who go home to "a place in the country for Jim, a city apartment for Keith, [and] a sunsprayed suburban hillside for Martin." Yet another paired a bookstore manager and a steelworker who "each has achieved, in substantial measure, the good life as they see it."[19]

Unlike *Amerika*, whose economic articles focused on particular industries, *America Illustrated* included many stories about how "people's capitalism" touched people's everyday lives. "Revolution in the Kitchen" described how the American housewife spent "less than half the time in the kitchen than her mother did a generation ago, yet her family is getting a better-balanced diet and a bigger and better variety of foods than ever before." The cornucopia of consumer goods was featured in articles such as "City of Stores for the Suburbs," which described America's new shopping centers as offering "a vast variety of goods and services to satisfy the whole family's needs," and "Shopper's Paradise," which told of the miracles of the modern American department store. America's abundant leisure was highlighted in "Leisure in a Changing Society." "Vacation Time" wasn't just about most people taking a trip; it also touted vacation opportunities ("Boats for Everybody"; "Second Homes for Family Vacations"). "Teenagers' Economics" told of "the billions of dollars pouring into their hands every year," and "Assembly Line Home-Building" boasted that standardized construction "gives the homeowner a better house at a lower price." Articles about U.S. fashion, home decorating, and new car models contributed to the image of America as the consumer's paradise. Several late-1950s articles celebrated that Americans could afford to buy twice as much food as they could thirty years before, that the population had 61 million phones, and that Americans had so much leisure that long and varied summer vacations were a commonplace.[20]

Bigger-picture articles about America's remarkable economic growth were especially common by the late 1950s. "Ten Amazing Years" and "Decade of Growth" lavishly described America's advances on every imaginable indicator—from "medicine and automation" to "rising worker's wages and family income, increased farm productivity, higher school enrollment, stronger old-age protection, and wider automobile ownership." As the author of "Ten Amazing Years" wrote: "This picture of a vigorous United States, drawn in text and charts, shows how the restless energy that has characterized the American people continues to find and conquer new frontiers of economic and social well-being." "Facts about the U.S. Income" trotted out economic statistics to prove that "the redistribution of income is a significant fact of American life today." The 1959 article went on to claim that taxes make the accumulation of great wealth difficult, labor legislation has improved the bargaining position of workers, and steadily rising income levels have been accompanied by a shorter work week and a wide variety of supplementary benefits, paid by employers and government."[21]

"The Changing American Society," by *Fortune* writer Robert Seligman, made clear that the United States had achieved the communists' purported goal of classless, measurable prosperity. "The traditional concept of class divisions has become totally inaccurate. In contemporary America, occupational distinctions are blurred, incomes increasingly cluster at the middle range, and families of diverse social and economic backgrounds are ever freer to choose their styles of living. . . . No longer burdened with the struggle for economic survival or rankling under invidious social distinctions, more and more Americans have the security and leisure to experiment more freely in taste and idea."[22]

Amid this panoply of tributes to America as a great economy, *America Illustrated* largely eschewed any articles on America's political heroes or the country's history.[23] Instead of the ideals-filled seven-part U.S. history featured in *Amerika*, readers of *America Illustrated* would discover an America where every worker was a capitalist, had a comfortable home, sent his children to college, took vacations, had a boat or vacation home perhaps, and had a multitude of things to buy. To the extent that freedom was discussed, it was mostly in the context of describing the freedoms that enabled America to prosper. The shift in U.S. propaganda emphasis can be seen in the subtly different conclusions to a 1953 edition and a 1957 edition of a fifty-page comic book, "A Picture Story of the United States," which went through huge print runs in multiple languages for distribution to Asia, Latin America, and the Middle East. The first edition concluded that America's "story has been one of quest . . . quest for opportunity, material happiness, quest for better ways of doing things, and above all, quest for freedom, freedom of mind and spirit, for all men are created equal in the sight of God." Four years later, the story ended with America's "economic transformation," in which "92 percent own real estate," and workers are "enjoying the fruits of people's capitalism." The final line again mentions the "quest for more opportunity, material well-being and better ways of doing things," and the need to make "freedom secure" but no longer talks about the "quest for freedom," "freedom of mind and spirit," or of all men being created equal.

A host of late 1950s pamphlets, with hundreds of thousands of copies printed in a multitude of languages, repeated these themes: *The American Consumer: Key to an Expanding Economy* (1960) approvingly quoted French observer André Siegfried describing the new American economy as "surely one of the great achievements in the history of mankind." Reprising the argument from his book *People of Plenty,* David Potter provided a similarly grand historical patina in *The American Economy* (1960): "When Americans saw that for the first time the possibility of having more than enough to go around was a reality and not a dream, they set themselves another goal which fitted well with the goal of democracy. This was the goal of creating a rich economy with a wide distribution of material benefits."[24]

Trade Fairs

The idea that U.S. economic abundance was the best way to sell America led to a raft of trade fair exhibitions in cities around the world between the mid-1950s and early 1960s. Amid concern that the Soviet Union was besting the United States in the propaganda war of the early 1950s, Eisenhower created a Special Emergency Fund in 1954 for government to partner with corporations to exhibit their wares and the new American image. The Departments of Commerce and State and USIA collaborated with major U.S. companies, the National Association of Manufacturers, and leading designers on scores of fairs. After fifteen fairs in 1955 under this "emergency" authority, Congress passed the International Cultural Exchange and Trade Fair Act in late 1956 to demonstrate "the contributions being made by the United States economic and social system toward a more peaceful and fruitful life for its own people and other people throughout the world." AFL-CIO leader George Meany spoke of the inseparability of "material abundance" and freedom in America. The trade fair program was ratcheted up at fever pitch, to the point that ninety-seven exhibits in twenty-nine countries were sponsored in 1960 and seen by an estimated 60 million people.[25]

Most exhibits featured a model American home, complete with the latest appliances, together with films and displays of other consumer goods. Lawnmowers, color TVs, juke boxes, synthetic fabrics, not to mention free blue jeans, Pepsi, and cornflakes became the ambassadors of the American way of life from the first "people's capitalism" exhibition in Bogotá in late 1956 to Kabul, and Poznan to Moscow. An entire U.S.-style supermarket was installed at a 1957 Zagreb fair. Child-oriented exhibits at the 1957 Barcelona and Milan fairs and the 1958 Brussels fair emphasized the link between an abundant economy and healthy, happy children. The connection between abundance, technology, and domesticity was emphasized in the fairs' appliance-bedecked kitchens. Frequent fashion shows were used not only to juxtapose svelte U.S. models with their more matronly Soviet counterparts but also to demonstrate that America's economy allowed all of its people to enjoy the latest fashions. A monthly magazine and exhibit on the New York Stock Exchange at the 1958 Brussels World's Fair expressly paired the voting machine and stock exchange as twin expressions of America.[26]

Trade fairs became the object of intense cold war rivalry. In the much reported-on "battle of Brussels," the U.S. government poured resources into the American exhibition. Noted architect Edward Durrell Stone designed a huge circular pavilion, and a "House of Tomorrow" like one recently opened at Disneyland was installed. The best known example of U.S. trade-fair diplomacy and the people's capitalism argument came with the 1959 American National Exhibition in Moscow—made famous by the Nixon-Khrushchev "kitchen debate." The Moscow exhibition, made possible by a cultural agreement that also facilitated a parallel Soviet display in New York's Coliseum, was open in late July and early August in Sokolniki Park. Organized by USIA and Commerce, the American pavilion was a huge geodesic dome designed by Buckminster Fuller—an icon of overseas displays of U.S. abundance through Expo '67 eight years later in Montreal. The exhibition included short films on the American workday by Charles and Ray Eames and on American leisure by Billy Wilder, fashion models enacting lavish American weddings and casual American barbecues, endless technology, and free Pepsi that generated long lines of curious, thirsty Russians. The centerpiece was a prefabricated fourteen-thousand-dollar ranch house contributed by Long Island developer All-State Properties and furnished by Macy's and General Electric, displayed as the average American's palace of comfort and technology. The home featured an RCA Whirlpool "miracle" kitchen, a robot cleaner, foods from General Mills and General Foods, and a home workshop.[27]

In the often-told story, Nixon and Khrushchev toured the exhibit together. Nixon then delivered a speech, "What Freedom Means to Us," in which he said little about American rights and liberty but instead emphasized the "extraordinarily high standard of living" in the United States, America's achievement of "prosperity for all in a classless society," and suggested that the Sears catalog was the best book about America for Soviets to read. Khrushchev—who had vowed to surpass the United States economically by the late 1960s—basically shared Nixon's belief that the cold war would be won by which economy could bring abundance to the most people. As the two men paused in the model kitchen, Nixon proudly argued that the kitchen's cornucopia of consumer goods—emblematic of general U.S. prosperity—was the essence of America; that democracy meant the ability to choose from limitless goods; and that America had advanced to a new level of freedom. Indeed, the American Way was clearly conflated with the American Standard of Living. Although the Soviet newspaper *Izvestia* lambasted the American pavilion—asking, "What is this—a national exhibit of a great country, or a branch department store?"—Nixon easily "won" the kitchen debate.[28]

6
Beyond Civics and the 3 R's

The U.S. economy in 1962 is something of a miracle. . . . [It] is an awesome wealth-creating machine of incomparable magnitude. It is difficult for an American to describe it without sounding like a pompous braggart.

Scholastic magazine, 18 April 1962

In the quarter century after World War II, American children increasingly were taught to understand their nation, its history and greatness in economic, rather than political, philosophical, social, or moral terms. School children learned that the U.S. economy was an unprecedented marvel of productivity and a facet of Americanness of which to be proud. During this period, economics became a much more prominent part of social studies, history, and other classes, and an economic education movement emerged to develop and promote the understanding of America as an "economy." By the late 1950s and 1960s, a broad consensus developed that learning about the economy's workings, the roles of various economic actors, and U.S. economic achievements was critical for young Americans. Truman's first Council of Economic Advisers (CEA) chairman Edwin Nourse referred to economic education as a "high calling." Solomon Fabricant, research director of the National Bureau of Economic Research, called it "capital formation," and AFL-CIO research director Stanley Ruttenberg said that economic education was "vital if our economic system is to survive."[1]

During the first half of the twentieth century, as attitudes toward children and child rearing changed, child-labor laws took effect, public education began to expand, and the first flickering of a children's consumer market appeared, Americans began to think of children as citizens and not as insensate appendages to their parents. Early public education in the nineteenth century had generated textbooks and "readers"—many which instilled patriotic values and told narratives of the "American story." However, it was only after World War II, as universal K–12 education became a reality and children increasingly became Spock-pampered, business- and cold war–inspired "American leaders of tomorrow," that opinion-leaders considerably ratcheted up their efforts to influence America's children. There were many messengers—the educational system, advertisers, popular culture, and child-oriented "movements" such as scouting. Likewise, many messages were conveyed—ranging from what is good behavior and the need to oppose communism to what commodities and experiences are desirable and what is the essential nature and meaning of the United States. American freedoms remained central to social-studies lesson plans, but the idea that America's exceptionalism also resided in its measurable abundance was new. Older children were hardly oblivious to the messages of a new "classless abundance" presented to their parents by political leaders, business, and the media, but the very consistency of these classroom messages with broader societal discourse about America as an abundant economy is striking.

It is all but impossible to reconstruct what actually occurred in hundreds of thousands of classrooms with millions of teachers and tens of millions of students, but textbooks and other curricular materials provide a proxy, albeit imperfect, for what children learned about the United States. Thus, it is telling to compare school texts before and after the mid-twentieth century.

Learning about America, 1900–1940

In the late nineteenth and early twentieth centuries, schoolchildren consistently learned that the United States was exceptional because of its devotion to liberty and democracy, as well as its achievements in forging a great nation out of a supposedly virgin continent. While messages taught in schools always have been contested to various degrees, schoolbooks consistently celebrated America—though not always uncritically—as a great nation. That greatness had resided in the master narrative of hardy, pious, freedom-loving (white) settlers forging a new democracy, taming a continent, becoming a beacon of liberty to the world, and rising to world dominance. As an 1875 school textbook said, America is "the land designed by God for the home of liberty," and an 1879 McGuffey Reader insisted that patriotism be based on values of "equality and the principle of representation." The idea that school textbooks should promote national cohesion and a widely agreed-upon basis for American patriotism began in the aftermath of Reconstruction, when, as is often observed, the United States became a singular, rather than a plural, noun. Charles

Morris's *Young Student's History of the United States* (1900), for example, emphasized the importance of learning history for children to become citizens and Americans to "be made the noblest and happiest of all the people of the earth."[2]

The most famous textbook of the early twentieth century—and, perhaps, the most influential history textbook in U.S. history—was Barnard College professor David Saville Muzzey's *American History.* First published in 1911 but updated and reissued into the 1970s, Muzzey revered the Founding Fathers, the Enlightenment, and what Louis Hartz later described as an America cast in the image of Lockean liberalism. With a picture of George Washington on his frontispiece, Muzzey rooted American culture in Anglo-Saxon Europe and American politics in Jeffersonian idealism. Economic and social history were largely absent from the early editions, and Muzzey hearkened back to an agrarian, white ideal, condemning both the "heartless exploitation" of capitalism and the threat posed by "hundreds of thousands of aliens [who] come to our shores."[3]

Muzzey's Progressive contemporaries, in texts such as Willis Mason West's *American History and Government* (1913) and Albert Bushnell Hart's *School History of the United States* (1920), treated the Revolution and Constitution as the sacraments of American civilization, yet—like John Dewey—viewed learning about America as a vehicle for social reform. Charles and Mary Beard's *History of the United States* (1921) told America's teenagers about Jefferson's "Republican simplicity," invention as "the very warp and woof of American progress," and "the tremendous, irresistible energy of a virile people." Rivaling Muzzey, Connecticut schoolteacher Mabel Casner and Yale professor Ralph Gabriel's *Exploring American History* (1931) was primarily geared to junior high school students and survived in revised editions into the 1970s. Casner and Gabriel celebrated the United States as a model of virtue among nations, highlighting "nine fundamental ideas" about "how the U.S. has promoted world peace," the marvels of how "the machine changes the American way of living," and how America "offers an opportunity to start life again" to the "suffering peoples of Europe."[4]

Yet these and other texts of the 1920s and 1930s also reflected a sense of America not fully living up to its ideals of equality. Such qualities largely disappeared from schoolbooks of the late 1940s, 1950s, and early 1960s. No works expressed this better than Harold Rugg's 1930s textbooks. *A History of American Civilization: Economic and Social, Man and His Changing Society,* and *An Introduction to Problems of American Culture,* with 5 million in print, were the single most popular U.S. history texts of the New Deal era. Rugg celebrated the drama of America's settlement, urged children to be "tolerant, understanding and cooperating citizens," and his *History of American Government and Culture* came to the startling conclusion that "industrial civilization" had brought seven benefits but sixteen "difficult problems." He wrote of better living standards, greater longevity, shorter working hours, and expanded education and leisure but also of "unequal distribution of the national income," most Americans' inability to attain a "minimum comfortable standard of living," increasing commercialism and materialism, growing "indifference" to public life, and increasing conformity. Not surprisingly, Rugg became a bête noire, as the American Legion, the National Association of Manufacturers, and the Hearst newspapers vilified him. He was brought before the anti-communist Dies Commission, his loyalty questioned, and his textbook publishing career was all but ended.[5]

Telling America's Story in the Postwar Era: A Teleology of Abundance

After World War II, history and social studies textbooks changed dramatically, reflecting the new influence of the economics profession and the rise of a postwar political consensus that economic growth could solve all problems, and echoing the sophisticated business public relations led by the Committee for Economic Development, the Advertising Council, and a new business journalism. The years from V-J Day until the end of the Korean War and McCarthyism were a time of transition. Dissenting books such as Rugg's disappeared, but the most important change was in the image of America to which millions of schoolchildren were taught to pledge their allegiance. Frances Fitzgerald has noted that history and social-studies textbooks' portrayal of U.S. homogeneity was greatest in their "reporting of economics in American life," although they virtually never hinted at any economic inequality or injustice, or any relationship between economics and power. Ralph Volney Harlow and Ruth Elizabeth Miller's 1947 *Story of America* presented U.S. history as showing "how our predecessors triumphed over difficulties, solved major problems [and have] given us our freedom." Beginning to reflect the emerging postwar emphasis on American economic success, the authors noted that, while it was long "fashionable to condemn" business leaders, "American business has brought great advantages."[6]

It is noteworthy to see this shift by examining subsequent editions of the same text. The 1950 edition of Fremont Wirth's *The Development of America* opened with a description, illustrated with a drawing of covered wagons, of the book as about "American ideals and institutions." Like many texts, it lionized America's creation and the elaboration of its fundamental principles by its revered Founding Fathers. The twentieth century received short shrift, with little or nothing said about the emergence of a consumer society, rising living standards, or even the New Deal. Forebodingly, the 811-page tome ended with Americans feeling "a sense of grave responsibility." By contrast, seven years later, an updated version of Wirth's popular text discussed U.S. economic might throughout the book and opened with an almost poetic paean to prosperity: "America is a strong and wealthy nation." A sixteen-page opening color spread on American ideals, subsumed under "the American way of life," now included Freedom of Enterprise and Individual Ownership of Property. Instead of his 1950 image of covered wagons lumbering across the prairie, Wirth began his 1957 book with a portrait of modern abundance: "Powerful cars moving smoothly along superhighways; swift ocean liners plowing through great harbors; skyscrapers pushing up into the blue; wide acres of wheat waving across the prairies; fields of cotton ripening in the sun; busy little shops lining Main Street; factories turning out thousands of products; and all across and up and down the land, millions of students like yourselves hurrying back and forth to school. This is America today."

Even more remarkably, the Jefferson who was lauded for his commitment to "equal and exact justice" in 1950 had become the man who "emphasized the importance of free enterprise." John D. Rockefeller, a villain of Wirth's 1943 textbook, was now a hero, as tables on rising corporate profits and consumer spending prominently were featured. Finally, the twentieth century, the subject of two of forty chapters in Wirth's 1950 book, warranted a dozen chapters in 1957. Instead of facing "grave responsibilities," contemporary Americans now had TV, atomic energy, and prosperity for all. Highlighting the country's "tremendous economic growth," Wirth described the change in American capitalism from the exploitative robber barons to a "popular capitalism" that had given "the American Consumer a high standard of living, which in turns makes possible mass production and mass consumption."[7]

A similar change can be seen in the continuing series of Muzzey textbooks. His 1945 *A History of Our Country* echoed the strongly moralistic tone of his earlier books, insisting that the United States is not about the false gods of money but its enduring ideals of liberty, democracy, union, and the achievements of the pioneers. Critical of "worshipping the golden calf," not giving all Americans their "fair share," and "our preoccupation with material success," Muzzey hailed "the threefold motto of the American republic as 'Liberty, Democracy, Union'" and concluded by urging students to be "more faithful" to the Founders' ideals of liberty. By 1955, Muzzey not only had changed his frontispiece from a somber-looking George Washington to a collage of progress from a tepee and explorers to giant office buildings and factories. He also apparently had changed his mind about the beneficence of business. The Constitution was still a "wonderful achievement" and Jefferson was still lionized—albeit now more for the Louisiana Purchase than the Declaration of Independence—and the robber barons were now "our great captains of industry" who "could hardly help growing rich" and brought "our modern industrial prosperity." Moreover, he added four chapters on "How Our Reunited Country Increased in National Wealth and Power."[8]

An even more dramatic transformation is evident in the succeeding postwar editions of Howard Wilder, Robert Ludlum, and Harriett McCune Brown's *This Is America's Story*. The 1954 edition opened with a catalog of America's leadership in production of refrigerators, cars, radios, and washing machines, despite a conclusion titled "What Can Each Citizen Do to Help Build a Better America and a Better World?" Whereas the 1954 edition called for collaborative effort to address national problems, by 1963 the authors felt confident enough to declare that business, labor, and government had "solved the problems" of modern America. Moreover, the hierarchy of American qualities of which to be proud had been inverted, as the 1963 edition featured a fourteen-page introduction highlighting seven defining attributes. The first four emphasized America's demographic and economic size and power, while republican government and the global defense of liberty were relegated to the last spots. The very scale of American abundance was such that if anyone had predicted it, they "would have been thought completely mad." Unit eight, which focused on the first half of the twentieth century in both texts, metamorphosed from 1954's long disquisition on the arrival and contributions of immigrants to become a story of "growth and change . . . [of] modern conveniences and labor-saving machinery . . . greater leisure and increased opportunities [and] reduced working hours."[9]

By the mid-1950s and early 1960s, school textbooks seemingly could not get enough of the story of America's transformation into an abundant land of popular capitalism. But transformation from what? Was this a change from high-minded ideals of liberty and equality—to which lip service was still paid—to an economy whose dominant characteristic was its growing prosperity? No one said it quite so bluntly, but the role and meaning of the older ideals were no longer what they had been in texts prior to about 1950. Less and less did the word *freedom* connote the ideals of the Bill of Rights. Free enterprise was now the backbone of the American system. Rarely did a textbook of the 1950s or early 1960s chastise the nation for not living up to its ideals, or implicitly challenge students to make their land what the Founders or Lincoln had called for—a land of liberty, justice, and equality for all. The ideals were now like wallpaper—a pretty background adornment that was not pondered too deeply, and not the big story.

Henry W. Bragdon and Samuel P. McCutchen's *History of a Free People* (1954), for example, opened with the statement: "In terms of wealth and strength the U.S. is one of the great nations of the world—probably the greatest. . . . Amazing productive capacity has given it the world's highest standard of living." Number one on the authors' list of ten qualities of "Americanism" was economic opportunity, and chapter 1 began with the Reverend John Higginson declaring: "Lord thou hast been a gracious God, and exceedingly good unto thy servants. . . . We live in a more comfortable and plentiful manner than ever did we expect." Although the authors extolled the virtues of freedom, the first of three freedoms described was "freedom of enterprise," which "encourages the production of goods which Americans enjoy in abundance."[10]

Freedom still figured prominently in 1950s titles, but this may have been an artifact of the cold war. Like Bragdon and McCutcheon's *History of a Free People,* however, Gertrude Hartman's *Land of Freedom* (1959) presented American history as if it were a two-act play—the first about the "adventure" of the nation's early history, the second about "a century of industrial progress." The teleology is clear—from "Land of Promise" in chapter 4 to "Land of Plenty" in chapter 27. After graphically illustrating this in terms of the hundred-fold growth in ice-cream production between 1900 and 1957, Hartman told her students:

> Today, the standard of living of the people of this country is the highest in the world. They have better food, better clothes, better houses than any other people. The majority of American homes are equipped with a host of modern household appliances and labor-saving devices. There are more electric lights, more telephones, automobiles, radios, television sets, and other con-

veniences than in other countries. The people have more leisure, with all that this means in the way of recreation, education, and opportunity for cultural improvement.

Students were encouraged to work hard to create ever more abundance for all: "This is the challenge which our democratic society must meet." Historian Allan Nevins contributed his two cents in a foreword to Hartman's book with a summation of U.S. history: "It is a story of the conquest of material wealth . . . to create a standard of life such as the world had never before known."[11]

Cold war themes jostled with abundance for prominence in 1950s textbooks. Edna McGuire and Thomas B. Portwood's *Our Free Nation* (1954) told students "how fortunate you are to be living in a free land" and that "there exists today a mighty struggle between the free nations and those whose freedom is not allowed." A few textbooks, highlighting American freedoms, even touched on the still unsecured rights of African Americans, and offered a puritanical critique of the material "selfishness" and "wastefulness" of a people who should be devoted to higher ideals.[12] The liberal winds that began blowing in mid-1960s America were evident in texts that started to note such problems as racism and environmental degradation alongside their cheerleading about the nation's GDP growth. Lewis Paul Todd and Merle Curti's *The Rise of the American Nation* (1966) mentioned the contemporary "age of anxiety" and the challenges of civil rights and poverty, and introduced women as worthy of a sidebar in an eight-hundred-page text.

However, Todd and Curti cited Frederick Lewis Allen, describing the mid-twentieth century's "democratization of our economic system, or the adjustment of capitalism to democratic ends." The final chapter described "Americans building an economy of abundance" and ushering in "a new epoch in human history." In "Where Karl Marx Was Wrong," Todd and Curti pointed out how "the great majority of Americans share material comforts and recreational and cultural advantages undreamed of by even the wealthiest people a half century ago." Another mid-1960s textbook, Johns Hicks, George Mowry, and Robert Burke's *A History of American Democracy* (1966), also told students that a new era had dawned in their lifetimes. "The abundance produced by business, and its widespread distribution among all classes" characterized modern America, and "the new business system was described as a people's capitalism and a democratic capitalism." Likewise, Princeton historian Arthur Link's 1968 *The Growth of American Democracy: An Interpretive History* ended with "storm clouds" in Vietnam, juvenile delinquency, and the "Negro Revolution." However, his book, completed in 1966, remains a basically optimistic story of reforms addressing problems throughout U.S. history and the advent of "breathtaking" prosperity that had nearly solved the age-old problem of poverty, citing statistics that led him to ponder whether the nation was headed toward a "classless society."[13]

Scholastic Reports on the "Sweep and Power of the American Economy"

Scholastic magazine, another venerable source of social-studies learning in America's schools, reinforced these messages with its distillations of contemporary journalism. *Senior Scholastic, Junior Scholastic,* and the company's stable of magazines for younger children seem to have been cribbed from Luce magazines such as *Fortune* and *Life,* the CEA's Economic Reports of the President, and the CED's or Twentieth Century Fund's reports. It is noteworthy that the upbeat reportage on American abundance was so thoroughly replayed for teenagers and children. "Scholastic Teacher," the section at the back of each week's issue, featured ads for largely business-produced educational films such as the Arrow shirtmakers' *Enterprise,* General Motors' *American Miracle,* U.S. Rubber's *Finding People for Products,* and the Institute of Life Insurance's *American Portrait,* as well as booklets such as the Ad Council's *The Better We Produce, the Better We Live,* the CED's *Toward More Production, More Jobs, and More Freedom,* and the Pure Oil Company's *Fifty Fabulous Years.* The importance of understanding economics was emphasized in a 1956 article on "Requisites for Economic Literacy," and a 1961 report included a forty-five-page appendix for teachers, featuring "Study Materials for Economic Education in the Schools." Schoolchildren and their teachers also were treated to periodic, glossy, sixteen-to eighteen-page General Electric supplements such as a 1950 comic book showing a progression from Colonial Williamsburg to the present, when, "Yes, Jane, inventive industry is working harder than ever to bring us wonderful new things tomorrow," and a 1956 ode to "the overall [technological and economic] progress of the American people."[14]

Even if *Scholastic* was not exactly original, it was a sophisticated forty-eight-page publication that offered fifteen-year-olds a more complex understanding of the world than many early-twenty-first-century media do for adults. Foreign news, U.S. political news, science, and world religions, not to mention economics, were given prominent play, together with features on sports and a "Boy Dates Girl" advice column. Recognizing its audience's rapidly growing buying power, *Scholastic* also featured ever more ads—for everything from Coke, cars, and the U.S. Air Force to Breck, Cover Girl, and even engagement rings. A 1953 Chrysler ad touted the company's role in "helping to bring about the miracles of tomorrow."[15]

The special features and weekly coverage devoted to the economy are notable for their messages about America. The first major feature, in 1950, included seven articles and twenty-one pages about "America's Economic System." The magazine opened with the familiar trope of American socioeconomic exceptionalism: "In this half century, the United States became the richest and most productive nation in the history of man. With only 7 percent of the world's people and 6 percent of its land area, we produce about 50 percent of the world's industrial products and about 40 percent of the world's goods and services." Praising "America's miracle workers" for their productivity, the magazine quoted GE president Charles E. Wilson that "there are undoubtedly fewer real economic distinctions between rich people and poor people in the U.S. than in any other country in the world. . . . Truly we are a nation of wealthy people." Two articles summarized the Twentieth Century Fund's *Productivity—Key to Plenty* film and *U.S.A.: Measure of a Nation* book, telling youth that poverty and other social problems soon would be washed away in a tide of prosperity. "How We Can Make America Better?" pondered ridding the country of slums, poor health, racial problems, and the rapid depletion of resources but ended optimistically, concluding that "the marvelous progress America has made in the past 50 years demonstrates that these things are not only possible—they are within our grasp." A special issue, "A Look into the Future, 1950–2000," included articles by Paul Hoffman, David Sarnoff, and others predicting "ever increasing abundance" and a "Golden Age," suggesting that such wealth would make questions of life's meaning central, and even predicting a "radio mail system" that foreshadowed many attributes of the Internet.[16]

In 1951, *Scholastic* reviewed the Brookings Institution's play for children, *The Dynamic Economy: A Dialogue in Play Form,* reprinted a Twentieth Century Fund–NBC radio play on business and citizens working together (*Partners in Velvet*), and announced America's "Production Miracle." An article by AFL president William Green noted the many areas where "management and labor are in complete agreement . . . that ours is a dynamic, expanding industrial system based on free competition. . . . It has produced the greatest output of consumer's goods and the highest level of general welfare for the common man of any nation in the world." After the Korean War, *Scholastic,* like the news magazines, even published an annual economic issue, touting the U.S. economy's achievements. Eisenhower's and Kennedy's Economic Reports were given prominent play. Ike was quoted as saying that "high levels of production, employment, and income will be broadly sustained. . . . We have broken through to new and higher ground."[17]

Also featured was the idea of America representing a "middle way" between collectivism and robber-baron capitalism, or achieving a new form of "democratic capitalism." One article digested a speech, praised by Eisenhower, by Smith College history professor Massimo Salvadori that noted the disparity in earnings between the average executive and farmer was much less in the United States than in the Soviet Union. A 1959 special series, "Americans at Work—Case Studies in Economics," celebrated worker productivity as the font of American prosperity, and a special issue, "The American Economy 1962—From Main Street to Wall Street," featured ten dense articles that provided sweeping characterizations of American abundance and strikingly detailed topical coverage of the economy. The special issue examined government's broad powers to stimulate the economy, misconceptions about excessive corporate profits, and the benefits of "slashing the tariff" while worrying about the "hard-driving and effective [Soviet] economic system" and whether the prospect of doubling living standards in twenty-five years would leave Americans "soft, jaded, and corrupt." But the chief takeaway message of "The Sweep and Power of the American Economy" was that "the U.S. economy in 1962 is something of a miracle. . . . [It] is an awesome wealth-creating machine of incomparable magnitude."[18]

The Economic Education Movement

History textbooks and *Scholastic* magazines were not the only vehicles used to teach American schoolchildren to think about their nation as a marvel of abundance and, more generally, about the United States as an economy. The perceived importance of viewing the world through an economic prism led a coalition of business leaders, educators, economists, and politicians to advance the idea that schoolchildren deserved special training in "economic education" to cultivate "economic literacy" and appreciation for the American "free enterprise system." Postwar economic education was not just for kids. Many employers provided workplace education on "the American free enterprise system." Several efforts were made to use the new medium of television to teach economics to the public. And college economics curricula expanded with the profession's newfound prestige. However, the most elaborate aspect of the economic education movement focused on secondary and elementary students.

The earliest forays into explicitly teaching children economics, with a twist, were part of the National Association of Manufacturers' and U.S. Chamber of Commerce's late-1930s and World War II–vintage efforts to link "the American way" with the "free-enterprise system." Despite the culturally inhospitable climes of the Depression and the New Deal, the NAM launched a "You and Industry" series of primers and filmstrips for schools in 1936. One film, *America Marching On,* narrated by Lowell Thomas, described the United States as "marching" upward to higher living standards and more leisure under the greatest politico-economic system ever known. During the 1940s, a revived "You and Industry" series emphasized industry's role in U.S. material and social progress. The NAM's free monthly newsletter, *Trends in Education-Industry Cooperation,* was mailed to nearly fifty thousand K–12 educators and administrators. The chamber's school materials, like many NAM efforts of the time, smacked more of anti-FDR propaganda than economic pedagogy. The NAM also produced and presented *Industry on Parade* each week on NBC-TV from 1950 to 1960, and *The American Economy,* produced by the CED and others, was broadcast on CBS from 1962 to 1964.

While the NAM-chamber efforts did reach many schoolchildren, and "Business-Education Days" were launched in 1946 in Michigan and other states by local chambers for teachers to learn about business, the economic education movement is generally dated to the creation of the Joint Council on Economic Education (JCEE) in 1949. G. Derwood Baker, an education professor at New York University, began meeting with CED leaders after the war to devise ways of getting economics into the school curriculum. Their efforts led to a first, three-week workshop in August 1948 at NYU that brought together administrators of thirty-three city school systems, seven state departments of public instruction, CED leader Beardsley Ruml, Twentieth Century Fund president J. Frederic Dewhurst, union representatives such as International Ladies' Garment Workers' Union education director Mark Starr, and even CEA chairman Edwin Nourse. Baker, who headed the JCEE from 1949 to 1955, described the workshop as "a first attempt to help teachers, curriculum developers and school administrators develop a realistic understanding of the functional operation of our economy." However, Dewhurst captured what was to be the true flavor of much economic education. Reprising his massive 1947 report, *America's Needs and Resources,* he spoke of "America's fame" stemming from "our immense standard of living" in which one-fifteenth of the world's people produced one-third of its goods. The link to national goals was made explicit by the dean of NYU's School of Education, Ernest O. Melby: "If we are interested in the survival of our way of life, there is no kind of education more important than that which seeks to make the average American intelligent about our economic system and effective as a citizen in relation to it."[19]

Yet there was tension in the movement's objectives. Baker, Nourse, and many economists believed that economics education was critical for students to better understand their world and become better citizens. The CED and the Twentieth Century Fund—later joined by the Ad Council, the NAM, the Chamber of Commerce, the Ford Foundation, and others, and which paid many of the bills—agreed that economic education was for the sake of better citizenship. However, they partially defined better citizenship as greater productivity, output, and consumption, and an understanding of America predicated on its prodigious economic capacity. The heavy cold war overlay that American freedom depended on growth and prosperity, which brought both power and its citizens' happiness and loyalty, was often explicit. JCEE economist Lawrence Senesh described the four goals of economic education as the promotion of "growth, stability, security, and freedom." Similarly, a 1949 Michigan State College workshop report stated these overlapping goals: The purpose of the "American economic system . . . is to enable every individual to become a happy and useful citizen." The underlying message was of urgency to increase U.S. economic production and strength and ensure a society of abundance. As an educator told Congress, "First graders can learn that the faster and better men can produce goods and services, the more wishes and dreams can be fulfilled."[20]

The movement was a decentralized network of local committees, with workshops around the country to provide teachers and school administrators with in-service professional development. By the mid-1960s, there were forty-five state, local, and regional councils of economic education. Efforts also were made to get schools of education, economics departments, and business to collaborate to provide preservice training for teachers and develop curricular materials. Despite the strong backing of the CED, the movement grew slowly at first. Many economists initially

balked at simplifying their work for students, although figures ranging
from Nourse to *Fortune* journalist Todd May advised the JCEE and partici-
pated in their workshops during the mid-1950s. The American Economic
Association (AEA) only deigned to lend its support in 1957, but its, and
others', support grew substantially over the succeeding decade. After a
1955 conference on the training of future teachers at Saranac Lake, New
York, the JCEE established a College and University Program in 1957 to
foster collaboration between schools of education and economics departments to teach aspiring teachers. With the AEA's backing, about fifteen
"centers of economic education" were created at colleges such as the
State University of Iowa and Purdue University. By the 1970s, there were
more than two hundred such centers.[21]

Shortly after M. L. Frankel succeeded Baker in 1955, the JCEE began
publishing extensive bibliographies of supplementary materials for classroom use. The first thirty-six-page bibliography included an eclectic array of materials produced mostly by business associations and companies
such as the Advertising Council (*The Miracle of America* and *An Examina-
tion of the American Economic System*), the chamber (*Free Markets and Free
Men*), the American Institute of Management, the Conference Board, the
NAM (*Industry's Goal: Building a Better America*), the CED, the American
Bankers Association, Chase Manhattan, Standard Oil of New Jersey, U.S.
Steel, Ford, and Chrysler (*Modern Industry and Human Values*). Reprints of
New York Times, Fortune, Saturday Review, Life ("U.S. Growth: Our Biggest
Year"), and *Business Week* ("25 Years That Remade America") articles also
were included, as was the Twentieth Century Fund's *U.S.A.—Measure of a
Nation* (1949). Seeking to be nonpartisan, a few publications by the AFL,
the CIO, the American Farm Bureau Federation, the National Planning
Association, the National Council of Churches, and the Methodist church
(*Christianity and Wealth*) also were included.[22]

U.S.A.—Measure of a Nation (1949), a text intended for student and public education, spent 101 pages boasting that no people had ever been so
wealthy. Americans had more and spent more than anyone else, yet "few
Americans appreciate how prodigious our performance has been." Its
twenty-one brief chapters provided a sector-by-sector picture of American
abundance, illustrated by colorful graphs. The Twentieth Century Fund's
1957 sequel, *U.S.A. in New Dimensions: The Measure and Promise of America's
Resources,* followed the same format but reflected the mid-1950s euphoria
about the economy. According to the fund, not only had America made
"giant advances," bringing it five times the per capita wealth of the world

as a whole, but it had a society in which people of all economic strata had the same goods. Barring atomic warfare, the U.S. economy was capable of anything. This 124-page illustrated booklet included the fund's oft-repeated assertion that only the United States was able to provide "abundance for all in a classless society."[23] The Twentieth Century Fund also produced the twenty-minute film for schools called *Productivity—Key to Plenty.*

Succeeding bibliographies between the late 1950s and early 1960s grew to become lengthy tomes, underwritten by the CED, the Ford Foundation, the Alfred P. Sloan Foundation, the Crown-Zellerbach Foundation, the Sidney Hillman Foundation, the Reader's Digest Foundation, the Twentieth Century Fund, the W. Alton Jones Foundation, the Whirlpool Foundation, the AFL-CIO, and the Calvin J. Kazanjian Economic Foundation. (Kazanjian, of the Peter Paul Mounds candy fortune, was a particularly active supporter.) While specialized reports on housing statistics and foreign aid were included among hundreds of titles, most materials—and those produced in greatest number for mass distribution—were statistics-laden celebrations of American abundance and the economic system that made it possible. When not reciting the macroeconomic litany of American successes—as in *Fortune's The Amazing Secret of Economic Growth* (1957) and *What a Country* (1956) or the New York Stock Exchange's *America Embraces a People's Capitalism* (1956)—the imperative to produce and spend were drilled into students in materials such as General Motors' *American Battle for Abundance* (1955) and *Business Week's For Americans Today—Money Is to Spend.* Many publications offered a gee-whiz picture of America's future, driven by technology and economic growth, such as the chamber's *The World of Tomorrow: What Will It Be Like?* (1956) and Peter Drucker's *Harper's* series, "America's Next 20 Years" (1955). The chamber's 1960 *Promise of Economic Growth* devoted fifty-five pages to the beneficence of growth and its *Goals of Economic Policy* enumerated five "consensus" goals—free enterprise, growth, efficiency, stability, and security. The near unanimity of mid-1950s America's faith in the abundant society was evident in pamphlets such as the AFL-CIO's *Pioneers of Progress: Higher Living Standards* (1956) and the National Council of Churches of Christ's *American Abundance* (1956).[24]

The NAM and the CED published their own catalogs of study materials that schools could order. In late 1940s pamphlets such as *The Free Enterprise System* and *Our Material Progress,* NAM writers emphasized that the U.S. economic system and business leadership were providing Americans with the world's highest living standards—which they promised would

only rise higher. The NAM's annual *Ed Aids for High Schools* and compan-
ion volume for colleges, included booklets such as *A Comparison of Three
Economic Systems* (1958), which proclaimed: "The amount of economic
freedom we enjoy in the United States has brought us many rewards,
among them our very high standard of living." Between 1959 and 1963,
the NAM distributed 3.5 million copies of its eleven-booklet "Industry and
the American Economy" series to schools. It also distributed posters such
as "You Sure Can Go Places in America!" and films such as *Tomorrow's
America, The American Business System* (a ten-part, six-hour production),
and all two hundred *Industry on Parade* TV episodes. By 1960, the CED
was distributing three hundred thousand of its publications a year to high
school and other educators.[25]

Many other groups jumped onto the economic education bandwagon.
Leonard Reed's right-wing Foundation for Economic Education, supported by Sun Oil Company chairman J. Howard Pew, distributed its libertarian monthly, *The Freeman,* and Henry Hazlitt's *Economics in One Lesson* to thousands of high school principals. While the Americans for the
Competitive Enterprise System tried to get their anti-collectivist message
into schools, liberal organizations such as the National Planning Association, unions, and the Brookings Institution also distributed materials to
teachers.[26]

By the late 1950s, other educators had begun to develop their own materials. The State University of Iowa, a hotbed of economic education,
developed a "Primer of Economics" series. They also produced curricular
materials such as *How the American Economy Is Organized* (n.d.) and *Measuring the Performance of the Economy* (1956), a thirty-nine-page pamphlet that
explained GNP and national income accounting to high schoolers. Commercial curriculum developers such as Curriculum Resources published
America and the World Economy (n.d.) and the eighty-four-page *Our Labor
Force* (1961), and Oxford Social Studies Pamphlets produced the seventy-
six-page *Business and the American Way* (1955) and a ninety-two-page *Labor
and the American Way* (1960). The Council for Advancement of Secondary
Education produced a 116-page text, *American Capitalism: An Introduction
for Young Citizens* (1958), which told students that understanding America's
free-market economics was essential. Calling the American system "modified free enterprise," the book emphasized the nation's disproportionate
share of the world's wealth, its rapid growth, and its "substantial progress"
toward achieving equity. In addition, the JCEE and the National Council
for the Social Studies began producing "Economic Life" resource units in

1955. JCEE economist Lawrence Senesh created a 150-frame filmstrip, *Our Growing America,* in 1956. Although it recognized problems of unemployment and low incomes for some, its concluding frames proclaimed: "We have a good and growing economy—an economy that is good to people by providing them with material abundance."[27]

At a tenth-anniversary banquet at the Waldorf-Astoria Hotel, the JCEE celebrated its progress not only with educators from around the country but also economic luminaries such as past CEA chairmen Edwin Nourse and Arthur Burns, foundation and union leaders, and a host of businessmen from companies such as Standard Oil of New Jersey and the management consulting firm McKinsey. Held in the aftermath of Sputnik and Khrushchev's challenge to economically overtake the United States by 1970, several speakers explicitly linked economic education to America's survival. Donald David, CED chairman and vice chairman of the Ford Foundation, insisted that economic education was vital because "we are engaged in a life and death economic struggle with those who do not believe in our form of free society. The side that wins this war is going to be the side that demonstrates its ability to find people the greatest satisfactions, the best hope of fulfilling their noblest aspirations. This means economic growth, stability, and security."[28]

Building on these successes, the 1960s were a time of heady expansion. In July 1960, the CED and AEA established a task force of five economists, including Paul Samuelson, the JCEE's M. L. Frankel, Stanford economist G. L. Bach, and two secondary-school educators to chart the future teaching of economics. Fourteen months later, the task force issued its seventy-eight-page report, *Economic Education in the Schools,* calling on the nation to step up its educational efforts vastly. The report criticized the "dry and sterile" treatment of economics in history or Problems of American Democracy courses, teachers' poor understanding of economics and biases, and most students' lack of awareness that a paramount national goal was "how to obtain stable economic growth." The report reflected faith in a mixed economy and general agreement on "goals [such] as higher living standards, maximum economic freedom for the individual, and less inequality of opportunity." It recommended, not surprisingly, that more time in high school be devoted to economics, and that schools should build "economic understanding from the time the child enters first grade." It also urged that all social studies teachers be required to take college-level economics courses for certification, that professional development be expanded, economists play a larger role in developing curricula, and that government and the public should join the private and nonprofit sectors in supporting economic education. An estimated 129,000 copies of the report were distributed, and the National Education Association, the National School Board Association, and many local school boards and state education agencies pledged to adopt its principles. In addition, the CED distributed kits containing forty-seven recommended teaching materials to 24,500 principals. The task force marked a turning point for the movement and professional economists' involvement in it. The AEA created its own textbook-review committee, supported by the Ford Foundation, and published a report in 1963, with an introduction by Samuelson and Oberlin economist Ben Lewis. The organization also created an internal task force on economic education, and devoted the May 1961 and May 1963 issues of the *American Economic Review,* and much of the association's annual meetings in both years, to the effectiveness and role of economic education. As longtime economic-education proponent and University of Wisconsin professor Leon Schur said, the task force report made economic education more respectable among economists.[29]

Perhaps the single most ambitious effort was the remarkable 160-part television series *The American Economy* produced by the CED, AEA, JCEE, the Learning Resources Institute, the Ford Foundation, and eighty-five companies, which aired on CBS's College of the Air and fifty-nine educational TV stations in 1962–63 and 1963–64. Aimed at high school teachers but reaching an unprecedented weekly audience of 1.25 million households, each half-hour show was narrated by economist John Coleman, president of Haverford College and the Philadelphia Federal Reserve Bank. The extraordinarily detailed series included episodes devoted to the workings of the market economy, GNP, twentieth-century economic history, the role of money, how corporations operate, poverty and income security, unions, government's role, trade, competing economic systems, and "America's unfinished business." Star-studded expert "lecturers" included economists such as Robert Heilbroner, Joseph Fisher, Paul Samuelson, Walter Heller, Solomon Fabricant, Milton Friedman, Arthur Burns, Theodore Schultz, Robert Solow, Jacob Viner, and Joseph Pechman, as well as Presidents Eisenhower and Kennedy, businessmen such as Henry Ford II and David Rockefeller, and labor leader Walter Reuther. The splendors of America's productivity and wealth were intertwined with a conceptual tour d'horizon of economic concepts. McGraw-Hill published an accompanying textbook, and thousands of teachers earned course credit from 350 colleges. JFK's secretary of commerce, Luther Hodges, lauded the series in a 15 January 1963 speech, urging all adults to watch. The series was widely sold to schools for classroom instruction well into the 1970s.[30]

The JCEE developed and broadly disseminated a curriculum framework, the Developmental Economic Education Program (DEEP), which outlined a progression of economic concepts that could be learned from kindergarten through high school. One curriculum sequence instructed kindergartners that goods and services depend on income; first graders of the interdependence of the businessman, producer, and consumer; second graders of America's broad distribution of ownership; and third graders of the interdependent "loop" between businesses and households. Another urged that first graders learn about the division of labor, trading, the complexity of the market, and the importance of government, with second graders ready to move on to the advanced concepts of "the social and economic significance of market price" and the workings of competition. By 1989, DEEP was in 1,836, or 39 percent, of America's school districts.[31]

In April 1967, the congressional Joint Economic Committee's subcommittee on economic progress, chaired by Wright Patman, held three days of hearings on economic education. Witnesses, who included economist and CEA member James Duesenberry, several businessmen, a union official, school officials, and economic education leaders such as M. L. Frankel, Lawrence Senesh, and Leon Schur, bemoaned Americans' economic illiteracy, and the inaccurate and biased economics being taught. They emphasized that good, widespread economic education was crucial to enhance the "wealth and physical strength of the United States." McKinsey's Marvin Bower told the committee that economic education was important for children to learn how the American system "has made ours the most productive and powerful nation in the world with the highest standard of living."[32]

Economic education continued to expand after the 1960s, although the focus on the U.S. economy's measurable achievements diminished. Yet economic education has lived on. The number of children taking economics courses increased significantly by the 1980s, particularly after California and other states began requiring economics, and about two million high school students were taking such courses at any given time by the early twenty-first century. A Test of Economic Understanding was developed in 1964, and a *Journal of Economic Education* was launched in 1968. High school textbooks were published, film series such as *Trade-Offs* and *Give and Take* were produced, a Test of Economic Literacy was developed in 1979, 29 percent of high school students were taking some economics by 1987, and the College Board introduced an Advanced Placement economics test in 1989.[33] However, a shift in emphasis began in the 1970s. As in journalism, personal finance and a focus on the "world of work" increasingly gained the upper hand. Courses such as Financial Fitness for Life became popular. The Securities Industries Association (SIA) developed a stock-market game to "teach the role of markets," which was widely played in late-twentieth-century high schools. In the Internet era, other economics games and simulations became popular. Junior Achievement, which had long instructed schoolchildren about business, sent businesspeople into schools as guest speakers, to teach how American businesses operate. The JCEE changed its name to Economics America/the National Council on Economic Education in 1992. By the early twenty-first century, financial-services organizations such as the NASDAQ as well as the U.S. Treasury and new foundations such as the Peter G. Peterson Foundation were especially active.[34]

While economic education as a way of teaching how to "keep score" for the nation and oneself remains, the period between the early to mid-1950s and the mid-1960s was unique in the way that American schoolchildren learned about their country. Despite insisting on the "objectivity" and nonpartisanship of economic education activities and materials, the movement and its materials clearly had a message that went far beyond supply-and-demand curves and savings-investment-consumption functions. Tens of millions of children born between the latter years of the Depression and the first half of the baby boom were taught that theirs was not only the country of the Declaration of Independence and the Bill of Rights, of brave settlers and a melting pot that made e pluribus unum, but also the wealthiest, most productive society in history, and that this was what made America distinctive and great. It was a nation—thanks to a new, system of "democratic capitalism"—that had solved the age-old problem of economics: Scarcity was no more; abundance was here to stay. And everybody in America could share in it. As Galbraith would have argued, messages about "people's capitalism" bestowing classless, ever-increasing abundance on Americans were "conventional wisdom." These assumptions were not to be questioned. Even if the notion of shared abundance has become frayed by the early twenty-first century, the idea of America as an economy has not.

Amid the babel of messages of the era, including anti-communism, a key source of patriotic pride for American youth was their economy, not ideals tarnished by McCarthyism and the threat of thermonuclear war. As textbook and economic education writers said, America's greatness lay in its wealth and standard of living. And as *Scholastic* had said, it was "difficult for an American to describe [the economy] without sounding like a pompous braggart."

7

A Flawed Measure: Critics and Realities

As a nation we spend an inordinate amount of time feeling our indices, trembling when freight car loadings drop and rejoicing when they rise. Apparently as our supply of reassuring statistics increases, our need for reassurance grows.

ROBERT LEKACHMAN

What good is happiness; it can't buy money.

HENNY YOUNGMAN

Economic metrics may have become a dominant way to gauge America's success as a nation and culture and its people's worth in the decades after World War II, but not everyone bought this message. And by the late twentieth and early twenty-first centuries the U.S. economy itself no longer churned out such unambiguously positive data suggesting that America—a nation measured in economic terms—was an across-the-board success.

Some intellectuals, politicians, and economists had chipped away at various aspects of this equation of America with its economy since the mid-twentieth century. Critics of consumerism and the idea that material riches are the measure of an individual or nation can be found from the Puritans to Thorstein Veblen in the early 1900s to the present. The Puritans took to heart Jesus' injunction that "a man's life consisteth not in the abundance of his possessions." Quakers and others preached the virtues of the simple life. The word *consume* emerged in fourteenth-century England as a pejorative meaning to "waste, devour, or use to the point of exhaustion." The Puritans and early republican theorists such as Benjamin Franklin valued hard work; luxury and consumption were viewed as wasteful vices throughout the eighteenth and nineteenth centuries. Max Weber's famous discussion of the Protestant ethic spoke of the value placed on work and thrift—or what some have called a "producerist" orientation.

Radicals and hippies of the 1960s certainly criticized it in spades. Some conservatives, especially since the late 1970s, have taken aim at the idea

164

that government's role is to ensure an ever stronger economy, and many have returned to a neo-Puritan distaste for unbridled consumption. Critics from the left and right, secular and religious, have found common ground in arguing that the economy and abundance are not the true measure of America or the paramount goal or concern of public policy or individual striving.

After World War II, some criticized abundance as a shallow national obsession, and others, who addressed poverty and unmet national needs, saw it as a national illusion. By 1960, questions of what defined America's "national purpose" beyond expanding incomes and consumption, as well as a new awareness of poverty and what John Kenneth Galbraith called "public squalor," percolated up into broader public debate. Such ideas began to dim the view of the United States as a model of economic plenty and success. Many poorer Americans undoubtedly saw this as a chimera, if not a downright lie.

Some critics had considerable influence. However, their messages were not widely or clearly heard by most Americans and they hardly expressed the dominant visions of American culture. The premise that America could and should be measured in economic terms was entirely plausible during these good years. Whether or not one subscribes to Gramscian ideas of hegemony or C. Wright Mills's conception of a power elite, there is no question that those singing the praises of rising GNP and classless abundance had overwhelmingly greater social and cultural power. The stellar performance of the U.S. economy and its macroeconomic maestros from the 1940s through the 1960s obviously made it easier, if not natural, for elites and citizens to equate American success with economic success and America with its economy.

Postwar critiques of the equation of America with its economy largely fall into four often overlapping categories: moral criticism of American materialism, selfishness, and a shallow preoccupation with status, at the expense of "higher" values of the spirit, art, the community, and democratic, civic engagement; attacks on capitalist manipulation of public buying and beliefs; a focus on poverty and unfulfilled public needs in the midst of abundance; and questioning of the priorities, metrics, methodologies, and assumptions of the economics profession. The first and third categories were not entirely dissonant with visions of America as an economy becoming ever richer through careful economic management, as many critics believed that abundance held the key to eliminating poverty, meeting all public needs, and giving Americans leisure to cultivate spiritual and cultural pursuits—positions held by Truman, Eisenhower, Kennedy, Johnson, the Ad Council, the CED, Time Inc., and even some New Leftists, among others.

Critics from the Left

Critiques of consumer and mass culture picked up steam during a golden age of social criticism in the 1950s and early 1960s that included public intellectuals such as David Riesman, John Kenneth Galbraith, William H. Whyte, Daniel Bell, Vance Packard, Paul Goodman, Dwight Macdonald, Theodor Adorno, Herbert Marcuse, Beat writers and other novelists, dissident theologians, and the early civil rights movement. Economists expressing alternative views ranged from Galbraith, James Duesenberry, Tibor Scitovsky, Leon Keyserling, Robert Lekachman, and Robert Heilbroner to Mollie Orshansky, who questioned whether "private affluence" was the ultimate measure of social well-being.

An important link between earlier and post-1945 critics were the exiled German scholars of the Frankfurt school. Adorno, Max Horkheimer, Walter Benjamin, and the more popular Erich Fromm and Marcuse drew on Marx's discussion of the "fetishism of commodities" and Hungarian Marxist Georg Lukacs's 1920s argument that capitalism transformed people from what they do into what they have. They saw the near universal adoption of consumer values and behavior as inculcated by the culture-industry minions of mass-production-era capitalism. Mass-mediated affluence, shaped by advertising and popular culture, pacified the populace to accept existing power relationships. The Frankfurt school analysis was a sophisticated elaboration of Werner Sombart's well-known 1904 statement that, in the United States, "all socialist utopias came to nothing on roast beef and apple pie." Horkheimer noted that it was no surprise that consumption should be seductive, for "in Utopia, production does not play a decisive part. It is the land of milk and honey."

The idea of the manipulative nature of postwar consumer society was popularized by freelance writer Vance Packard, who, in three best sellers during Eisenhower's second term—*The Hidden Persuaders* (1957), *The Status Seekers* (1959), and *The Waste Makers* (1960)—lambasted the "hidden persuaders" of advertising for advancing the notion that acquiring more material goods was Americans' overriding national purpose. Sombart's question was the basis for the original discussions of "American exceptionalism" in the 1920s. Picking up on pre-Depression critiques of advertising such as Walter Dill Scott's *The Psychology of Advertising* (1903) and Stuart Chase and F. J. Schlink's *Your Money's Worth* (1927), Packard floridly wrote about "large-scale efforts being made, often with impressive success, to channel our unthinking habits, our purchasing decisions, and our thought processes by the use of insights gleaned from psychiatry and the social sciences." In *The Waste Makers,* he chastised America for its "widespread commitment to use an increasing GNP as the mark of national success." Sociologist C. Wright Mills, in *The Power Elite* (1956), argued that decision-making power was vested in a political-corporate-military elite that manipulated the population into cheerful support through the seductive appeal of ever-rising consumption.[1]

David Riesman, best known for his 1950 tour de force, *The Lonely Crowd,* cast a lightning bolt across an otherwise cloudless sky in *Abundance for What?* (1964), saying that Americans felt a "compulsion" to prove their patriotism "by acquiring the standard package of goods." Others repeated these themes that America had plenty at the price of conformity, manipulation, and loss of meaning. Critics Paul and Percival Goodman declared that Americans "spend [their] money for follies." Novelist Henry Miller damned an "air-conditioned American nightmare." Dwight Macdonald bluntly denied the vision of a joyfully prosperous nation, saying, "We are an unhappy people." Even historian Daniel Boorstin decried a culture beholden to "the image," in which Americans were passive, malleable spectators and consumers of ideas and opinions, intriguingly prefiguring 1960s French radicals such as the Situationists. The Beats also broadly criticized American conformity, lack of creativity, militarism, and materialism, with Allen Ginsberg writing in his book-length poem "Howl" of a "Moloch whose blood is running money."[2]

By 1960, even Dwight Eisenhower and Henry Luce were troubled by an abundant yet seemingly complacent and purposeless America. These doubts were fueled by the twin traumas of the Soviets' 1957 Sputnik launch, which challenged the faith in American technological supremacy, and the 1958 Little Rock battle to desegregate public schools, which similarly challenged the faith that social conflict had been eliminated in a new, classless economy. Ike appointed a National Goals Commission during his last year in office, and *Life* published a series of articles by assorted luminaries collected in its 1960 book, *The National Purpose.* In it, Archibald MacLeish asked, "Are we lost in the blaze of our own prosperity?" Even *Fortune* opined in 1960: "In a society where the basic material wants have been met for almost everybody, and met in abundance for many . . . there is nothing quite like material satisfaction for convincing people that material satisfaction is not enough."[3]

The *Nation* criticized the "disease" and immorality of "galloping consumption." Some members of the clergy—ranging from Protestant theologian Reinhold Niebuhr, Methodist bishop G. Bromley Oxnam, and Episcopal priest Gibson White to Trappist monk Thomas Merton, Dorothy Day's Catholic Worker movement, and a group of one hundred Protestant, Catholic, and Jewish clergy who issued a 1955 statement, "American Abundance and World Need"—expressed worries about the pressures on Americans to find fulfillment in consumption, as well as the morality of "islands of abundance amid oceans of poverty, hunger and distress." Most clergy—from Protestants Norman Vincent Peale and Billy Graham to Catholic bishop Fulton J. Sheen, Rabbi Joshua Liebman, and theologian Will Herberg—went along for the ride, celebrating a feel-good abundance linked to a "Judeo-Christian," middle-class America. Herberg, in *Protestant, Catholic, Jew* (1955), articulated the idea that the melting pot had melted away differences among America's three principal faiths into a vague belief in the "American way of life."

Betty Friedan, in *The Feminine Mystique* (1963), damned the postwar socioeconomic system for imprisoning women in the "comfortable concentration camp" of the suburban home. Beyond the humanistic idealism of Martin Luther King's "Letter from a Birmingham Jail" or his "I Have A Dream" speech, there was also the strong message that America's economy had failed most African Americans. It is often forgotten that economics had the top billing over freedom in the August 28, 1963, March on Washington for Jobs and Freedom. During his speech that day, King said, "the Negro lives in a lonely island of poverty in the midst of a vast ocean of material prosperity." Two years later, in Selma, he reiterated this point more forcefully: "The Negro is still smothering in an air-tight cage of poverty in the midst of an affluent society." In short, King and other early civil-rights leaders did not so much reject the metric of an abundant economy as demand that African Americans be able to fairly share in it. As some have noted, the lunch-counter and other sit-ins were as much about the right to consume as about rights. Clearly, disparate parts of the U.S. population did not embrace the cheery official reports or upward-sloping economic graphs in the media. Some polling data provides a mixed picture, with the elderly least likely to buy the idea of perpetually rising growth curves, women also less enthused, and African Americans upbeat about their personal economic future, but less so about the nation's.[4]

These critiques grew louder in the mid to late 1960s, as the student, antiwar, feminist, and environmentalist movements denounced a culture seemingly founded on little more than the gaudy production and consumption of material goods. Of course, critics on both the right and left aptly observed that much of the counterculture's supposed rejection of materialism was simply a substitution of different types of consumption from the *Life* magazine/network TV norms of the 1950s and early 1960s. European critics such as Jurgen Habermas, Jean Baudrillard, and the French Situationists, whose work became influential among some American leftists, also argued that consumer society and the cult of GNP reduced civil society to little more than the pursuit of wealth. Habermas, in *The Structural Transformation of the Public Sphere* (1962), contrasted the active "public sphere" of the heyday of liberal democracy in the late eighteenth and nineteenth centuries with a debased public sphere in which citizens had given way to consumers, and opinion was manipulated by a political-cultural elite. Baudrillard, in his 1970 book, *The Consumer Society,* criticized the "imperative of consumption" and the "mystique of GNP." Economic output statistics, he said, failed to account for culture, household work, and many psychological needs, yet counted pollution and other "nuisances." In *The Society of the Spectacle* (1967), Situationist theorist Guy Debord spoke of the "degradation of being into having."[5]

To many others, "late capitalism" had run amok, producing a spiritually empty and manipulated society. Robert Kennedy, shortly before he was murdered, lamented that "for too long, we seem to have surrendered our personal excellence and community value in the mere accumulation of material things," noting that GNP measures cigarette advertising and air pollution but not children's health, wit, or courage. Books such as Christian fundamentalist Hal Lindsey's *The Late Great Planet Earth* (1970), which sold 28 million copies, and E. F. Schumacher's *Small Is Beautiful: Economics as if People Mattered* (1973) became bibles to many, while the macroeconomic problems apparent by the early 1970s led millions to hail the Club of Rome's 1972 manifesto, *The Limits to Growth,* as the new conventional wisdom.[6] Neo-moralist "communitarians" on the left and the rising Christian right criticized American culture for being excessively materialistic, giving short shrift to values such as community, beauty, creativity, and spirituality. Many continued to attack advertising as the mouthpiece of corporate capitalism, enticing people to want and "need" a forever expanding array of consumer goods. Another strand of criticism derided consumerism for leading Americans to become narcissistic and cultivate their own gardens at the expense of public participation in a democratic society.

No one was more of an heir to Riesman, and no work of social criticism came closer to its influence, than Christopher Lasch and his 1979 *The Culture of Narcissism: American Life in an Age of Diminishing Expectations.* Lasch denounced Americans' retreat from politics and social engagement to narcissistic consumerism, significantly blaming a postwar liberalism that sought "painless progress toward the celestial city of consumerism." Drawing on Freud, Riesman, and the Frankfurt school, Lasch described narcissistic Americans who measured themselves largely in terms of their ability to satisfy their material needs. To Lasch, advertisers were the villains, whose siren calls seduced Americans to consume. The University of Rochester historian influenced fellow moralist, President Jimmy Carter, who declared: "Too many of us now worship self-indulgence and consumption. . . . Owning things and consuming things do not satisfy our longing for meaning."[7]

Even more than Eisenhower's questioning of the "national purpose" in 1960, doubts in high places were especially evident with Carter, who declared in his Inaugural Address that "we have learned that more is not necessarily better, [and] that even our great nation has its recognized limits." Two and a half years later, in Carter's astute, but politically foolish "malaise" speech, he said: "We can measure GNP. . . . We can be grateful for material blessings. But we know that they are not the most important characteristics of a nation's life. They do not hold us together as a unique people. . . . We measure the real meaning of America in our intangible values."[8]

A less dark critique of Americans' focus on economic satisfaction was offered seven years later by Robert Bellah and his colleagues in *Habits of the Heart: Individualism and Commitment in American Life.* Bellah argued that Americans were captivated by consumption as a form of self-fulfillment. More optimistic than Lasch and an early proponent of "communitarianism," Bellah decried Americans' abandonment of the altruistic, interdependent values of community and participatory democracy. Americans' loss of both small-scale community and political engagement was attributed to time and money pressures, suburban sprawl, TV, and the waning of the postwar era's "long civic generation" by Robert Putnam, in his similarly influential *Bowling Alone: The Collapse and Revival of American Community* (2000).[9] Even PBS devoted a 1997–98 series to what it called "affluenza."

Seeing a "culture of narcissism," as Lasch put it, or a "me decade," as writer Tom Wolfe described the 1970s, a rising critique identified a nation populated by self-obsessed, self-aggrandizing individuals who were "looking out for number one," as one best seller urged. Others saw the triumph of a "therapeutic" ethos in which therapists, support groups, and self-help books now held the keys to the kingdom of happiness. Psychotherapists became the experts du jour, and the language of psychology—from neurosis and depression to consciousness-raising, adjustment, personal growth, and striving to understand and realize one's inner needs—became, for many, the way to measure success (or failure) instead of rising per capita income. America was once again a nation of individualists—only they were not rugged pioneers or entrepreneurs—but seekers of an inner nirvana defined by "seven habits," "twelve steps," "self-actualization," or "emotional intelligence." For others, the barricades were raised under the spell of multiculturalism—whether in the rosier terms of former New York mayor David Dinkins, who called America a "glorious mosaic," or in the darker vision of Arthur Schlesinger Jr., who wrote of a "disuniting of America" into component ethnic [and other] subcultures.[10] Indeed, a new front was opened in the war to define America—between a politically correct embrace of the nation's many historically oppressed subcultures and those defending a supposedly lost, English-speaking, implicitly white Christian culture.

Early Dissident Economists

At the same time that cultural critics launched their assaults, some economists and popular economic writers deviated from the hymnal of Keynesian growth ushering in a new paradise measured by rising economic indicators.

Daniel Bell, an ex–*Fortune* writer, denounced America's worship of output and production in place of a concern for human needs. He seconded William H. Whyte Jr. in saying that Americans' compensation for meaningless jobs was consumption of goods and "escapist fantasies." Bell famously proclaimed the "end of ideology," with the rise of the seemingly post-ideological liberal consensus that focused on relentlessly achieving economic growth. Bell's notion of the "end of ideology" was widely accepted in the late 1950s and early 1960s as describing the intellectual consensus of a society geared to fine-tuning the technical problems of abundance. Similar ideas were expressed by Lewis Feuer in *Beyond Ideology*

(1955), Seymour Martin Lipset in *The End of Ideology* (1960), and Raymond Aron. Nonetheless, Bell lamented the "abandonment of Puritanism and the Protestant ethic," leaving only "hedonism" and the "secular religion" of economics. He also spoke of the "revolution of rising entitlements," in which Americans were conditioned to perpetually want more than they had.[11]

Galbraith, another veteran of *Fortune,* added a new political and economic twist in his 1958 blockbuster, *The Affluent Society.* He pointedly questioned America's all but universal preoccupation with increased productivity and output, denounced the "social imbalance" between private affluence and "public squalor," and criticized the premise that society's highest goal should be to "maximize output": "Production [is all that] Republicans, Democrats, right and left, white and colored, Catholic or Protestant could agree on. It is common ground for the general secretary of the Communist Party, the chairman of ADA, the president of the U.S. Chamber, and the president of NAM."

Often misconstrued as celebrating American abundance, Galbraith attacked what he called the "conventional wisdom" of an economics based on scarcity, saying that the real problem was an economy that produced private consumer goods excessively and efficiently but public goods such as schools, health care, and decent housing inadequately and inefficiently. At the same time, the apparent end of scarcity reduced the marginal gains from additional private goods. Moreover, excessive private consumption created problems of consumer debt and inflation, and emphasized output rather than leisure or cultural pursuits. In a line that sounded more like a Beat poet than a Harvard economist, Galbraith said: "The family which takes its mauve and cerise, air-conditioned, power-steered, and power-braked car out for a tour passes through cities that are badly paved, made hideous by litter, blighted buildings, billboards, and posts for wires that should long since have been put underground." Galbraith's criticism of private "waste" had been partly anticipated in Stuart Chase's 1929 best seller *The Tragedy of Waste.*[12]

Yet Galbraith was not "against" abundance or the economics that had fostered it. Rather, picking up the Institutionalist banner of Simon Patten, he wanted America's wealth to be redirected to provide for the needs of all Americans. In fact, he was later to hail the Keynesian revolution as one of the "great modern accomplishments in social design." Increasingly marginalized by his compatriots in economics, Galbraith became a superstar among public intellectuals. He quickly sold more than a million copies of *The Affluent Society* in several dozen languages, commanded seemingly unlimited space in the mass media, including television, and became a leading Democratic Party theoretician and confidant of John Kennedy. Aside from his service in the Roosevelt administration and influence as a popular writer during the Truman era, Galbraith headed the Democratic Party's domestic policy committee in the late 1950s, advised Democratic candidates and presidents from Adlai Stevenson to George McGovern, and was given the Presidential Medal of Honor by Bill Clinton.

William H. Whyte Jr., yet another *Fortune* journalist, in his best-selling *The Organization Man* (1956), portrayed an America where the Protestant ethic of hard work, thrift, and self-denial had given way to a "social ethic" in which people took their cues from the conformist tendencies of large organizations. Like Riesman, Whyte decried the absence of bold visions, which had been traded for the "modest aspirations" of good pay and benefits "and a nice house in a pleasant community populated with people as nearly like themselves as possible." In Americans' quest for "belongingness," they followed their co-workers and neighbors in perpetually redefining upward "the good-life standard." Whyte, whose Lucean sociology was based on his reportage on suburban Oak Park, Illinois, echoed themes that rumbled through Sloan Wilson's 1955 novel *The Man in the Gray Flannel Suit* and John Keats's 1956 anti-suburban diatribe, *The Crack in the Picture Window.*[13]

Whereas most American economists adopted the party line of Keynesian-induced abundance and growth, Galbraith was not entirely alone in criticizing his profession's conventional wisdom. James Duesenberry, the Harvard economist who later became a member of Lyndon Johnson's Council of Economic Advisers (CEA), coined the Veblenesque phrase of "keeping up with the Joneses" as an explanation of Americans' fevered consumption. Kenneth Boulding (*Towards a General Theory of Growth,* 1953) was an iconoclast who was sympathetic to the Institutionalist view that mathematical models and theories could not explain all economic behavior. He astutely noted that "if we want the wrong things," growth was not an unmitigated blessing. Robert Solow argued that growth could not be indefinitely stimulated, but few beyond a handful of economists were listening.[14]

Tibor Scitovsky, who later wrote *The Joyless Economy: The Psychology of Human Satisfaction* and *Consumer Dissatisfaction* (1972), agreed with Packard and Galbraith in the 1950s that consumers were manipulated. He also argued that life's true pleasures could not be measured in economic terms, and questioned mainstream economists' belief in "consumer sovereignty." Instead, he said that people make buying decisions based on inadequate and skewed information, and that "the American" should not be equated with "the consumer." Yet Scitovsky continued to believe that increased growth should be a social priority.[15]

Robert Heilbroner—an unconventional economist with the New School for Social Research and a former employee of Galbraith's at the Office of Price Control during the war—sounded many of these critiques in books such as *Quest for Wealth: Study of Acquisitive Man* (1956), popular articles, and *The Triple Revolution* (1964), an intriguing leftist tract written with Jan Myrdal, Bayard Rustin, Tom Hayden, Todd Gitlin, and Irving Howe. In it, they called for government to play a greater role in economic planning, and hailed a coming technocratic utopia in which science raised production so much that work would become obsolete.[16] In fact, it is noteworthy that early New Left authors such as Hayden and Gitlin essentially agreed with Paul Hoffman, Richard Nixon, and John L. Lewis that economic growth and abundance were the measure of a "good" America.

Robert Lekachman, a City University of New York economist, diagnosed America's obsession with economic statistics as "economic hypochondria." He wrote in *Harper's* that, "as a nation we spend an inordinate amount of time feeling our indices, trembling when freight car loadings drop and rejoicing when they rise. Apparently as our supply of reassuring statistics increases, our need for reassurance grows." Lekachman also urged economists to focus more on the all but ignored topic of the unequal distribution of economic power.[17]

Galbraith, who was criticized by Leon Keyserling for downplaying poverty, nonetheless essentially agreed with Keyserling—and the liberal consensus, for that matter—that American abundance could eliminate poverty once and for all. While Keyserling insisted that it required increased economic growth, Galbraith suggested that it was a matter of reallocating resources. Keyserling, in his post-CEA life heading the Conference on Economic Progress, offers a striking example of an economist at once obsessed with growth and a social critic who chastised America for "the gaps in our prosperity" that left so many on the economic sidelines. Declaring that one-fifth of the population was poor and another fifth "near poor," he saw the solution in policies geared toward achieving 5 to 6 percent growth. University of Chicago economist and later Illinois senator Paul Douglas also spoke out in the late 1950s about the need to reduce poverty. Even before serving as chairman of the Joint Economic Committee for six years in the late 1950s and early 1960s, Douglas decried the "dangerous fact that millions of Americans are shabbily sheltered and living in filthy, malignant slum areas."[18]

While Galbraith may have highlighted "public squalor," and Keyserling, Douglas, and the early civil-rights movement may have pressed the issue of poverty, it took Michael Harrington's *The Other America* (1962) to shock an America complacent about its economic successes. Harrington challenged the widely accepted belief that affluence had eliminated all but the residues of poverty. First published in *Commentary* in 1959, Harrington used U.S. government data to argue that at least a quarter of America's 180 million people were poor. He said that the poor were largely invisible in affluent America, as they were concentrated in urban slums and isolated rural areas. "There is a familiar America," he wrote. "It is celebrated in speeches and advertised on television and in the magazines. It has the highest mass standard of living the world has ever known." While Americans worried about the problems of abundance, "there existed another America. In it dwelt somewhere between 40,000,000 and 50,000,000 citizens of this land. They were poor. They still are."[19]

President Kennedy's declaration of a "war on poverty" was galvanized by Harrington's best seller (and JFK appointed the young socialist to a presidential antipoverty task force), as well as by the antipoverty writings of Galbraith, Keyserling, Douglas, and Social Security Administration economist Mollie Orshansky. In a series of articles between 1963 and 1966, Orshansky used data from the Department of Agriculture's Household Food Consumption Survey and the Census Bureau's Current Population Survey to develop the first poverty threshold. The CEA's 1964 Economic Report contained a chapter on poverty based on work by CEA economist Robert Lampmann. Shortly thereafter, as President Johnson launched his war on poverty in earnest, the new Office of Economic Opportunity adopted Orshansky's thresholds as a semi-official definition of poverty.[20]

Dissident economists and social critics may have tried to demolish the validity of the neoclassical idea of consumer sovereignty, attack excessive consumption and conformity, focus attention on poverty and public needs unmet by the market, and echo late New Deal and Western European ideas that government should provide for social needs. Such ideas contributed to a sense that all was not right in a land that prided itself on its economic prowess. These critiques—together with political, economic, and cultural developments beginning in the late 1960s—convinced more and more Americans that there was truth to the criticism of "mauve and cerise, air-conditioned" cars, the "disease" of "galloping consumption," "poverty in the midst of an affluent society," and a "Moloch whose blood is running money." While these and other cultural critics and dissident economists sought to puncture the idea of an America to be celebrated for its mighty and bounteous economy, many still bought a major piece of the postwar premise. Most only timidly questioned the economic equation of abundance and growth with the good society and the national purpose. For them, if only the United States could justly distribute the fruits of its abundance, America's promised land would be at hand. Egalitarianism and moral critiques of consumerism didn't necessarily negate the idea that a higher GDP and a stronger economy were desirable goals.

Critics from the Right

While progressives took aim at the soullessness of an economically defined America and the lies of "abundance for all" implicit in widespread poverty and economic injustice, the fire didn't come only from the left. And, like the leftist social critics, conservatives who attacked the policies and culture of the postwar consensus also embraced many aspects of a culture that measured America economically.

In the years between the late 1970s and early 2000s, conservatives provided the most potent political and cultural assaults on, and redefinitions of, ideas of how economics and national identity interacted. Conservatives drove the nail into the coffin of growth liberalism, the Keynesian consensus, and transformed America's obsession with all things economic. Keynes, on the cover of *Time* in 1965, was in the dustbin of intellectual history barely a decade later. Ronald Reagan and the neoconservatives dealt the final death blow to the liberal consensus that had reigned after World War II, and simultaneously squashed the ideas of left-liberal critics. After January 20, 1981, when fireworks over the Potomac heralded Reagan's inauguration, the conservatives—from the Club for Growth or the Cato Institute to Reagan's (and, later, George W. Bush's) policy advisers—had won politically and intellectually. Growth liberalism was dead.

Conservatives were emboldened in the 1970s to attack fiscal policy, leading to what Allen Matusow has described as the "unraveling of liberalism." "Rational expectations" theory turned Keynesianism on its head by returning to the classical economic argument that people seek to maximize utility and forecast their own economic outcomes. Thus, policymakers have no appropriate role in manipulating the economy and leading the populace to hold allegedly false expectations. Rational expectations theory, advanced by Robert Lucas and Richard Muth, also redirected economics to microeconomic rather than macroeconomic behavior—a shift that was consonant with the rising conservative temperament.[21]

In the mid-1970s, *Wall Street Journal* editor Jude Wanniski pulled together the ideas of conservative economists Arthur Laffer, Robert Mundell, and others to popularize "supply side" economics, which turned the clock back to argue that production, or supply, was more important than consumption or demand. By emphasizing the preeminence of private investment over consumption or public investment, supply-siders called for tax cuts, not to stimulate demand, but investment. Thus, began the anti-tax and anti-government crusade, whose signal event was California's 1978 Proposition 13 (also led by Laffer) but which culminated in President Reagan's supply-side-influenced tax and budget cuts of the early 1980s, and was followed by twenty years of intermittent tax-cutting.

Simultaneously, the perceived failures of fiscal policy under Presidents Nixon, Ford, and Carter gave Federal Reserve chairman Paul Volcker political license to use monetary policy to cure 1970s stagflation; the success of his harsh medicine in the late 1970s and early 1980s contributed to yet another conservative triumph—the preeminence of the Federal Reserve and monetary policy over fiscal policy since about 1980. This was what Milton Friedman and his disciples had been arguing for years—that the Federal Reserve should maintain an equilibrium in the supply and demand for money, and that market economies successfully self-regulate and avoid inflation if the money supply is not permitted to fluctuate significantly. Like rational expectations and supply-side advocates, the monetarists dismissed the need for macroeconomic demand management and stimulating consumption through measures to increase purchasing power and incomes for all.

"Social-issue" politics attacking legal abortion, alternative lifestyles, "welfare cheats," permissiveness, and criminality—couched in pre-twentieth-century terms extolling the family and individual responsibility—also deflected attention from the new economics that accepted broadly unequal outcomes. It is hard to know what traction these social issues would have had with a middle and lower-middle class whose economic fortunes were more secure and continued to expand in tandem with those in the top quintile. If the paradigm of America's mighty economy providing increasing prosperity for all remained plausible, would these Americans care so much about these social issues?

In sum, Keynesianism, the growth liberalism consensus, and the belief that shared abundance was a worthy national goal were demolished by a disparate band that, for a time, managed to squeeze together Ronald Reagan, George W. Bush, Jerry Falwell, Milton Friedman, Newt Gingrich, anti-abortion, anti-gay, xenophobic, and anti-multicultural conservatives. Right-wing critics of various stripes—from economists such as Friedman and Laffer to social-issue conservatives—attacked the conventional wisdom of the postwar era during the late twentieth and early twenty-first centuries from as many vantage points as the left-wing critics did from the late 1950s to the 1970s and beyond. Government's business was not managing the economy, or at least one with a semblance of equity. Markets, whatever economic, social, or moral failures they left in their train, ruled. Abundance for all and people's capitalism were hardly part of the neoconservative mantra.

Neoclassical Economics and Redefining American Economic Success

However, despite the right's attacks on the conventional economic wisdom, a strange thing happened with the rise of neoconservatism. Growth liberalism morphed into growth conservatism. Although there always were conservative elements to the postwar consensus, they coexisted—somewhat harmoniously, somewhat uneasily—with more progressive ones. In the late twentieth century, the postwar liberal consensus was bifurcated, with the belief in government support for business and economic growth retained, while the belief in government support for social welfare (even in the name of "purchasing power") was diminished. Under Presidents Reagan, Clinton, and George W. Bush, growth and prosperity remained the business of America, the business of government, and the chief rallying cry of politics. The fixation on economic growth did not go away, and opinion leaders hardly stopped extolling the virtues of the American economic system and the prosperity that it bestowed. Economics and their political handmaidens still pulled the marionette strings in Washington, on Wall Street, and on Main Street between the late 1970s and the second Bush administration, but it was economics in a new key.

The growth liberalism that underpinned postwar visions of classless abundance for all became transformed in the 1980s and after into a vision that still emphasized economic growth and American economic might, but tolerated rising living standards for some and wage stagnation, increased economic pressure on the middle class, and continued poverty for others. CED leader Sol Hurwitz's formulation of what's good for America is good for business had been supplanted by a credo of what's good for business, shareholders, and top executives is simply good. The patriotic patina of American economic strength remained, as U.S. leaders gloatingly compared America's economic performance to European and Japanese weaknesses in the 1990s. But, instead of classless abundance being a sign of national pride, aggregate macroeconomic puissance, stock-market or asset—rather than income—growth, and America's continued status as the world's largest and most powerful economy were what mattered. Economic success—in the form of assets, income, and consumption—became the measure of the new America. Business groups, the financial media, schoolbooks, public diplomacy, and politicians no longer spoke in the terms of the 1950s and early 1960s, and fewer economists claimed, or were accorded, the status of masters of abundance, although some conservative economists tried to argue that growth was dependent on their policy-driving ideas.

The economy, albeit differently conceived, was still a barometer of national success and economic statistics were still key figures in modern American numerology. The corollary also remained from the 1980s to the early 2000s—that accumulating ever greater wealth was a worthy national goal, regardless of other worthy goals that might be pursued. Even in choppier economic waters, this belief reinforced the desirability of using whatever means to ensure that economic indicators still rose—whether measuring consumption, household or national income, or, increasingly, stock-market and housing-market indices.

By the early twenty-first century, liberals and conservatives were probably more divided about the meaning of rights and freedoms than during the third quarter of the twentieth century, or at many other times in American history. Some reverted to a neo-Wilsonian idealism about America. Others made "moral" issues central to defining the nation. And still others have made particularistic, group identities the basis for their self-understanding and their understanding of American culture. Yet if there was a political common denominator from Reagan to Clinton to George W. Bush, it remained that the United States was an economic powerhouse (or must remain one)—an idea that may have been even less contested than during the 1950s and early 1960s. But, the apparent disuniting of America, fostered by multiculturalism and the psychological credo of "looking out for number one," made even more salient the culture's greatest unifying element—the grand notion of America as an unbounded market and economy where material wants can be satisfied and where material satisfaction, measured by economic indices, was the nation's greatest achievement. Measurable economic success, differently defined than in the 1950s and early 1960s, was still the cultural coin of the realm.

Moreover, the language of economics and the conception that economics is the best way to "keep score," if anything, remained pervasive. Trickling down through the other social sciences, policy and management theory, and the media, economic paradigms were still transplanted—or implanted—into many corners of American life. For example, public choice theory has used the tools of economics to examine political processes. Best-sellers such as Steven D. Levitt's and Stephen J. Dubner's *Freakonomics* (2005) took microeconomic theory to explain behaviors ranging from cheating to naming children. As they wrote: "Incentives are the cornerstone of modern American life. And understanding them—or, often, ferreting them out—is the key to solving just about any riddle, from violent crime to sports cheating to online dating. . . . Knowing what to measure and how to measure it makes a complicated world much less so." Steven Landsburg's *Armchair Economist* (1993) applied the economic logic of costs and benefits, with a libertarian spin, to everyday issues of courtship and entertainment choices (including reading his own book). Tyler Cowen, in *Discover Your Inner Economist* (2008), turned economic concepts into material for a Dale Carnegie–style self-help book, proclaiming that one should "use incentives to fall in love, survive your next meeting, and motivate your dentist." Cowen argued that human behavior and desires can be understood and measured with the tools and language of economics.[22]

The economic measurement revolution launched by Simon Kuznets and others, and that was stoked by everyone from Eisenhower and the National Association of Manufacturers to *Fortune* journalists and school textbook writers, hardly was discarded. If anything, the number of economic statistics—and the numbers of official, academic, and unofficial purveyors of them—were greater than ever by the early 2000s. A day does not go by without new Department of Commerce, Labor, and Treasury, OMB, CBO, or Federal Reserve economic statistics. The constant economic pulse-taking and measurement mania are more prevalent than ever. The consumer and business "confidence" indices pioneered by George Katona, continue to make news under Conference Board auspices, and economically oriented research institutions issue a raft of reports in print and on the Internet. Moreover, in an era of "globalization," World Bank, Organization for Economic Cooperation and Development, World Trade Organization, United Nations, and other international organizations, as well as intergovernmental and business entities such as the G-8 (or G-20), the Davos World Economic Forum, and many international banks and investment firms, issue their own, endless reports on economic performance. If anything, stock-market indices became more watched with the long bull market that began in the mid-1980s, stoked by the proliferation of 24/7 cable TV and the Internet. For a globalized elite, a rising Dow Jones, NASDAQ, and non-American market indices are increasingly more important measures of aggregate and individual success than national output or living-standards statistics.

The new, neoclassical economic consensus that emerged in the last two decades of the twentieth century reestablished but changed the idea that America's business is, and meaning can be found in, economic growth. It fostered the idea that "morning in America" had been lit by the klieg lights of a renascent economy. For market-oriented conservatives, since the 1980s, there were two key differences with their postwar precursors. First, government, in theory, had a lesser role in ensuring prosperity, and, second, the fruits of abundance no longer needed to be broadly shared. In some ways, the rejection of government was more rhetoric than reality, as government continued to play a huge role in steering the U.S. economy in the late twentieth century, grew faster during George W. Bush's administration than at any time since Lyndon Johnson, and expanded greatly with the economic crisis that unfolded in 2008–2009, although the welfare/regulatory state was significantly pared back. Second, tolerance for increasing inequality has been a marked departure from the perspective of the postwar decades.

Reagan, Gingrich, George W. Bush, and other conservatives—drawing on motley forbears including Friedman and von Hayek to Margaret Thatcher and modern supply siders—successfully repackaged neoclassical economics to argue that if taxes were cut, it would spur investment and create employment. At the same time, with deficit spending discredited as a positive fiscal tool to stimulate demand, conservatives called for a balanced budget, which became a proxy for cutting domestic spending. The Reagan tax cuts did not restore the growth and high employment of the early 1960s, and contributed to the rise of socioeconomic inequality and soaring federal deficits under Republican presidents Reagan, George H. W. Bush, and George W. Bush. The national debt rose from $1 trillion when

Ronald Reagan became president to $11 trillion when George W. Bush left office, increasing rapidly under President Barack Obama, with another $45 trillion in unfunded liabilities for Medicare and Social Security.

The rise of a seemingly more free-market politics and political economy and a re-glorification of consumption since the Reagan "revolution" and the near blind faith in markets of the 1990s were seen as marking a new era. Market "liberalization" with limited government "interference" replaced the idea of a Keynesian, government-business-labor partnership in a mixed economy as the route to prosperity. Government-led growth, spurred by fiscal demand management and public investment, at least rhetorically and before the Obama administration, became a thing of the past. Phrases such as "classless abundance for all" and "a rising tide lifting all boats" were not on the lips of many political or business leaders.

Economically—despite some neo-Keynesian fiscal policy under Clinton (tax increases, budget cuts, and the Earned Income Tax Credit's expansion), and again with the financial crisis that exploded in 2008—the post-Reagan, post–Berlin Wall triumph of a market-oriented consensus coincided with growing distortions in the American economic pie. By rejecting demand management and activist fiscal policy, the neoliberal consensus not only rejected government economic intervention but also, by stealth, the postwar consensus that the purpose of economic growth was to raise living standards for all. The tax and spending cuts and more lax regulation of the Reagan and Bush II eras helped enable the rich to get much richer, while miring a sizable chunk of the population in poverty or near poverty and shifting the fruits of growth from the middle class and some of the poor largely to the top quintile—and, particularly, the top few percentage points—of the income and wealth distributions. As we have seen, the pie was growing, but aside from the late 1990s, it wasn't growing for everyone, as the United States became, by the early twenty-first century, the most socioeconomically unequal developed nation.[23]

Faith in "the market" altered American political economy, but by the mid-1980s and during the Clinton era, the belief that faster growth and rising GDP were paramount national goals was very much back in the saddle. Of course, neoliberal market economics differed from the "free enterprise" and "people's capitalism" advocated by Eisenhower, Kennedy, Keyserling, Burns, Heller, the CED, the Ad Council, Henry Luce, and the USIA. From the late 1940s to the 1960s, the visible hand of government, held open to labor and the poor, added a helping hand to the market's invisible hand, boosting individual well-being and national economic growth. Since 1980, the invisible hand was culturally accepted as the primary, legitimate operating principle for the U.S. economy. And many millions of Americans who were helped by the public and private policies of growth liberalism and the cultural optimism in the wake of rising abundance were left to flounder and suffer in a new and turbulently changing economy. The aggregate tide may have continued to rise, but some experienced such spectacular rises that the Forbes 500 became a billionaires' club, while too many others desperately tread water in tide pools of economic insecurity.

The collapse of communism in 1989–91 made the free-marketeers even more gleefully triumphalist. The American economic way was now clearly the only way. Even by the anemic Brezhnev era, there was no longer a communist enemy with which to fight an economic cold war. Nineteen eighty-nine was more than a geopolitical victory; it was the triumph of America's economic system and ideas, which, unlike communism, successfully provided prosperity and economic growth. A new neoclassical "Washington consensus" reigned—not only in American policy and culture but also in the economic model exported to the world by the United States, the IMF, and the World Bank. Once again, ideology (and even history) was purportedly at an end. As in the Christian Middle Ages, there was one clear, reigning faith.

Even in 1980, with Reagan's successful campaign question—"Are you better off than four years ago?"—the message was that rising living standards were the metric of America's success. To Reagan, a growing economy was key to what defined American success, much as it was to earlier, postwar leaders. Sounding like Eisenhower or Kennedy, in his 1990 Economic Report, President George H. W. Bush said: "Our living standards remain well above those of other major industrialized nations. . . . The primary economic goal of my Administration is to achieve the highest possible rate of sustainable economic growth. . . . Growth is the key to raising living standards, to leaving a legacy of prosperity for our children, to uplifting those most in need, and to maintaining America's leadership in the world." President George W. Bush's 2006 State of the Union mentioned the economy twenty-three times and liberty four times.[24] Economic comparisons to the rest of the world still provided a powerful basis for defining what was unique about the nation.

With the United States experiencing 4.5 percent average annual economic growth in the late 1990s, Bill Clinton often echoed much of the postwar rhetoric, even quoting Kennedy's "rising tide" line in a 1999 speech. In his Second Inaugural Address, Clinton boasted that "our economy is the strongest on the earth." As the dot.com bubble again led to talk of a "new" economy, he told 1999 MIT graduates that America was "the most powerful engine of prosperity the world has ever known." At the start of his administration, after campaigning that "it's the economy, stupid," he decried the Carter-like talk of limits: "We simply cannot go gently into a good night of limited economic expectations, slow growth, no growth in living standards, and a lesser future for our children. It is not the American way."[25] With a Republican Congress, otherwise limited domestic-policy successes, and a second-term scandal, Clinton seized on rapid U.S. growth and economic successes to burnish his image. Such pronouncements by Reagan, George H. W. Bush, Clinton, and others were a far cry from Carter's late-1970s comments. On the surface, they certainly sounded much like the rhetoric of Truman, Eisenhower, Kennedy, Johnson, and other postwar leaders, yet the subtext, economic realities, and cultural context all were quite different.

Beyond the neoclassical triumph, recent years also have seen something of a backlash against critics of consumer culture, with postmodernists and neoliberals "on the same side of the barricade," as Don Slater has noted. Postmodernists have argued that critics of consumer culture downplay the positive valences of consumer values. "Functionalist" observers such as Mary Douglas and Baron Isherwood, James Twitchell, Michael Schudson, Gary Cross, Dinesh D'Souza, and others have emphasized both the psychological needs fulfilled by consumption and the active role that people play in constructing meanings and personal identity from consumption. Douglas and Isherwood argued in their 1979 book, *The World of Goods: Towards an Anthropology of Consumption,* that consumer choices are not so much the dictated reflection of "false needs" as a natural social process that expresses and generates culture. They took issue with many critics of consumer culture and many economists, whom they said avoid the question of why people want goods and fail to explain how tastes are shaped. Like Douglas, Jean Baudrillard argued that consumption provides a system of values, meaning, and signs by which people communicate. He questioned the Marxist and producerist belief that people's dominant nature is as a producer, saying that people are fundamentally consumers.[26]

Claiming that people have always enjoyed consuming, Twitchell and Schudson, as in the latter's cleverly titled "Delectable Materialism," said that people are not manipulated into consuming but rather find meaning and order in their lives through consumption. Cross carried these arguments further, saying that mass consumption reinforces liberal ideals of participation and equality. Sounding in the first half of his quote like many postwar apostles of "people's capitalism," he called consumer culture "democracy's highest achievement, giving meaning and dignity to people when workplace participation, ethnic solidarity, and even representative democracy have failed."[27] Indeed, many counter-critics, despite their efforts to sound iconoclastic, have provided little more than an intellectual rehash of the Ad Council–*Fortune* magazine vision of the 1950s, at best—sans the encomia to broad-based abundance, together with an apolitical apologetic for fetishized "markets" and growing inequality. So, the economic metric of consumption was defended as not only a definition of success but also of psychological fulfillment.

But Ronald Reagan certainly said it better than the postmodernists. As he declared in 1985: "With a future beckoning so brightly, we must move forward on the optimistic path of economic growth and expanding opportunity. Isn't that, after all, what it means to be Americans?"[28]

The Rise of Some People's Capitalism: New Realities and Critics

Critics from the left and right may have influenced many Americans' thinking about their nation, their economy, and the wisdom of seeing life through an economic lens. However, changes in the U.S. economy itself had at least as powerful an effect on Americans' thinking. The very numbers that so buttressed the faith in American greatness as an economy began to tell a radically different story: Instead of ever-increasing abundance, growth, and a "rising tide," there was stagflation, rising inequality, economic crises, and increasing hardship not only for the poor but for much of the bottom three, or even four, quintiles of the population.

However, beginning in the 1970s, the very idea of America as "number one" economically came into question, as the Japanese juggernaut and, to a lesser extent, the European Community demonstrated that growth and prosperity could be achieved elsewhere, by other means, and seemingly more successfully. While productivity, growth, and living standards stagnated in America for many of the same socioeconomic strata that had seen them rise in the 1950s and 1960s, Japan surged ahead in the 1980s, other nations passed the United States on a variety of economic indicators, and by the second decade of the twenty-first century China was riding a spectacular growth trajectory that made the glory days of post-war U.S. growth look paltry.

Indeed, many of the very numbers that were eagerly trotted out in the 1950s and early 1960s turned unmercifully against America after the early 1970s. Average wages no longer rose, but inequality did. A rising tide no longer lifted all boats. Productivity growth slowed to a crawl. Working hours stopped declining. The United States seemed to have less and less to export. GDP growth only inched forward as more Americans—particularly women and new immigrants—joined the labor force. Americans made do by going deeper into debt. And the pretty, reassuring, upwardly sloping graphs of 1950s and early 1960s America now characterized first, Japan, other Asian "tigers," and, then, China. In place of upward-marching economic indicators, Americans saw "stagflation," "malaise," a "misery index," waning global "competitiveness," stock-market crashes, burst asset bubbles, and a once rock-solid financial system in tatters. The optimistic faith that growth and abundance could solve the nation's problems and bring better lives to all Americans waned. Whereas pollsters in the late 1950s and early 1960s regularly found overwhelming majorities saying that life was getting better, polling since the 1970s has tended to find majorities saying that things are getting worse, with more than 80 percent saying that the country was "on the wrong track" during the deep recession that began in late 2007 and the 2008 election campaign, with the numbers not much better early in the Obama administration.[29]

Statistics are hotly debated, but many have pointed to a relative stagnation in the living standards of a large portion of the middle class, falling real incomes for the low-skilled, thirty years without a net rise in the male wage (known to the postwar decades as the "family wage"), a poverty rate that has been stuck between 11 and 15 percent since the 1970s, and declining average incomes during the George W. Bush years. Much has been made of the economic insecurity of a once-secure middle class. Long, two-income household working hours, multiple jobs, dwindling benefits, and soaring costs for the three "H"s of housing, health care, and higher education have turned the rosy optimism of the early 1960s into the nervous angst of the early twenty-first century. Many have talked about the savings crisis, as personal savings fell into negative territory around 2005. Americans held more than $11 trillion in mortgage debt and another $2.6 trillion in nonmortgage debt in 2008, equal to about 135 percent of disposable income, an increase of more than 130 percent in a decade. Unfunded pension and health-care liabilities totaled more than

$2 trillion in 2007. Average household credit-card debt rose from about $2,700 in 1989 to $10,700 in 2008. Personal and business bankruptcy filings rose sharply in 2009, an estimated one in four home owners had negative equity in their homes in 2009, and the financial crisis and housing bust led to a record 2.5 million home foreclosures in 2008.[30] This is not to mention another $13 trillion in federal debt in mid-2010 and growing state and local government deficits, which have soared since about 1980, and huge current-account deficits. Likewise, individual Americans and politicians have expressed growing worries about job insecurity and "outsourcing" of service as well as manufacturing jobs in an age of globalization, layoffs, short trading and share-value driven CEOs who no longer see that American well-being is the business of American business. Extraordinarily mobile global capital markets and the capacity to produce and distribute goods and many services globally makes many "American" businesses simply borderless profit-seekers with their headquarters incidentally planted somewhere within the fifty states or with their roots traced to a U.S.-founded past.

In short, the vaunted "people's capitalism" of the late 1950s had given way to a harsher "some people's capitalism" a half century later. Demographers, headline writers, and some politicians made much of the astronomical compensation of a wealthy elite that was economically pulling farther and farther away from the mass of Americans. Average CEO compensation rose from 35 times the average worker's pay in 1978 to 275 times average worker pay in 2007. Since the late 1970s, while average, real, after-tax household income for the highest-earning 1 percent of Americans grew by 176 percent, and the top 20 percent of households saw their incomes rise by about 69 percent, the bottom 20 percent of households experienced income growth of 9 percent. The highest-earning 1 percent of Americans took home as much in after-tax pay as the bottom 40 percent put together. And average household income has mainly risen because of the increasing number of households with multiple wage-earners and jobs. Inflation-adjusted paychecks for the average American male in 2009 were no higher than a generation earlier. By the early twenty-first century, the richest 1 percent of the population owned 33.4 percent of the nation's wealth, with the richest 5 percent owning 58.2 percent, compared with the bottom 40 percent of the population owning just 0.3 percent of national wealth. And that wealthiest 1 percent, or about 3 million Americans, commanded twice as much wealth as the bottom 80 percent, or some 240 million Americans.[31]

Mansions of seven thousand to fifteen thousand square feet prolifer-
ated, and the ranks of decamillionaires soared, as the merely well-to-do,
with no longer spectacular seven-figure assets, accounted for several million Americans. This cascade of wealth at America's economic summit
provided a trickle down to the upper middle class in the top 20 percent
of the wealth and income distributions. But as many spoke of the vast,
old middle class "hollowing out," tens of millions struggled to pay their
bills and afford an ever-growing number of "necessities," all the while anx-
iously looking in life's rearview mirror to watch out for an employment
ax to fall or debt collector to appear. And then there is that one-quarter
of working Americans—eerily similar to the percentage in poverty that
Michael Harrington cited half a century earlier—who in 2007 were earning eight dollars an hour or less. This is not a living wage, and it is not the
measure of a successful, broadly abundant economy. Other than an up-
tick in personal savings, income, debt, and wealth statistics remained on
a worsening trajectory as the twenty-first century moved into its second
decade.

Instead of "classless abundance for all," it was widely accepted at the
end of the Bush era and start of the Obama administration that abundance was really only the province of some Americans. The rise of so-
called "niche marketing" in some ways has been marketers' and academics' codeword for abandoning the implicit, postwar mass-market ideal of
classlessness, in favor of class-based marketing. Unlike the United States
of 1960, Americans recognized that theirs was no longer a land of broad-
based abundance and rising tides: A 2007 Pew Research Council poll found
that 73 percent agreed that "today, it's really true that the rich just get
richer while the poor just get poorer"—perceptions that were exacerbated
by tales of executive bonuses and money-mongering financiers during the
2008 economic meltdown. Wealth and consumption as personal measures
of success remained, whereas the idea of a rising tide for most Americans as a measure of societal success did not. As inequality widened, most
Americans no longer achieved the rising incomes, increased leisure, and
other fruits of abundance that were a hallmark of the postwar decades.
The perpetually rising incomes, increased leisure, and technotopia predicted in the late 1950s turned into a nostalgic dream that was never realized
for most Americans. In an era when stock options, megamansions, and a
panoply of luxury goods were juxtaposed against stagnant wages, middle-
class bankruptcies and foreclosures, and Wal-Mart discount shopping, the
United States certainly experienced what Robert Reich called "the seces-

sion of the successful," Robert Frank called the "winner-take-all" society, and Jared Bernstein termed the "you're on your own economy."[32]

Post-1970s America experienced not only growing social inequality but also declining, or "stickier," social mobility—not the kinds of economic facts to be broadcast proudly. Instead, many European and other countries had higher rates of social mobility than the United States by the early 2000s. Whereas all quintiles of the American population experienced similarly healthy income gains between the 1940s and early 1970s, and disparities in income and wealth modestly declined between the New Deal and the 1960s—key reasons for the near universal belief that economics was the elixir of abundance during these years—the trend lines began to diverge sharply in the 1970s. (These trends briefly reversed during the second Clinton administration.)[33] Although even left-liberals disagree on the causes and extent of social inequality in late-twentieth-century and early-twenty-first-century America, often-mentioned factors have included globalization and the downward mobility of less skilled American workers, the divergence between productivity growth and personal income growth, Reagan and Bush II tax policies, the decline of unions, cuts in the welfare state, and a culture that has rewarded greed.

Yet arguments about growing inequality and diminished social mobility are hotly debated. For example, some say that levels of consumption, rather than income, may be a better measure of living standards, and have not diverged as much, even though this has depended on plummeting savings and rising levels of debt. Others note that absolute incomes, for most households, have kept rising, albeit at very different rates for lower- and middle-income Americans in comparison to those at the top of the income scale. Some attribute greater inequality to the surge in immigration. In addition, more cheery economists point to bigger increases in household incomes, as opposed to individual incomes, although this has been dependent on increasing numbers of household members—women and even teen-agers—working, and people and families working longer hours outside the home and/or at multiple jobs. The one-breadwinner, forty-hour work week of the 1950s, and the predicted twenty-five- to thirty-hour work week, instead became two breadwinners together working seventy to one hundred hours a week, with a dearth of leisure, in the early 2000s.

This sense that the postwar bargain had been broken—and the data to back this up—have been increasingly addressed by academics, journalists, and politicians. MIT economist Frank Levy used government data to convincingly show a marked shift in income distribution in his *Dollars and Dreams: The Changing American Income Distribution* (1987). Journalist Barbara Ehrenreich gave this shift a human face in her description of a sea of minimum-wage workers without health or other benefits and little job security juxtaposed against an ever more affluent upper-middle class and a growing coterie of the stratospherically super-rich in her biting *Nickel and Dimed: On (Not) Getting by in America* (2001). Similarly, Jacob Hacker, in *The Great Risk Shift* (2006) demonstrated that strikingly large numbers of Americans experience sharp income drops and periods without health insurance. In his *The Cost of Talent* (1993) former Harvard president Derek Bok said that diminished competition and the social acceptance of greed during the 1980s diverted talent toward questionably valuable tasks in the private sector, reducing the nation's supply of competent teachers and public servants. Economists Robert Frank and Philip Cook, in their provocative *Winner-Take-All Society: Why the Few at the Top Get So Much More Than the Rest of Us* (1995), argued that many labor markets have come to resemble those of entertainment and professional sports, in which a handful of stars win exorbitant compensation, while most workers fail to win the rewards of a Pavarotti, Tom Cruise, or a Michael Jordan. A torrent of reports in the first decade of the twenty-first-century found that the top decile, and top 1 percent, of the income and wealth distribution pocketed most of the nation's economic gains.[34]

Another aspect of the broken bargain, taken up by sociologist Juliet Schor, has been the decline of leisure. For a century, until World War II, working hours steadily declined from sixty or more hours until the forty-hour week became the postwar-era norm. Despite many 1950s predictions of further declines—by figures ranging from Richard Nixon to George Meany—average working hours have increased by at least 10 percent since 1970. Schor argued that rising consumption in the late twentieth century has been facilitated by increased work, dwindling private savings, and a Veblenesque "competitive consumption" in which Americans have shifted their reference group for consuming to ever more upscale, upper-middle-class norms. Echoing Betty Friedan's quote that "housewifery expands to fill the time available," economists Valerie Ramey and Neville Francis found that the time Americans spend doing housework is higher today than in the early twentieth century as leisure has declined.[35]

The rise in individual working hours masks the much sharper rise in household working hours. While the postwar emphasis on domesticity and discrimination against working women until the late twentieth century made women less-than-equal Americans, much of the tremendous influx of women into the workforce since about 1970 has been driven by individual or household economic need. Elizabeth Warren and Amelia Warren Tygi have argued, in *The Two-Income Trap: Why Middle-Class Mothers and Fathers Are Going Broke* (2005), that while two-income families earned about 75 percent more at the beginning of the twenty-first century than single-income families did in 1970, they actually had about 10 percent less discretionary income because of rising costs of housing, health care, child care, taxes, and other expenses. They calculated that inflation-adjusted discretionary income for middle-class, two-income families was an average of $18,110 around 2000—a number that hadn't budged in a decade—compared with $19,560 for middle-class single-income families in 1970.[36] The male "family wage" of the postwar decades may have been sexist, but it did provide for greater aggregate and family well-being and "leisure," and less harried lives for tens of millions of American households.

In short, economic facts no longer painted the pretty picture of the United States that they did in the 1950s and 1960s. Given this, and the growing sense that the economy inspired more fear than pride, how tenable was the very idea of an America defined economically?

8

Measuring America in the Twenty-first Century

We can measure G.N.P. . . . But we know that they are not the most important characteristics of a nation's life.

JIMMY CARTER, 1979

A decade into the twenty-first century it is difficult to see the appeal of framing U.S. identity in economic terms. At this juncture in our nation's history, why would Americans embrace such a framework for thinking about their country, its success and greatness, and their personal success? The economic failures that began in 2008, extreme and seemingly surprising, came in the wake of a U.S. economy that has performed unevenly at best for several decades. As we have seen, the moderate economic growth of the quarter century beginning in the early 1980s has masked widening inequality, a growing middle-class "squeeze," increased privation and economic insecurity for millions, a ravaged industrial base, a tattered "social contract," and diminished U.S. economic clout in a rapidly globalizing economy. The Wall Street, asset-bubble, and credit-market catastrophes of 2000 and 2008– only make the picture more grim. As poll upon poll have revealed for more than a generation, Americans are cynical, anxious about their futures, more angry than happy, and more inward-looking and alienated from the public sphere than David Riesman or Christopher Lasch could have imagined. As is often noted, many believe that the historic American promise of our children living better lives than their parents has become a thing of the past.

Postwar ideas about America as an economy had to do with the nation's identity—defining what the United States was, what made it tick, and what made it unique. Some threads of identity are more central than others—and the preceding pages have laid out the argument that, after the Depression and World War II, the United States wove a new garment with which to drape itself with threads that emphasized things economic and measurable. Like most healthy conceptions of identity, these ideas focused on the positive—what was good and great. It is important to understand what was emphasized, why such emphases were placed, what psychological and cultural meanings they had for Americans, and what effects these messages about America had on U.S. politics, policy, and the economy itself. The postwar economic "measure of America"—never monolithic, always nuanced, often challenged—nonetheless profoundly changed how the American people saw their country and themselves in both positive and less positive ways.

The abundant economy and rising economic indicators defined national and personal identity and self-worth, and framed conceptions of the United States during the latter part of the twentieth century. Long after economists were lionized as "masters of abundance," the idea that economics is how you score America certainly has not disappeared. The United States was a remarkably growing and rich nation beginning in the 1940s. By most aggregate economic measures, it still is. But this measure of America never primarily has been an economic story, even though it was infused with the language and metrics of economics. Instead, it has been largely about culture and a conception of the United States that permeated the thinking of the American people. Such ideas didn't arise sui generis. Opinion-shaping elites helped give voice and credibility to them, but they were not imposed on Americans. The American people were not victims of propaganda, brainwashing, or what Marxists have called "false consciousness." The United States was, and is, an open society, with differing views; ideas and beliefs are cast into the mix. Some messengers have more cultural power than others, but some ideas also simply have more truth value than others. They are plausible, compelling, and appealing, and thus are adopted by large segments of the population. This is merely how a culture works.

During the mid-twentieth century, broad-based abundance and the quest for it united Americans. This was the essence of the postwar social contract, not only politically—in terms of the liberal consensus on the "mixed economy"—but also as a cultural motif. The postwar ethos of a mighty economy providing better lives for all Americans was the cultural expression of the social contract and a revamped American dream that endured from World War II until at least the early 1970s. Since then, the United States has lost the near unity of purpose—the alliance of business, workers, and government, Republicans and Democrats—to strive for not only economic growth but also turning the fruits of that growth into better lives for more than 300 million people. The idea that business

generally sought Americans' best interests has all but vanished in an age
of corporate and financial-industry mismanagement and greed, downsiz-
ing and offshoring, and the Wal-Mart/McJob economy. CED-like efforts
to promote America's greater good succumbed to the view that "greed
is good," a value only somewhat caricatured in the 1987 film *Wall Street*
and its 2010 sequel. And the idea that government was the people's beneficent helpmate in securing ever-rising prosperity has given way to a
wave of cynicism about political leaders in Washington and throughout
the country.

While the cultural commitment to measurably increasing abundance
united Americans for decades, the excessive focus on measures of material wealth since World War II has been facile and shallow. Life is not primarily about economics and prosperity, despite the hubristic statements
of economists, business leaders, politicians, journalists, and others. Economic growth and rising living standards are important, and measuring
them is essential in a modern, complex society, but they are not the full
measure of any nation. Life, of course, is richer than that. As the striking
1912 Lawrence, Massachusetts, textile workers famously are said to have
said: "Hearts starve as well as bodies; give us bread, but give us roses."[1]
Americans, who historically have been an idealistic and religious people
influenced by many nonmaterialistic values, at some levels, realize that
there is more to success, happiness, and the good life than rising GDP, individual or household incomes, asset values, consumption, or Wall Street
indices.

Moreover, in light of falling stock and housing values, sluggish growth,
stagnant incomes, and sticky social mobility, the idea of delineating what
makes America unique or great, using much contemporary economic
data, is hardly a recipe for pride, patriotism, or cultural cohesion in the
early twenty-first century. Likewise, the case for American exceptionalism based on economic measures becomes rather implausible when the
story behind the data is less than stellar. The economic crisis that began
in 2008, amplifying the already straitened economic conditions of many
Americans over several decades, is hardly grist for being a "pompous braggart," as *Scholastic* long ago wrote. It does not help that the nation is also
being challenged by rising economic powers such as China or that its very
model of capitalism has come into question. Indeed, the United States is
no longer the leader of the pack when it comes to most of the economic
rankings in which it was once number one. Contemporary America's
economy is not so exceptional in either sense of the word. It goes without

saying that the public reverence for do-no-wrong economists that brought Saint Keynes to the cover of *Time* in 1965 has long since dissipated. Indeed, by 2009, many were proclaiming—without too many tears shed—the death of neoclassical economics. In sum, to see early-twenty-first-century America through an economic lens is to peer through a glass darkly.

Nonetheless, that is precisely what most Americans continue to do. A decade into the new century, economics—national and personal—is at least as much a cultural metric of identity, and of success and failure, as it was during the Eisenhower or Kennedy eras. Deluged and obsessed by economic data, we remain convinced that who we are as Americans can best be described by a raft of quantitative economic measures. Whether we look at macroeconomic data or financial-market indicators, or gauges of personal wealth, income, and consumption, quantitative economic measures remain the ways by which we largely understand ourselves and our progress. Each daily statistic is overanalyzed to determine whether we (our economy being a proxy for Americans) are getting better or worse.

Economics has remained the measure of America in the Bush and early Obama eras. We judge our nation as failed or flawed if GDP, the stock market, wealth, and incomes decline; if debt and unemployment increase; and if the trend lines on our forest full of economic graphs point the wrong way. We are not necessarily wrong to do so, but we are still much more likely to see these as the ways to take America's pulse than whether we are achieving greater equity or justice; successfully cultivating the life of the mind and the spirit; being a force for peace and international understanding; or bequeathing a healthier and more sustainably habitable planet for future generations. At the same time, we too little measure our nation by the cultural qualities cited in the 1940s by Lee Coleman, in the 1830s by Tocqueville, or by our Founders—that we are generally a free, democratic, altruistic, tolerant, creative, and entrepreneurial people. Our freedoms and other values are too often taken for granted as cultural wallpaper, while what remains first and foremost in our minds are the furnishings of our cultural home, which are material and economically quantifiable.

Economics remains America's measure in a darker, more personal sense as well. "Keeping up with the Joneses" may have been a mid-twentieth-century construct, but it continues in such post-1980s ideas for measuring individual success as "It's all about the Benjamins" and "Whoever dies with the most toys wins." These formulations were economic, materialistic, competitive, and desirous of "more," but the earlier one suggested satisfaction with parity (albeit at rising levels), whereas the more recent ones are explicit about economic one-upmanship. Forget the idea of all boats being lifted on a swelling economic sea, and think instead of catching the biggest economic wave and riding it solo the farthest. "Bling" captures our consciousness. Having the most money and the most that money can buy continue to resonate as primary cultural symbols of one's individuality and station in contemporary America. For all too many, "success" and "failure" are calibrated in these terms—a recipe for widespread disappointment, anxiety, and unhappiness. The common quest and social contract of the middle decades of the twentieth century were something quite different from today's lemming-like personal pursuit of wealth and consumption, which author Samuel Barber has said is Americans' only remaining purpose as a people.[2] While money and material well-being always, and reasonably, have mattered to Americans, and to all people, so too have less tangible assets, the broad array of personal attributes and assets that Martin Luther King spoke of as "the content of our character."

The conception of America as an economy has changed how we think, relate to others, and view our roles in society, and it has shaped our policy predilections in many ways. This mind-set has helped supplant moral, ethical, and idealistic ways of thinking about life. Such ideas have given a green light to an almost frenzied imperative for the nation and individuals to earn and consume more, with too little thought for environmental or moral consequences, the future, or other worthy values and goals. It has colored our policymaking for sixty years. It is Hamiltonianism with a vengeance when what matters most is economic growth. Government domestic policy should concern itself with much more than ensuring that economic indicators rise; this, however, has not been the case for many decades. Americans' thinking about success, happiness, and goals also should concern itself with much more than economically measurable achievements.

Measuring America as an economy also has led to the application of economic models to other aspects of political and social-science thinking, a trend furthered by the advent of public choice theory and by a raft of popular economic commentators. From politics and social science to everyday thinking, we live in the shadow of myriad economic metaphors. Even our personal lives are framed, seriously or tongue-in-cheek, as cost-benefit calculations.

At the same time, the ways in which the postwar economic vision changed after 1980 from "people's capitalism" to "some people's capitalism" hardly has been neutral in its effects on either our policymaking or our culture. The postwar era's egalitarian, if propagandistic, idea of "abundance for all in a classless society" has all but disappeared. With the dwindling of this belief in rising, broad-based prosperity, the contemporary United States has given up a great deal in terms of a commitment to socioeconomic justice. The Jeffersonian belief—but also that of Harry Truman, Dwight Eisenhower, John Kennedy, Lyndon Johnson, and even Richard Nixon—that the United States should be a land of opportunity and improving outcomes for every American, not just a privileged minority, has had little cultural currency since the late 1970s or 1980. Gone is the idea that pervaded the culture from the 1940s through the mid-1960s—from schoolbooks and glossy magazines to politicians' speeches and America's public diplomacy—that the United States is a great nation because, as the economists' charts showed, economic well-being was improving for the vast majority of its people and not just the well-to-do.

During the postwar decades and throughout much of its history, the United States not only was philosophically and politically predicated on equality, but it also functioned best economically, and people were more optimistic, when Americans felt that relative equality was real. Millions of Americans obviously would be better off than they are but also less bitter about the gross income disparities that leave many in the dust and far fewer in Guccis and Mercedeses. Even if economist Richard Easterlin was right, that happiness only rises to a certain threshold income, evidence suggests that happiness also rises when most people feel that they are not faring demonstrably worse than a cosseted elite. Moreover, more equal societies may well experience stronger overall growth, as the postwar era suggests—holding constant myriad other factors from labor and capital markets or demography to legal and regulatory frameworks.

Economists are divided about the relationship between inequality and growth, but studies have suggested that more unequal societies may hinder growth in several ways: They may reduce potential investment in education and health, or "human capital," for all but the relatively wealthy, resulting in a lower marginal return on investment. They may reduce savings and, hence, capital for investment, and create incentives for the disadvantaged to drop out of the market economy, opting for black-market or criminal activities or dependence on the state. Thus, a more equal distribution of resources gives more people a greater interest in participating in the economy in a variety of ways, leading to higher effort and output.[3]

As economic measures of ever-rising, measurable, and broadly shared abundance have become harder to come by, not only personal happiness has been affected but also the cultural zeitgeist. Accepting the precepts of a growing, bounteous economy as a cultural measure of America fed deep strains of popular optimism and confidence about Americans' national and personal futures. The idea that Americans could quantify how life perpetually was getting better fueled an underlying happiness and hope. They, and their nation, were thriving, and life only would get better. This affected individuals' psychological outlook and a sub rosa historical faith that perfectibility was possible. Utopia was just around the corner.

Instead, the United States has lost much of the almost utopian idealism and giddy optimism of the quarter century after World War II that prosperity could be ensured by well-meaning, respected government and business leaders, and that this, in turn, could solve the nation's great problems. The postwar story line of the United States as an ever more perfect economy fueled most Americans' faith that their lives continually would get better. It also increased pride in their country as making good on its founding promise to provide its citizens with the opportunity to pursue happiness with success. Whereas technological progress and economic growth remain American preoccupations into the twenty-first century, gone is the stunning postwar vision that a growing economy and the abundance generated by technology and wise economic policymaking would bring a paradise of material wealth, science fiction–like leaps in the very nature of life, and a surfeit of leisure in which to cultivate cultural, interpersonal, and spiritual pursuits. Eisenhower- and Kennedy-era pundits talked about an abundant society in which the life of the mind and spirit would flourish. That is about as au courant as the personal gyrocopters at early 1960s world's fairs.

In many ways, figures ranging from Henry Luce and (the 1950s-vintage) Richard Nixon to Leon Keyserling and Walter Heller were liberal utopians. America's future-oriented spirit, amplified in the postwar decades, was beautifully captured in Robert Kennedy's deservedly remembered line, borrowed from the work of Irish playwright George Bernard Shaw: "Some men see things as they are and say, 'Why?' I dream of things that never were, and say 'Why not?'" Since the 1970s, mainstream utopians simply have not existed in American life. Americans may continue to imagine making personal fortunes and partaking of a consumer bonanza. But the belief in an ever more perfect macroeconomy as a proxy for the nation—and one that can bestow noneconomic benefits—has slipped from popular consciousness. As novelist Kurt Vonnegut said before his death in 2007, "The America I loved is gone. It was an optimistic place. [When you asked people what class they belonged to] practically everybody said 'middle,' and there was always a job you could get that was enough to live on."[4] The ascendant mass comfort depicted in 1950s and 1960s TV sitcoms has given way to a lottery-like view of hitting the jackpot on reality shows or in casinos. And the starry-eyed vision of a technotopian future portrayed in *The Jetsons* has been displaced by the casual cynicism of *The Simpsons.*

So, in Barack Obama's America, what, if any, aspects of these cultural markers are worth preserving, reinforcing, or even gently modifying? Does an economic mirror to view the United States still make sense in a country that, as Galbraith said, is rich in private goods and not so well off in public goods? Does it make sense when only selective economic metrics suggest success, while too many others do not? Is such an economic looking glass something of an anachronism—a throwback to an era of industrial might and the wondrous newness of abundant mass production and consumption? Is taking our national temperature with thermometers to measure GDP, personal income, and consumption relevant when we might better measure our national well-being by the knowledge and skills of our children, the sustainability of our environment, the physical security and peace of our world, and the "content of our character"? We mistake macroeconomic might or personal economic success for greatness at our peril. Even in recession, we still may be the world's largest and productive economy, but that won't last forever. China is nipping at our heels to surpass us in GDP; other countries do better than the United States on other economic metrics. We still may be the world's "greatest" economy, but what does that mean if more and more Americans aren't sharing in the fruits of that greatness? Perhaps greatness, happiness, and the success of a society and individual lives—as Robert Kennedy and Martin Luther King said so eloquently—are best measured by more intangible things like heroism, compassion, values, and character, not economic statistics.

If a narrow, economically defined measure of America is neither factually and culturally viable nor morally desirable, what can or should replace or supplement it? How can the United States and its people evaluate whether they are succeeding and be hopeful about their futures? An economic measuring of America is neither wrong nor right. Nor is it entirely bad or good. The philosophical, political, and moral questions are large and broadly ramifying. However, any efforts to reshape America and how it conceives of itself and its goals must take into account culture and psychology as much as policy, politics, and, yes, economics. If, as a nation, we want to restructure or tinker with how our citizens live, we need to be cognizant, artful navigators of culture. In policy arenas, this can be cast not only in terms of investments in "people" or "the future" but also as efforts to invigorate our minds and spirit. Any attempts to achieve socioeconomic change to build a truly "great society" for the twenty-first century must go hand in hand with cultural and moral change to build a truly good society at the level of beliefs, values, and behavior.

Identity matters. Cultures and peoples require definition for cohesion, self-understanding, and hope. That is why, despite its conceptual problems, it is important to recognize, analyze, define, and even try to redefine American identity and what it means to thrive as a nation and as citizens. The beliefs and values embedded in a culture and how individuals appropriate them are amorphous yet not wholly incoherent. A 2008 study that found a "weakening" sense of national identity in the United States concluded: "A sense of national identity is necessary to enable individuals to transcend self-absorption and commit to the common good."[5] And such an identity needs to be richly constructed, embracing much more than quantifiable, economic measures.

Philosophers may debate the validity of Thomas Hobbes's and Jean-Jacques Rousseau's formulations of a social contract, but their basic idea remains sound: To prevent social conflict and private interest from running amok, a society needs to establish and abide by reciprocal rights and duties, as well as privileges and responsibilities. As the twentieth-century philosopher John Rawls has added, a viable, healthy society also needs agreed-upon general principles of civil and social justice. These must have cultural and values-based underpinnings, as well as political and economic ones. And as economist Amartya Sen has argued, society's aim must be to extend human "capabilities"—some dependent on economic factors, but many not.

Many possible components of a new social contract are needed and can be hotly debated. But one underlying principle—and one from which we can learn from the postwar decades—is a need for collaboration among government, business, and citizens. Government can no longer be derided as "the problem"; greater responsibility also must be demanded of individuals and employers. Although the notion of reciprocal rights and responsibilities suggests that government should provide a more embracing—but not coddling—safety net, business should provide higher and more evenly distributed pay, and individuals need to take better care of themselves and their families with an eye to the long term. It may "take a village," but it also takes good, old-fashioned American individualism.

A new social contract must go together with new visions of what America is about, what makes for a good society, and what defines success for individuals and the nation. The powerful postwar idea that America's—and Americans'—principal national purposes and measures of success are economic ones will not vanish with the waving of a cultural, moral, or policymaking wand. But a broad array of social institutions can help Americans begin to think in other terms and value other things.

If, for example, we accept that economics will remain a key measure of America, we need to embark on public and private actions that, once again, make economic metrics a source of satisfaction and hope, rather than fear and discontent. We can strive to build a strong economy for all those now struggling and frightened. This requires policymaking that is both pro-growth and pro-justice, and that is engaged with business and citizens/workers/consumers. If we can begin to accomplish this, we then need to speak about economics differently and in broader contexts: Aggregate and individual wealth per se are not so important as how they are used and distributed. What our wealth buys, why we want growth—not wealth, income, or growth in isolation—are what matters. In our cultural messaging to this effect, we could take a page from Eisenhower and the Ad Council but also from the deeper wells of our political and spiritual traditions. Messaging—talking the talk—as we have seen, is important in achieving meaningful change in culture and values.

Similarly, if we want to place greater emphasis on service, knowledge, stewardship, justice, and civic engagement, this must entail not only laws and policies but also concerted efforts to change how Americans think about themselves and the meanings of their country. From the pioneers of national income accounting to those exploring the frontiers of an economics of happiness, economists and others have long recognized that economic data are far from a perfect measure of a society. As Robert Kennedy noted more than forty years ago, acts of kindness are not measured by GDP, while pollution-creating activities are. Perhaps, in our new cultural measuring of America, we should find ways to calculate, institutionalize, and disseminate such metrics. We could develop an index of overall contributions to our society and world—including our economic activity—that also would include such things as volunteer service, charitable giving, unpaid family care, participation in schools and community institutions, and other forms of giving. We also could measure ourselves by improvements in our health, our civility and courtesy, our knowledge and learning, our leisure and life satisfaction, and the cleanliness and greenness of our world. Perhaps, as some have attempted, we need a multifaceted, nuanced index of well-being, and we need to engage in serious discussion of what it means to thrive and succeed in life.

"Thriving," "well-being," and meaningful, satisfying measures for American cultural identity are elusive, values-laden concepts with different meanings for different people. Thus, we need to measure our country's successes and what it essentially is about, as well as individual success, in many ways. Are measures of success cultural and historical constructs, or are there elements that are basic to human nature? Is success a process—of growth, of attaining goals, of achieving? Is it akin to Abraham Maslow's theory of self-actualization, of first meeting basic needs in order to be able to reach one's full potential? Or can it be seen in a more steady-state, Zen-like manner?

The postwar conventional wisdom equating success and American-ness with rising economic indicators clearly masks a host of other ways of thinking about what makes the United States or individual Americans who they are and happy and optimistic about their lives and nation. Even though spirituality and materialism are generally viewed as antonyms, Americans are increasingly captivated by emerging trends that merge the two concepts, from minister Joel Osteen's "prosperity gospel" to money guru Suze Orman's financial/spiritual advice. Can spirituality be a means to prosperity? Or perhaps the converse is closer to Americans' concept of thriving, more in keeping with Somerset Maugham's vision, in *Of Human Bondage:* "It is not wealth one asks for, but just enough to preserve one's dignity, to work unhampered, to be generous, frank and independent"?

Ever since Richard Easterlin questioned the sacrosanct link between wealth and happiness in the mid-1970s, other economists and social scientists have tried to measure happiness or "well-being." Amartya Sen, with his focus on human capabilities, contributed to the U.N. Development Programme's attempt to replace economic metrics of societal success with a Human Development Index. The World Values Survey, conducted by the University of Michigan's Institute for Social Research, and other "happiness indices" have made stabs at asking whether people are happy, charting the vicissitudes of their feelings, and comparing countries and communities. But many of these efforts have been crude and superficial. More substantively, behavioral economist Daniel Kahneman and others have contributed to the "gross national happiness" construct, which includes wellness measured in economic, environmental, physical, mental, workplace, social, and political terms.

John Rowe and Robert Kahn, in the wake of the pioneering work of gerontologist Robert Butler, have written about "successful aging," and gerontologists have used indicators that include physical well-being, high cognitive and physical functioning, and active engagement with life and people. Physicians, particularly pediatricians, have cast thriving as a matter of healthy physical and, to a lesser extent, emotional development.

Thomas Jefferson, echoing eighteenth-century philosophes, said that people had an entitlement to happiness, or at least to the pursuit of it—but, as we have seen, this is open to multiple interpretations. Psychologists and self-help gurus have defined thriving and a healthy sense of identity in terms of a well-integrated ego, contentment, self-awareness, a sense of security, love and friendship, "centeredness," and freedom from the "demons" that the modern world has characterized as mental illness.

Others have rejected the one-dimensional conflation of thriving and subjective happiness, suggesting that "shiny happy people" are not necessarily doing well as fully developed human beings. From the ancient Greeks to the Talmud to Benjamin Franklin (who ascribed to the "healthy and wealthy" formula, too), wisdom has been a part of thriving. Artists have extolled the value of creativity. Achievement and recognition also may be benchmarks of success, but to what extent are these competitively driven or colored by a culture that values celebrity? Christians and others say that to grow spiritually as children of God is the key to thriving; many atheists would disagree. Freedom and independence have been posited by political philosophers as essential to a good life, while some consider these less important than connectedness with other people, or, once again, material abundance. (For instance, is China repeating America's postwar experience, albeit more rapidly, where economic growth trumps more basic freedoms?)

Indeed, how we measure America and its people's well-being not only looms larger on the research agenda of many disciplines but seems to hover above our political, economic, and personal lives like the big, unspoken question about our nation, its citizens, its goals, and its future. At a time of economic and geopolitical challenges, politicians are acutely sensitive to "how Americans are doing." This question cannot meaningfully be answered only by economic measures.

Twenty-first-century America needs a language laden not only with economic accounting but also with social and individual accountability for qualities that are essential to our humanity and were wisely embodied in much of America's early political theory and culture. One underlying principle that we can retain from World War II and the ensuing decades is the we're-all-in-this-together spirit, instead of the "you're on your own economy," of which Jared Bernstein, Vice President Joseph Biden's economic adviser, has spoken.[6] Throughout American history—from the efforts of Alexander Hamilton, Henry Clay, Abraham Lincoln, and the postwar "growth consensus" to foster economic and educational development to Lincoln's, Teddy Roosevelt's, FDR's, and LBJ's efforts to advance social justice—government has done many things to make life in the United States much better. Business and finance cannot be a lone rangers, out to maximize short-term shareholder value without responsibility for its workers, consumers, communities, and the nation that has given it the opportunity to succeed. Individual Americans cannot just tune out, tend their own gardens, and consume their way into financial and moral oblivion with little thought of their fellow Americans or of tomorrow. And those who shape our culture need to move—or be prodded to move—to extol values other than material ones about what America means and what it means to be a good, successful American.

If there are several lessons from the postwar story, one is that policy, including economic policy, cannot be divorced from culture. We cannot succeed as a people or as an economy without a compelling cultural vision of who we are and what our goals should be. We need to re-ask the early 1960s questions of "prosperity for what?" and probe deeply. Well-being, including economic well-being, is an admirable goal, but we need to define it more carefully and thoughtfully than as a function of economic output, income, growth, or consumption. And we need to define it in tandem with other goals. Economic metrics will remain important, but we must situate them in broader, more idealistic, more long-term and socially meaningful contexts. A sense of cultural identity is important for Americans—for national cohesion, national purpose, self-understanding, confidence, and the optimism that motivates the quest for better tomorrows. We just need to be careful that we frame, define, and measure the parameters of that identity in rich, multidimensional terms. Economics is an important way of measuring America or any society, but we must think more (or again) of the many other, non-economic ways of measuring the United States.

Notes

Introduction: A New Measure of America?

1. Lee Coleman, "What Is American? A Study of Alleged American Traits," *Social Forces* 19 (1941): 26–28.

2. Louis Hartz, *The Liberal Tradition in America: An Interpretation of American Political Thought since the Revolution* (New York: Harcourt, Brace and World, 1955), 10–11, 43, 292; Daniel J. Boorstin, *The Genius of American Politics* (Chicago: University of Chicago Press, 1953); Henry Steele Commager, *The American Mind: An Interpretation of American Thought and Character since the 1880s* (New Haven: Yale University Press, 1950); and Bernard Bailyn, *Origins of American Politics* (New York: Alfred A. Knopf, 1968).

3. Frederick Jackson Turner, "The Significance of the Frontier in American History," in *The Frontier in American History* (New York: Henry Holt, 1921); and David Potter, *People of Plenty: Economic Abundance and the American Character* (Chicago: University of Chicago Press, 1954).

4. Godfrey Hodgson, *America in Our Time* (New York: Vintage Books, 1976); Alan Wolfe, *America's Impasse: The Rise and Fall of the Politics of Growth* (New York: Pantheon Books, 1981); Robert Lekachman, *The Age of Keynes* (New York: Vintage Books, 1966); Robert Griffith, "Forging America's Postwar Order: Domestic Politics and Political Economy in the Age of Truman," in *The Truman Presidency*, ed. Michael J. Lacey (Cambridge: Cambridge University Press, 1989); Elizabeth Fones-Wolf, *Selling Free Enterprise: The Business Assault on Labor and Liberalism, 1945–1960* (Urbana: University of Illinois Press, 1994); Robert M. Collins, *The Business Response to Keynes, 1929–1964* (New York: Columbia University Press, 1981) and *More: The Politics of Economic Growth in Postwar America* (New York: Oxford University Press, 2000); and Lizabeth Cohen, *A Consumers' Republic: The Politics of Mass Consumption in Postwar America* (New York: Alfred A. Knopf, 2003).

5. U.S. House of Representatives, "Full Employment Act of 1945: Hearings," National Archives and Records Administration: RG 233: Records of the U.S. House of Representatives, 1945, 1143.

6. Murray Shields and Donald B. Woodward, *Prosperity: We Can Have It if We Want It* (New York: McGraw-Hill, 1945), 3, 8, and 9.

7. Thomas R. Carskadon and George Soule, *U.S.A. in New Dimensions: The Measure and Promise of America's Resources* (New York: Twentieth Century Fund/Macmillan, 1957), 2, 121.

8. The Gallup Poll–AIPO, Jan. 1956; George H. Gallup, *The Gallup Poll: Public Opinion 1935–1971* (New York: Random House, 1972), vol. 2, 1016, 1399, and vol. 3, 1749, 1829, 1923, 2046, 2072; The Gallup Poll–AIPO, 8 Dec. 1959; University of Michigan Survey Research Center, Economic Behavior Program, *Surveys of Consumer Attitudes and Behavior* (Ann Arbor, Mich.: Inter-University Consortium for Political and Social Research, 1965); Lloyd A. Free and Hadley Cantril, *The Political Beliefs of Americans: A Study of Public Opinion* (New Brunswick, N.J.: Rutgers University Press, 1967); and Robert Lane, *The Loss of Happiness in Market Democracies* (New Haven: Yale University Press, 2000), 74.

9. Stanley Lebergott, *The Americans: An Economic Record* (New York: W. W. Norton, 1984), 396; Robert L. Heilbroner and Aaron Singer, *The Economic Transformation of America* (New York: Harcourt Brace Jovanovich, 1977), 54; U.S. Department of Commerce, *Historical Statistics of the United States: Colonial Times to 1970, Part 1* (Washington, D.C.: GPO, 1975), 224; and Richard H. Steckel, "Nutritional Status in the Colonial American Economy," *William and Mary Quarterly*, 3rd ser., 56:1 (Jan. 1999): 45.

10. Heilbroner and Singer, *Economic Transformation*, 54; Hodgson, *America in Our Time*, 83, U.S. Department of Commerce, *Historical Statistics of the United States, Part 1*, 224; Lebergott, *The Americans*, 396; Wolfe, *America's Impasse*, 13; J. Frederic Dewhurst and Associates, *America's Needs and Resources: A Twentieth Century Fund Survey Which Includes Estimates for 1950 and 1960* (New York: Twentieth Century Fund, 1947), 4, 651; Stephen A. Marglin and Juliet B. Schor, *The Golden Age of Capitalism: Reinterpreting the Postwar Experience* (Oxford: Clarendon Press, 1990), 187; and U.S. Census Bureau, *Poverty Status of People by Family Relationship, Race, and Hispanic Origin, 1959–2003*.

11. Heilbroner and Singer, *Economic Transformation*, 322.

12. Lane, *Loss of Happiness*, 74, 24–25; David Blanchflower and Andrew Oswald, "Happiness and the Human Development Index," National Bureau of Economic Research Working Paper no. 11416; and Richard Easterlin, "Does Economic Growth Improve the Human Lot? Some Empirical Evidence," in *Nations and Households in Economic Growth*, ed. Paul A. David and Melvin W. Reder (New York: Academic Press, 1974).

13. Robert E. Weems Jr., *Desegregating the Dollar: African-American Consumerism in the Twentieth Century* (New York: New York University Press, 1998), 56–69.

14. Dwight D. Eisenhower, State of the Union address, 7 Jan. 1954, http://www.geocities.com/presidentialspeeches/1954.htm?200514.

15. J. Hector St. John de Crèvecoeur, *Letters from an American Farmer* (New York: Penguin Books, 1981); Alexis de Tocqueville, *Democracy in America* (New York: Alfred A. Knopf, 1994), 26, 119, 164–65, 198–99, 211; Turner, "Significance of the Frontier"; Margaret Mead, *And Keep Your Powder Dry: An Anthropologist Looks at America* (New York: William Morrow, 1942); Coleman, "What Is American?" 26–28; Hartz, *Liberal Tradition*, 10–11, 292; David Riesman with Nathan Glazer and Reuel Denney, *The Lonely Crowd: A Study of the Changing American Character* (New Haven: Yale University Press, 1950); Potter, *People of Plenty*; Samuel Huntington, *Who Are We? The Challenges to America's National Identity* (New York: Simon & Schuster, 2004); and Bradley Foundation, *E Pluribus Unum: The Bradley Project on America's National Identity* (Milwaukee: Bradley Foundation, June 2008).

16. Daniel Rodgers, "Exceptionalism," in *Imagined Histories: American Historians Interpret the Past*, ed. Anthony Molho and Gordon S. Wood (Princeton: Princeton University Press, 1998), 21–40; and Prasenjit Duara, "Historicizing National Identity, or Who Imagines What and Whom," in *Becoming National: A Reader*, ed. Geoff Eley and Ronald Grigor Suny (New York: Oxford University Press, 1996).

17. Antonio Gramsci, *Prison Notebooks* (New York: Columbia University Press, 1991); Georg Lukacs, *History and Class Consciousness: Studies in Marxist Dialectics* (Cambridge, Mass.: MIT Press, 1971); Herbert Marcuse, *One-Dimensional Man: Studies in the Ideology of Advanced Industrial Society* (Boston: Beacon Press, 1964); Raymond Williams, *Culture and Society, 1780–1950* (New York: Columbia University Press, 1950); T. J. Jackson Lears, "The Concept of Cultural Hegemony: Problems and Possibilities," *American Historical Review* 90:3 (June 1985): 568–73; Lears, "Making Fun of Popular Culture," *American Historical Review* 97:5 (Dec. 1992): 1420–23; and Richard W. Fox and T. J. Jackson Lears, *The Culture of Consumption: Critical Essays in American History, 1880–1960* (New York: Pantheon, 1983), x.

18. Lears, "Concept of Cultural Hegemony," 586; Lawrence W. Levine, "The Folklore of Industrial Society: Popular Culture and Its Audiences," *American Historical Review* 97:5 (Dec. 1992): 1365–99; and Clifford Geertz, *The Interpretation of Culture* (New York: Basic Books, 1973).

19. Ernest Gellner, *Nations and Nationalism* (Ithaca: Cornell University Press, 1983); and Benedict Anderson, *Imagined Communities: Reflections on the Origins and Spread of Nationalism* (London: Verso Editions and NLB, 1983).

20. T. H. Breen, *The Marketplace of Revolution: How Consumer Politics Shaped American Independence* (New York: Oxford University Press, 2004), xv, 24.

21. David Nye, *America as Second Creation: Technology and Narratives of New Beginnings* (Cambridge, Mass.: MIT Press, 2003), 16–18; Erich Fromm, introduction to *Looking Backward, 2000–1887,* by Edward Bellamy (New York: New American Library, 1960), v, x.

22. Reid Badger, *The Great American Fair: The World's Columbian Exposition and American Culture* (Chicago: Nelson Hall, 1979), 104, 113, 131; and Robert W. Rydell, *World of Fairs* (Chicago: University of Chicago Press, 1993), 15.

23. Andrew Carnegie, *The Gospel of Wealth and Other Timely Essays* (Cambridge, Mass.: Harvard University Press, 1962), 14, 25, 27, 95.

24. Henry George, *Progress and Poverty: An Inquiry into the Cause of Industrial Depressions and of Increase of Want with Increase of Wealth . . . The Remedy* (New York: Robert Schalkenbach Foundation, 1955), 3, 8–9; and "The Omaha Platform," in *Myth and Reality in the Populist Revolt,* ed. Edwin C. Rozwenc and John C. Matlon (Boston: D. C. Heath, 1967), 9, 31–32.

25. Christopher J. Cyphers, *The National Civic Federation and the Making of a New Liberalism, 1900–1915* (Westport, Conn.: Praeger, 2002), 19, 24, 177, 40, 54–56, 35–37, 51, 10. 65–66; John Judis, *Grand Illusion: Critics and Champions of the American Century* (New York: Farrar, Straus & Giroux, 1992), 24, 33–35; William Leach, *Land of Desire: Merchants, Power, and the Rise of a New American Culture* (New York: Pantheon, 1993), 6; and Gary Gerstle, "The Protean Character of American Liberalism," *American Historical Review* 99:4 (Oct. 1994): 1050.

26. Herbert Hoover, 11 Aug. 1928, *Campaign Speeches of American Presidential Candidates, 1928–1972* (New York: Frederick Ungar, 1976).

27. Fox and Lears, *Culture of Consumption,* xi, 17, 19; Warren J. Susman, *Culture as History: The Transformation of American Society in the Twentieth Century* (New York: Pantheon, 1984); Jean-Christophe Agnew, "Coming Up for Air: Consumer Culture in Historical Perspective" *Ladies' Home Journal,* Sept. 1929.

28. Edward Filene, *Speaking of Change: A Selection of Speeches and Articles* (New York: privately published, 1939), 102–3, 232–33; Herman Krooss, *Executive Opinion: What Business Leaders Said and Thought on Economic Issues, 1920s–1960* (Garden City, N.Y.: Doubleday, 1970), 43, 25; Rydell, *World of Fairs,* 125–26, 92–93, 117; Kim McQuaid, "Corporate Liberalism in the American Business Community, 1920–1940," *Business History Review* 5:52 (Autumn 1978); Gerard Swope, "The Engineer's Place in Society," *Survey,* 21 Mar. 1924; Colleen Ann Moore, "The National Association of Manufacturers: The Voice of Industry and the Free Enterprise Campaign in the Schools, 1929–1949" (Ph.D. diss., University of Akron, 1985), 276, 284–94; and Hagley Museum and Library, Wilmington, Del., Chamber of Commerce Records, Accession 1960, Series II, Box 14.

29. George Soule, *Prosperity Decade: From War to Depression, 1917–1929* (New York: Holt, Rinehart & Winston, 1962).

30. Herbert Hoover, *On Recent Economic Changes (Including the Reports of a Special Staff of the National Bureau of Economic Research)* (New York: McGraw-Hill, 1929), 841.

31. Daniel Fox, *The Discovery of Abundance: Simon Patten and the Transformation of Social Theory* (Ithaca: Cornell University Press, 1967), 44–45, 58, 178, 158.

32. Kathleen G. Donohue, *Freedom from Want: American Liberalism and the Idea of the Consumer* (Baltimore: Johns Hopkins University Press), 118, 131–32, 5; Fox, *The Discovery of Abundance,* 155; Leach, *Land of Desire;* and James Truslow Adams, *Our Business Civilization: Some Aspects of American Culture* (New York: A. & C. Boni, 1929), 35, 56, 191, 282.

33. William Trufant Foster and Waddill Catchings, *The Road to Plenty* (Boston: Houghton Mifflin, 1928); *Business without a Buyer* (Boston: Houghton Mifflin, 1928); and Filene, *Speaking of Change,* 226, 102–3.

34. Stuart Chase, *The Economy of Abundance* (New York: Macmillan, 1934), 11–12, 308–10, 16, 18, 109, 51, 21, 302; Alan Brinkley, "The New Deal and the Idea of the State," in *The Rise and Fall of the New Deal Order,* ed. Steve Fraser and Gary Gerstle (Princeton: Princeton University Press, 1989), 85–121; Alan Brinkley, *The End of Reform: New Deal Liberalism in Recession and War* (New York: Alfred A. Knopf, 1995), 96; and Michael A. Bernstein, *A Perilous Progress: Economists and Public Purpose in Twentieth-Century America* (Princeton: Princeton University Press, 2001), 76.

35. National Resources Planning Board, *Security, Work and Relief Policies* (Washington, D.C.: GPO, 1942) and *National Resources Development Report for 1943, Part 1* (Washington, D.C.: GPO, 1943), 3–6, 16–17, 60–65; Henry Wallace, *Sixty Million Jobs* (New York: Simon & Schuster, 1945) and *Paths to Plenty* (Washington, D.C.: Home Library Foundation, 1938).

Chapter 1. The Economics Profession and the Changing Discourse

1. Michael A. Bernstein, *A Perilous Progress: Economists and Public Purpose in Twentieth-Century America* (Princeton: Princeton University Press, 2001), 7, 3; "Does Economics Ignore You?" *Saturday Review*/Committee of Economic Development (CED) (Jan. 1972); and Howard R. Bowen, "Graduate Education in Economics," *American Economic Review* 43:44 (Sept. 1953).

2. John F. Kennedy Presidential Library (JFKPL), Boston President's Office Files, Departments and Agencies: Council of Economic Advisers Box 76; Edwin G. Nourse, *Economics in the Public Service: Administrative Aspects of the Employment Act* (New York: Harcourt Brace, 1953); Harry S. Truman Presidential Library, Independence, Mo.: Leon Keyserling Oral History, 3, 10, and 19 May 1971; and Edwin E. Witte, "Economics and Public Policy," 1956 presidential address to the American Economic Association, *American Economic Review* 47:1 (Mar. 1957).

3. Robert Sobel, *The Worldly Economists* (New York: The Free Press, 1980), 5; Bowen, "Graduate Education in Economics"; and "The Economy's Scouts," *Fortune,* Dec. 1955.

4. "The Economy's Scouts," *Fortune,* Dec. 1955; Richard Parker, *John Kenneth Galbraith: His Life, His Politics, His Economics* (New York: Farrar, Straus and Giroux, 2005), 170; interview with Raymond Saulnier, Chestertown, Md., 14 Oct. 2000; and Herbert Stein, "Are Economists Getting a Bum Rap?" *Southern Economic Journal* 51:4 (Apr. 1985).

5. Robert Sobel and Bernard S. Katz, *Biographical Directory of the Council of Economic Advisers* (New York: Greenwood Press, 1988); "The President's Prophets," *Life,* 4 Jan. 1954; Edward S. Flash Jr., *Economic Advice and Presidential Leadership: The Council of Economic Advisers* (New York: Columbia University Press, 1965), 163; Fortune, *The Economists,* Dec. 1950; Nourse, *Economics in the Public Service,* 20, 77; Ewan Clague and Morton Levine, "The Supply of Economists," *American Economic Review* 52:2 (May 1962); "Structure of Economists' Employment and Salaries, 1964," *American Economic Review* 55:4 (1965); and Sobel, *The Worldly Economists,* 114, 107.

6. Paul A. Samuelson, *The Collected Scientific Papers of Paul A. Samuelson,* vol. 2 (Cambridge, Mass.: MIT Press, 1966), 89; interview with Paul A. Samuelson, 19 Oct. 2000; and Samuelson, *Economics: An Introductory Analysis,* 6th ed. (New York: McGraw Hill, 1958), 782, 3–4.

7. A. W. Coats, "The American Economic Association and the Economics Profession," *Journal of Economic Literature* 23 (Dec. 1985); Bernstein, *A Perilous Progress,* 10–15, 32, 45, 48; Richard T. Ely, "The Founding and Early History of the AEA," *American Economic Review* 26:1 (Mar. 1936); and Daniel Fox, *The Discovery of Abundance: Simon Patten and the Transformation of Social Theory* (Ithaca: Cornell University Press, 1967).

8. Interview with Martin Feldstein, 2 Mar. 2005; Bernstein, *A Perilous Progress,* 42–43, 54–60; Witte, "Economics and Public Policy"; Wesley Mitchell and Arthur Burns, *Measuring Business Cycles* (New York: NBER, 1946); and Herbert Hoover, President's Conference on Unemployment, *Recent Economic Changes in the United States; Report of the Committee on Recent Economic Changes (Including The Reports of A Special Staff of the National Bureau of Economic Research)* (New York: McGraw-Hill Book Company, 1929), vol. 1, 3–6, and vol. 2, 841.

9. Simon Patten, *Theory of Prosperity* (New York: Macmillan, 1902), 140–48.

10. A. W. Coats, "The American Economic Association, 1904–1929," *American Economic Review* 54:3 (June 1964): 261–85, and "The American Economic Association and the Economics Profession," *Journal of Economic Literature* 23:4 (Dec. 1985): 1697–1728.

11. Robert Lekachman, *The Age of Keynes* (New York: Vintage Books, 1966); and J. M. Clark, "Some Current Cleavages among Economists," *American Economic Review* 37:2 (May 1947).

12. National Resources Planning Board, *Security, Work and Relief Policies* (Washington, D.C.: GPO, 1942) and *National Resources Development Report for 1943* (Washington, D.C.: GPO, 1943); Richard Parker, *John Kenneth Galbraith: His Life, His Politics, His Economics* (New York: Farrar, Straus and Giroux, 2005), 163; interview with Lincoln Gordon, Washington, D.C., 6 June 2005; and Gordon and Merle Fainsod, *Government and the American Economy* (New York: W. W. Norton, 1941).

13. Karl Schriftgiesser, *Business and Public Policy: The Role of the Committee for Economic Development, 1942–1967* (Englewood Cliffs, N.J.: Prentice Hall, 1967), 2, 6, 29; CED, "The Economics of a Free Society" (Oct. 1944); interview with Bob Holland, Bethesda, Md., 16 Sept. 2004; John Davenport, "Baron Keynes of Tilton," *Fortune,* May 1944; and Parker, *John Kenneth Galbraith,* 157–58.

14. Bernstein, *A Perilous Progress,* 78–79; and Simon Kuznets, *Economic Change: Selected Essays in Business Cycles, National Income, and Economic Growth* (New York: W. W. Norton, 1953), 145–215, *National Income: A Summary of Findings and National Product Since 1869* (1946), *National Income, 1929–32* (Commerce Department, 1934), *National Income and Its Composition, 1919–38* (New York: NBER, 1941), *National Income: A Summary of Findings* (New York: NBER, 1946), and "Measurement of Economic Growth," *Journal of Economic History* Supplement (1947).

15. Godfrey Hodgson, *America in Our Time* (New York: Vintage Books, 1976), 80; and Robert L. Heilbroner and Aaron Singer, *The Economic Transformation of America: 1600 to the Present,* 2nd ed. (San Diego: Harcourt Brace, 1984), 322.

16. Bernstein, *A Perilous Progress,* 101–2.

17. Bowen, "Graduate Education in Economics"; Clague and Levine, "The Supply of Economists" and "Structure of Economists' Employment and Salaries, 1964"; and interviews with Paul Samuelson, 19 Oct. 2000, and Lincoln Gordon, Washington, D.C., 6 June 2005.

18. Herman Krooss, *Executive Opinion: What Business Leaders Said and Thought on Economic Issues, 1920s–1960* (Garden City, N.Y.: Doubleday, 1970), 266; interviews with Todd May, 24 July 2004, and Sol Hurwitz, 13 Apr. 2005; Conference Board, *Publications Index,* Hagley, Conference Board Records, Accession 1057, Series I, V, Chamber of Commerce of the United States Papers, Accession 1960, Series II, Box 15, and National Association of Manufacturers Records, 1917–1970, Accession 1411, Series I, Boxes 110, 147.

19. "7,000 Ways to Cure the Economy," *Business Week,* 9 Jan. 1960.

20. Samuelson, *Economics,* 2.

21. Seymour Harris and Alvin Hansen, *New Republic,* 15 Jan. 1945; Hansen, "We Must Grow or We Sink," *New York Times Magazine,* 18 Mar. 1962; Moses Abramovitz, "Resource and Output Trends in the United States since 1870," *American Economic Review* 46:2 (May 1956); Simon Kuznets, "Economic Growth and Income Inequality," 1954 AEA Presidential Address, and "Modern Economic Growth: Findings and Reflections," 1971 Nobel Memorial Lecture.

22. Interview with Charles L. Schultze, Washington, D.C., 3 Aug. 2005; James Tobin Papers, Box 1, JFKPL; Henry W. Spiegel and Warren J. Samuels, eds., *Contemporary Economists in Perspective* (Greenwich, Conn.: JAI Press, 1984), vol. 1, 152–55; and Tobin, "Economic Growth as an Objective of Government Policy," *American Economic Review* 54:3 (May 1964).

23. Spiegel and Samuels, eds., *Contemporary Economists in Perspective,* vol. 1, 110–15; and Kuznets, *Six Lectures on Economic Growth* (Glencoe, Ill.: Free Press, 1960), 38.

24. W. W. Rostow, *The Process of Economic Growth,* 2nd ed. (New York: W. W. Norton, 1959), 103–4, and "The Problem of Achieving and Maintaining a High Rate of Economic Growth: A Historian's View," *American Economic Review* 50:2 (May 1960).

25. Fortune, *Markets of the Sixties* (New York: Harper & Brothers, 1960); J. F. Dewhurst, *America's Needs and Resources: A Twentieth Century Fund Survey Which Includes Estimates for 1950 and 1960* (New York: Twentieth Century Fund, 1947) and *America's Needs and Resources: A New Survey* (New York: Twentieth Century Fund, 1955); Marshall Robinson, Herbert C. Morton, and James D. Calderwood, *Economic Growth* (Washington, D.C.: Brookings, 1959); Rockefeller Brothers Fund, *The Challenge to America: Its Economic and Social Aspects: America at Mid-Century* (Garden City, N.Y.: Doubleday, 1958), 254, 260, and *Prospect for America: The Rockefeller Panels Reports* (Garden City, N.Y.: Doubleday, 1961); Thomas R. Carskadon and Rudolf Modley, *U.S.A. Measure of a Nation: A Graphic Presentation of America's Needs and Resources* (New York: Twentieth Century Fund/Macmillan, 1949); Thomas R. Carskadon and George Soule, *U.S.A. in New Dimensions: The Measure and Promise of America's Resources* (New York: Twentieth Century Fund/Macmillan, 1957), 2, 120–24; and Samuelson, "American Economics" (1960), in *The Collected Scientific Papers of Paul A. Samuelson,* vol. 2, 1654.

26. Daniel Horowitz, *The Anxieties of Affluence: Critiques of American Consumer Culture, 1939–1979* (Amherst: University of Massachusetts Press, 2004), 59, 69–71; and George Katona, *The Mass Consumption Society* (New York: McGraw-Hill, 1964), 4, 7, 27, 320, 327.

27. George Katona, *The Powerful Consumer: Psychological Studies of the American Economy* (New York: McGraw-Hill, 1960), 42, 173; University of Michigan, Survey Research Center. Economic Behavior Program: *Surveys of Consumer Attitudes and Behavior* (Ann Arbor: Inter-University Consortium for Political and Social Research, Fall 1953, Fall 1957, Fall 1961, Fall 1965); and Horowitz, *The Anxieties of Affluence.*

28. "The Role and Interests of the Consumer," *American Economic Review* 41:2 (May 1951); "Consumers in the American Economy," *American Economic Review* 47:2 (May 1957); and "Research on Income, Consumption, and Savings," *American Economic Review* 50:2 (May 1960); Mary Jean Bowman, "The Consumer in the History of Economic Doctrine," *American Economic Review* 41:2; May 1951); Ruth S. Mack, " Trends in American Consumption and the Aspiration to Consume," *American Economic Review* 46:2 (May 1956); Elizabeth W. Gilboy, "Elasticity, Consumption, and Economic Growth," *American Economic Review* 46:2 (May 1956); James Duesenberry, "The Increase-of-Consumption Part of Economic Growth," *American Economic Review* 46:2; F. Thomas Juster, "Prediction and Consumer Buying Intentions," *American Economic Review* 50:2 (May 1960); John Kenneth Galbraith, *The Affluent Society* (Boston: Houghton Mifflin, 1958), 128; and Tobin, "Economic Growth as an Objective of Government Policy."

29. Milton and Rose Friedman, *Free to Choose: A Personal Statement* (New York: Harcourt Brace, 1980), 64, 127; and Friedman, *Capitalism and Freedom* (Delanco, N.J.: Classics of Liberty Library, 1999).

30. Parker, *John Kenneth Galbraith,* 237, 288, 292, 294, 311, 333–34, 436, 663, 667; and Galbraith, *The Affluent Society,* xxiv, 113, 233–41, 268.

Chapter 2: Economists Come to Washington

1. Alan Brinkley, *The End of Reform: New Deal Liberalism in Recession and War* (New York: Alfred A. Knopf, 1995), 250–54; 25 Apr. 1945, *Records of the U.S. Senate,* 79th Congress, Committee on Banking and Currency, RG SEN 79A-E1, Box 31, File S.380 #5, National Archives and Records Administration, Washington, D.C.; and Alvin Hansen and Seymour Harris, "The Price of Prosperity," *New Republic,* 15 Jan. 1945.

2. Marshall Field, *Congressional Record* (microfilm) 1945 Appendices, A1267; AFL statement, 25 Oct. 1945, *Congressional Record* (microfilm) 1945 Appendices, A4501; Franklin Roosevelt, State of the Union (7 Jan. 1945); and Stephen Kemp Bailey, *Congress Makes a Law: The Story Behind the Employment Act of 1946* (New York: Vintage Books, 1950), 42, 34–35.

3. Gallup, *The Gallup Poll: Public Opinion 1935–71,* vol. 1, 478, 481, 521; Bailey, *Congress Makes a Law,* 9, 19; Rep. Frank Hook, *Congressional Record* (microfilm), 1945 Appendices, A1650; Hansen

and Harris, "The Price of Prosperity"; Sen. James Murray, *Congressional Record* (microfilm) 1945, 380; Alan Brinkley, "The Late New Deal and the Idea of the State," in *The Rise and Fall of the New Deal Order*, ed. Steve Fraser and Gary Gerstle (Princeton: Princeton University Press, 1989), 98–99; 18 Sept. 1944 Hansen Memo, cited in Crauford D. Goodwin, "Attitudes Toward Industry in the Truman Administration: The Macroeconomic Origins of Microeconomic Policy," in *The Truman Presidency*, ed. Michael J. Lacey, 95; *Congressional Record* (microfilm) 1945 Appendices, A3177; "Full Employment: Report to the Congress and Currency" (Washington, D.C.: GPO, 1945); Leon Keyserling Papers, Box 28, and Leon Keyserling Oral History, 3, 10, and 19 May 1971, Harry S. Truman Library (HSTL); *New York Times*, 29 Mar. 1945; U.S. Senate, "Bibliography on Full Employment: Report to the Committee on Banking and Currency" (Washington, D.C.: GPO, 1945); *New York Times*, 12 Aug. 1945; and *New York Times*, 7 Sept. 1945.

4. CIO PAC, "People's Program for 1944;" Donald Montgomery, "Purchasing Power for Prosperity" (UAW, 1945); and United States Senate, 79th Congress, First Session. Full Employment Act of 1945: Hearings Before a Subcommittee of the Committee on Banking and Currency on S.380 (Washington, D.C.: GPO, 1945), 236.

5. Sir William Beveridge, *Social Insurance and Allied Services* (New York: Macmillan, 1942) and *Full Employment in a Free Society* (New York: W. W. Norton, 1945); United States House of Representatives, 79th Congress, Full Employment Act of 1945: Hearings Before the Committee on Expenditures in the Executive Departments, First Session on H.R. 2202 (Washington, D.C.: GPO, 1945), 8967.

6. Harris and Hansen, "Targets for Tomorrow's Economy," *New Republic*, 19 Mar. 1945; House, Full Employment Act: Hearings, 921–27, 756; and *New York Times*, 26 Aug. 26 1945, and 29 Jan. 1945.

7. American Presidency Project, http://www.presidency.ucsb.edu/index.php; Senate, Full Employment Act of 1945: Hearings, 511, 461–2; and William Green, "Jobs for All" (Washington, D.C.: AFL, 1945).

8. Gallup, *The Gallup Poll: Public Opinion, 1935–1971*, vol. 1, 519–83; Alonzo L. Hamby, *Beyond the New Deal: Harry S. Truman and American Liberalism* (New York: Columbia University Press, 1973), 60; and Brinkley, "The Late New Deal and the Idea of the State," 87–103.

9. Robert B. Carson, "Changes in Federal Fiscal Policy and Public Attitudes Since the Employment Act of 1946," *Social Studies* 58:7 (1967): 310; Edwin G. Nourse, "The Employment Act and the 'New Economics," *Virginia Quarterly Review* 45:4 (1969): 596; *Congressional Record* (microfilm) 1945, 11981, 12093; House, Full Employment Act of 1945: Hearings, 183, 548–54; and Senate, Full Employment Act of 1945: Hearings, 467, 602, 605, 521.

10. Edwin G. Nourse, *Economics in the Public Service: Administrative Aspects of the Employment Act* (New York: Harcourt Brace, 1953), 596; James Tobin and Murray Weidenbaum, *Two Revolutions in Economic Policy: The First Economic Reports of Kennedy and Reagan* (Cambridge, Mass.: MIT Press, 1988), 89; Leon Keyserling, "The Strength of the U.S. Economy," *U.N. World*, July 1949, in Leon Keyserling Papers, Box 29; HSTL; Wallace, 4 Mar. 1946, *Congressional Record* (microfilm) 1946, Appendices, A1289; Joint Economic Committee (JEC), *Twentieth Anniversary of the Employment Act of 1946: An Economic Symposium*, 23 Feb. 1966 (Washington, D.C.: GPO, 1966), 1, 3; Arthur F. Burns, "Some Reflections on the Employment Act," *Political Science Quarterly* 77:4. (Dec. 1962): 484; and Arthur F. Burns, *Prosperity without Inflation* (New York: Fordham University Press, 1957), 40.

11. Flash, *Economic Advice and Presidential Leadership: The Council of Economic Advisers* (New York: Columbia University Press, 1965), vii; and interview with Raymond Saulnier, 14 Oct. 2000.

12. Francis H. Heller, ed., *Economics and the Truman Administration* (Lawrence: Regents Press of Kansas, 1981), xvi; and Student Research File: Economic Growth, #1, Box 1, HSTL.

13. Edwin Nourse Oral History, Student Research File: Economic Growth #1, Box 1, Leon Keyserling Oral History, and Leon Keyserling Papers, Box 78, HSTL; and interview with Lincoln Gordon, HSTL.

14. Harry S. Truman, 16 Jan. 1952, American Presidency Project, http://www.presidency. ucsb.edu/index.php; Harry S. Truman, 24 Feb. 1949, in Clark Clifford Papers, Box 38, HSTL; and *Time*, 16 Jan. 1950.

15. Robert Sobel, *The Worldly Economists* (New York: The Free Press, 1980), 5; Leon Keyserling Oral History, HSTL; interviews with Charles L. Schultze, 3 June 2005, and Raymond J. Saulnier, 14 Oct. 2000; and CEA, *Economic Report of the President* (New York: Reynal & Hitchcock, 1947), 1, and *Economic Report of the President* (New York: Reynal & Hitchcock, 1948), 56.

16. Sobel, *The Worldly Economists*, 23; Hugh S. Norton, *The Employment Act and the Council of Economic Advisers, 1946–1976* (Columbia: University of South Carolina Press, 1977); Flash, *Economic Advice and Presidential Leadership*, 162, 291; Burns, *Prosperity without Inflation*, 30; interviews with Martin Feldstein, 2 Mar. 2005, and with Charles L. Schultze, 3 June and 3 Aug. 2005; Godfrey Hodgson, *America in Our Time* (New York: Vintage Books, 1976), 72; Herb Stein, *The Fiscal Revolution in America* (Washington, D.C.: American Enterprise Institute Press, 1969); and Robert Solow, "The Kennedy Council and the Long Run," in *Economic Events, Ideas, Policies: The 1960s and After*, ed. George L. Perry and James Tobin (Washington, D.C.: Brookings, 2000), 122.

17. Michael A. Bernstein, *A Perilous Progress: Economists and Public Purpose in Twentieth-Century America* (Princeton: Princeton University Press, 2001), 110, 129; Flash, *Economic Advice and Presidential Leadership*, 5, 13; interviews with Charles L. Schultze, 3 June 2005, and Martin Feldstein, 2 Mar. 2005; Feldstein, "The Council of Economic Advisers and Economic Advising in the United States," *The Economic Journal* 102 (Sept. 1992); Leon Keyserling Oral History, 3, 10, 19 May 1971, HSTL; President's Office Files: Speech Files, Box 42, John F. Kennedy Presidential Library (JFKPL).

18. Bertram D. Gross and John P. Lewis. "The President's Economic Staff During the Truman Administration," *The American Political Science Review* 48:1 (Mar. 1954): 116.

19. Nourse, *Economics in the Public Service*, 105; Edwin Nourse Papers, Box 6, Edwin Nourse Oral History, Leon Keyserling Oral History, Leon Keyserling Papers, Boxes 6, 17, 28, 29, 30, and Student Research File: Economic Growth, #1, Box 1, HSTL.

20. Heller, ed., *Economics and the Truman Administration*, 85; Council of Economic Advisers (CEA), *The Economic Report of the President* (Washington, D.C.: GPO, 1949), 1, 3, 63; Robert M. Collins, *More: The Politics of Economic Growth in Postwar America* (New York: Oxford University Press, 2000), 20–21; Harold Vatter, *The U.S. Economy in the 1950s* (New York: W. W. Norton, 1963), 7; Sobel, *The Worldly Economists*, 23; Flash, *Economic Advice and Presidential Leadership*, 28.

21. CEA, *Economic Report of the President* (Washington, D.C.: GPO, 1949), 1, 3, 63; CEA, *The Economic Report of the President* (Washington, D.C.: GPO, 1951), 4; CEA, *The Economic Report of the President* (Washington, D.C.: GPO, 1952, 40; and CEA, *The Economic Report of the President* (Washington, D.C.: GPO, 1953), 88.

22. See, for example, Joint Economic Committee (JEC), *Joint Economic Report on the Jan. 1948 Economic Report of the President* (Washington, D.C.: GPO, 18 May 1948), 2–3, 31; *Potential Economic Growth of the United States During the Next Decade* (Staff Study), 27 Oct. 1954; *The American Economy: Problems and Prospects*, 20, 23, 24, and 25 Mar. 1959; *The Low Income Population and Economic Growth*, by Robert L. Lampman; *The Adequacy of Resources for Economic Growth in the United States*, by Joseph L. Fisher and Edward Boorstein, 16 Dec. 1959; *Staff Report on Employment, Growth, and Price Levels*, 17 Dec. 1959 and 26 Jan. 1960; *The Potential Economic Growth of the United States*, by James W. Knowles, 30 Jan. 1960; and *Measuring the Nation's Material Wealth. Report of the Subcommittee on Economic Statistics*, 27 Aug. 1965.

23. JEC, *Joint Economic Report: Report of the Joint Committee on the Economic Report on the January 1949 Economic Report of the President* (Washington, D.C.: GPO, 1949), 28–29; *Joint Economic Report on the January 1950 Economic Report of the President* (Washington, D.C.: GPO, 1950), 3, 1, 5, 10; and *Joint Economic Report on the January 1951 Economic Report of the President* (Washington, D.C.: GPO, 1951), 18.

24. Delos C. Johns, "Address of the President of Federal Reserve Bank of St. Louis," 8 Nov. 1956; http://fraser.stlouisfed.org/historicaldocs/dcj1956/download/51959/johns_19561108.pdf.

25. Robert Sobel and Bernard S. Katz, *Biographical Directory of the Council of Economic Advisers* (New York: Greenwood Press, 1988), 209; Papers of Arthur S. Burns, Box 103, Dwight D. Eisenhower Library (DDEL), Abilene, Kans.; 7 Jan. 1954, State of the Union, in *State of the Union Messages of the Presidents, 1790–1966*, ed. Fred L. Israel (New York: Chelsea House, 1966), vol. 3; and Robert Griffith, "Dwight D. Eisenhower and the Corporate Commonwealth," *American Historical Review* 87:1 (Feb. 1982).

26. Raymond J. Saulnier, *Constructive Years: The U.S. Economy Under Eisenhower* (Lanham, Md.: University Press of America, 1991), 33; Oral History with Raymond J. Saulnier, DDEL; Flash, *Economic Advice and Presidential Leadership,* 163; Edwin C. Hargrove and Samuel A. Morley, eds., *The President and the Council of Economic Advisers: Interviews with CEA Chairmen* (Boulder, Col.: Westview Press, 1984); Dwight D. Eisenhower 1956 State of the Union Address, Paul Hoffman Papers, Box 27, HSTL; and Dwight D. Eisenhower, 3 Sept. 1956. *Public Papers of the Presidents: Dwight D. Eisenhower, 1956* (Washington, D.C.: GPO), 730.

27. *Newsweek,* 13 July 1953; 30 Dec. 1953 letter from Eisenhower to Burns, Papers of Arthur F. Burns, Box 103, DDEL; "How Prosperous Is Prosperous?" *Business Week,* 27 Oct. 1956; and *New Republic,* 8 Nov. 1954.

28. Hedley Donovan, *Right Places, Right Times: Forty Years In Journalism, Not Counting My Paper Route* (New York: Holt, 1989), 132; Eisenhower, 23 Aug. 1956, in *Public Papers of the Presidents: Dwight D. Eisenhower, 1956,* 709–14; and Eisenhower, 20 Jan. 1955, in *Public Papers of the Presidents: Dwight D. Eisenhower, 1955* (Washington, D.C.: GPO), 200–201.

29. JEC, *Joint Economic Report* (Washington, D.C.: GPO, 1954), 2, 20; and *Joint Economic Report* (Washington, D.C.: GPO, 1956), 1, 2, 6, 8; *Wall Street Journal,* 5 Sept. 1956; Oral History Interview with Heller, Gordon, Tobin, Ackley, and Samuelson, JFKPL; Leon Keyserling Papers, Boxes 31, 32, 333, 34, 65, HSTL; Eric Hodgins Oral History, DDEL; and Nelson Lichtenstein, *The Most Dangerous Man in Detroit* (Urbana: University of Illinois Press, 1997), 286.

30. Dwight D. Eisenhower, Second Inaugural Address, 20 Jan. 1957, in *Inaugural Addresses of the Presidents of the United States from George Washington 1789 to George Bush 1989* (Washington, D.C.: GPO, 1989).

31. Papers of Arthur Burns, Boxes 99 and 103, and Gabriel Hauge Oral History, DDEL.

32. Burns, *Prosperity without Inflation,* 40.

33. Arthur Burns, "As White House Sees Business Future," 18 June 1954, 73–74; "Good Times Ahead: $400 Billion Economy," 6 Oct. 1955, 48–51; "Business Future of America," 6 May 1955, 54–60.

34. CEA, *Economic Report of the President* (Washington, D.C.: GPO, 1954), iii, 3, 4, 114, 118; *Economic Report of the President* (Washington, D.C.: GPO, 1955), 4; *Economic Report of the President* (Washington, D.C.: GPO, 1956), 11, 12, 72, 126; and JEC, *1956 Joint Economic Report* (Washington, D.C.: GPO, 1956).

35. Burns, *Prosperity without Inflation,* 23; *Business Week,* 19 Jan. 1960; Richard Parker, *The Myth of the Middle Class* (New York: Liveright, 1972), 23; and Raymond Saulnier, *The Strategy of Economic Policy* (New York: Fordham University Press, 1962), 2, 5–6.

36. CEA, *Economic Report of the President* (Washington, D.C.: GPO, 1958), 2, and *Economic Report of the President* (Washington, D.C.: GPO, 1960), 1; and interview with Raymond Saulnier, 14 Oct. 2000.

37. Oral History with Raymond Saulnier; Saulnier, "National Economic Growth," *Business Horizons,* winter 1959, and "Learn to Live with Prosperity," *Nation's Business,* Mar. 1957, in Papers of Raymond Saulnier, Box 7, DDEL; Saulnier, *The Strategy of Economic Policy* (New York: Fordham University Press, 1962), 5–6; interview with Raymond Saulnier, 14 Oct. 2000; CEA, *Economic Report of the President* (Washington, D.C.: GPO, 1957), 1; *Economic Report of the Presi-*

dent (Washington, D.C.: GPO, 1958), 1, 2; *Economic Report of the President* (Washington, D.C.: GPO, 1960), 1 and Appendix, "The Diffusion of Well-Being, 1946–1959"; and *1957 Joint Economic Report* (Washington, D.C.: GPO, 1957), 1.

38. *Public Papers of the Presidents: Dwight D. Eisenhower, 1958* (Washington, D.C.: GPO, 1958), 6; JEC, *1957 Joint Economic Report* (Washington, D.C.: GPO, 1957), 1, 2; *Employment, Growth and Price Levels—Hearings, The American Economy: Problems and Prospects* (Washington, D.C.: GPO, 1959), 94–5, 100; *1959 Joint Economic Report* (Washington, D.C.: GPO, 1959), 4–5; JEC, *1960 Joint Economic Report* (Washington, D.C.: GPO, 1960), 2, 5–6, 29; *Hearings on Comparisons of U.S. and Soviet Economies* (Washington, D.C.: GPO, 1959); and Rockefeller Brothers Fund, *The Challenge to America: Its Economic and Social Aspects: America at Mid-Century* (Garden City, N.Y.: Doubleday, 1958) and *Prospect for America: The Rockefeller Panels Reports* (Garden City, N.Y.: Doubleday, 1961).

39. "7,000 Ways to Cure the Economy," *Business Week,* 9 Jan. 1960, 36; and "Fiscal Strategy: Ike Aims to Offer Balanced Budget, Put Kennedy on the Spot," *Wall Street Journal,* 28 Nov. 1960.

40. White House Staff Files: Papers of Pierre E. G. Salinger, Press Briefings, Box 45, and John Kenneth Galbraith Papers, Box 77, JFKPL.

41. Hodgson, *America in Our Time,* 70–71; Flash, *Economic Advice and Presidential Leadership,* 181–82; and W. W. Rostow, "The Problem of Achieving and Maintaining a High Rate of Economic Growth: A Historian's View," *American Economic Review* 50:2 (May 1960).

42. "Kennedy's Economic Mixture," *Business Week,* 25 Feb. 1961; "What Kind of Economy Is It?" *New York Times Magazine,* 23 Jan. 1961; Oral History Interview with Heller, Gordon, Tobin, Ackley, and Samuelson, 305, 260, and Reflections on the New Frontier: Oral History Interview with Members of JFK's Staff, JFKPL; interview with Charles L. Schultze, 3 June 2005; and Richard Parker, *John Kenneth Galbraith: His Life, His Politics, His Economics* (New York: Farrar, Straus and Giroux, 2005), 332.

43. President's Office Files, Departments and Agencies: CEA, Boxes 74 and 76, and Speech Files, Box 42, JFKPL; Flash, *Economic Advice and Presidential Leadership,* 222, 342; Bernstein, *A Perilous Progress,* 131, 138; CEA, *Economic Report of the President* (Washington, D.C.: GPO, 1962), 95; Hodgson, *America in Our Time,* 80; Arthur Okun, *Political Economy of Prosperity* (Washington, D.C.: Brookings, 1970); and Tobin and Weidenbaum, *Two Revolutions in Economic Policy,* 11, 29.

44. President's Office Files, Departments and Agencies: CEA, Boxes 74, 75, 75A, 76, and Walter Heller Papers, Boxes 7, 8, JFKPL; and James Tobin, "Economic Growth as an Objective of Government Policy," *American Economic Review* 54:3 (May 1964).

45. President's Office Files: CEA, Boxes 73–76, JFKPL; "Kennedy Economics," *Life,* 10 Feb. 1961; and Hobart Rowen, "Kennedy's Economists," *Harper's,* Sept. 1961.

46. Oral History Interview with Heller, Gordon, Tobin, Ackley, and Samuelson, 49, 53, 32, JFKPL; Tobin and Weidenbaum, *Two Revolutions in Economic Policy,* 6, 90; Flash, *Economic Advice and Presidential Leadership,* 180–81; CEA, *Economic Report of the President* (Washington, D.C.: GPO, 1963); President's Office Files: Speech Files, Box 42, JFKPL; Hodgson, *America in Our Time,* 80; and Tobin and Weidenbaum, *Two Revolutions in Economic Policy,* 195.

47. Theodore Sorenson Papers, Box 73, and President's Office Files, Departments and Agencies: CEA, Box 75, JFKPL; *Public Papers of the Presidents: John F. Kennedy, 1961* (Washington, D.C.: GPO), p. 45.

48. John F. Kennedy, 11 June 1962, President's Office Files: Speech Files, Box 39, and C. Douglas Dillon Papers, Box 60, JFKPL.

49. John F. Kennedy, 25 May 1961; 13 Aug. 1962; 26 Sept. 1962; and 14 Dec. 1962, in President's Office Files: Speech Files, Boxes 34, 39, 40, 42, JFKPL.

50. John F. Kennedy, 11 Jan. 1963; 13 Aug. 1962, Papers of Pierre E. G. Salinger, Box 102, and 25 Feb. 1963, President's Office Files: Speech Files, JFKPL.

51. Bernstein, *Perilous Progress,* 138; Alan Wolfe, *America's Impasse: The Rise and Fall of the Poli-*

tics of Growth (New York: Pantheon Books, 1981), 67; Hodgson, *America in Our Time,* 81; "Business in 1965: The Keynesian Influence on the Expansionist Economy," *Time,* 31 Dec. 1965.

52. CEA, *Economic Report of the President* (Washington, D.C.: GPO, 1964); Lyndon B. Johnson, 8 Jan. 1964; 23 Mar. 1964; 22 Apr. 1964; and 7 Sept. 1964, American Presidency Project, http://www.presidency.ucsb.edu/index.php; and 1964 Democratic Party Platform, "One Nation, One People," in Walter Heller Papers, Box 7, JFKPL.

53. Lyndon B. Johnson, 22 May 1964, and 4 Jan. 1965, Lyndon Baines Johnson Library and Museum, http://www.lbjlib.utexas.edu/johnson/archives.hom/speeches.hom/selected_speeches.asp.

54. Lyndon B. Johnson, 30 Oct. 1965, American Presidency Project, http://www.presidency.ucsb.edu/ws/index.php?pid=27341&st=abundance&st1=.

55. JEC, *Twentieth Anniversary of the Employment Act of 1946,* 1–2.

56. Wolfe, *America's Impasse,* 49.

Chapter 3: Business's New Paradigm, "People's Capitalism"

1. "U.S.A.: The Permanent Revolution," *Fortune,* Feb. 1951, 62–83; Father J. N. Moody, "The Future of Capitalism," *Commonweal,* 12 Sept. 1958, 587–90; Frederick Lewis Allen, "The Unsystematic American System," *Harper's,* Feb. 1952, 21–26; and "Wanted: A New Name for Capitalism," *Reader's Digest,* May 1951, 3–4.

2. Robert Griffith, "The Selling of America: The Advertising Council and American Politics, 1942–1960," *Business History Review* 57 (Aug. 1983): 402–3; and National Association of Manufacturers (NAM) Records, 1917–1970—Accession 1411, Series I, Box 110; "It's a Favorable Wind . . . Sail with It," and Chamber of Commerce Records, Accession 1960, Series II, Boxes 17, 15, Hagley.

3. Stuart Ewen, *Captains of Consciousness: Advertising and the Social Roots of the Consumer Culture* (New York: McGraw-Hill, 1976), 18, 90–91; Roland Marchand, *Advertising the American Dream: Making Way for Modernity, 1920–1940* (Berkeley: University of California Press, 1985); and Jackson Lears, *Fables of Abundance: A Cultural History of Advertising in America* (New York: Basic Books, 1994), 2.

4. Herman Krooss, *Executive Opinion: What Business Leaders Said and Thought on Economic Issues, 1920s–1960* (Garden City, N.Y.: Doubleday, 1970), 43; Filene, "Mass Production Will Make a Better World," *Atlantic,* May 1929; Kim McQuaid, "Corporate Liberalism in the American Business Community, 1920–1940," *Business History Review* 5:52 (Autumn 1978); Gerard Swope, "The Engineer's Place in Society," *Survey,* 21 Mar. 1924; and Edward Filene, *Speaking of Change: A Selection of Speeches and Articles* (New York: privately published, 1939), 102–3, 232–33.

5. Krooss, *Executive Opinion,* 25; Colleen Ann Moore, "The National Association of Manufacturers: The Voice of Industry and the Free Enterprise Campaign in the Schools, 1929–1949" (Ph. D. diss., University of Akron, 1985), 276, 284–94.

6. Chamber of Commerce Records, Accession 1960, Series II, Box 14, Hagley.

7. NAM Records, 1917–1970, Accession 1411, Series I, Box 147, Hagley.

8. Kim McQuaid, "The Business Advisory Council of the Department of Commerce," in *Research in Economic History, 1976,* ed. Paul Uselding (Greenwich, Conn.: JAI Press, 1976); and Henry S. Dennison et al., *Toward Full Employment* (New York: Whittlesey House, 1938).

9. Marion B. Folsom, Columbia Oral History Project Memoir, Eisenhower Administration Volume 55–56, Columbia University Libraries, New York.

10. Interview with Sol Hurwitz, 13 Apr. 2005; and James T. Howard, "Improving Economic Understanding in the Public Schools" (CED, 1950), 17.

11. CED, "Toward More Production, More Jobs, and More Freedom" (Oct. 1945) and *1958 Annual Report;* interviews with Sol Hurwitz, 13 Apr. 2005, and Robert Holland, 16 Sept. 2004; James T. Howard, "Improving Economic Understanding in the Public Schools" (CED, 1950), 17;

Schriftgiesser, *Business Comes of Age* (New York: Harper and Brothers, 1960), 27, 201; Elizabeth Fones-Wolf, *Selling Free Enterprise: The Business Assault on Labor and Liberalism, 1945–1960* (Urbana: University of Illinois Press, 1994), 28; and CED, "Jobs and Markets" (Feb. 1946).

12. CED, "Taxes and the Budget: A Program for Prosperity in a Free Society" (Nov. 1947), 75; Robert M. Collins, *The Business Response to Keynes, 1929–1964* (New York: Columbia University Press, 1981), 130–31; Schriftgiesser, *Business Comes of Age,* 5–8, 10; personal communication, Van Ooms, CED research director; and CED, "The Economics of a Free Society" (Oct. 1944), 5–7, 12, 17.

13. CED, *A Postwar Federal Tax Plan for High Employment;* Harold Groves, *Postwar Taxation and Economic Progress* (CED, 1946), 373; CED, *American Industry Looks Ahead* (1945), *Jobs and Markets* (Jan. 1946), 114, 123–24, 125, " *Taxes and the Budget: a Program for Prosperity in a Free Economy* (1947), and *How to Raise Real Wages* (June 1950); *New York Times,* 29 May 1945, 23; Senate, *Full Employment Act of 1945: Hearings,* 602, 605; interview with Robert Holland, 16 Sept. 2004; and CED, *1959 Annual Report.*

14. CED, *1957 Annual Report, 1960 Annual Reports, Toward More Production, More Jobs and More Freedom* (Oct. 1945); and *CED and Economic Research in College-Community Centers* (Nov. 1952).

15. Schriftgiesser, *Business Comes of Age,* 55–56, 139.

16. CED, *1958 Annual Report;* and *1957 Annual Report,* 6–7; and *New Role of the Soviets in the World Economy* (1958).

17. CED, *Economic Growth in the United States: Past and Future* (1958); *Problems of U.S. Economic Development: Papers by 49 Free World Leaders on the Most Important Problems Facing the United States,* vol. 1 (Jan. 1958), 79; and *Problems of U.S. Economic Development: The 50 Winning Papers in CED's Free-World-Wide Competition on the Most Important Problems to Be Faced by the United States in the Next 20 Years,* vol. 2 (May 1958), 39.

18. Advertising Council, *Matters of Choice: Advertising in the Public Interest; The Advertising Council, 1942–2002;* and Daniel L. Lykins, *From Total War to Total Diplomacy: The Advertising Council and the Construction of the Cold War Consensus* (Westport, Conn.: Praeger, 2003).

19. Hagley, Accession 1960, Series II, Box 17.

20. Griffith, "The Selling of America," 400.

21. Lykins, *From Total War to Total Diplomacy,* 68–75; and Charles Jackson Files, Box 8, Harry S. Truman Library (HSTL).

22. Charles Jackson Files, Box 15, HSTL; Griffith, "The Selling of America," 400; and Eric Foner, *The Story of American Freedom* (New York: W. W. Norton, 1998), 263.

23. Lykins, *From Total War to Total Diplomacy,* 98–103; Charles Jackson Files, Box 15, HSTL; "The Miracle of America," *Look,* 25 May 1948; and C. W. McKee and H. G. Moulton' *A Survey of Economic Education* (Washington, D.C.: Brookings, 1951).

24. James M. Lambie Jr. Records, 1952–61, Box 12, Dwight D. Eisenhower Library (DDEL); and Robert Griffith, "Dwight D. Eisenhower and the Corporate Commonwealth," *The American Historical Review* 87:1 (Feb. 1982): 87–122.

25. Advertising Council, "The American Roundtable Discussions on People's Capitalism" (1957); and "Condensed Record of a Round Table Discussion on the Basic Elements of a Free, Dynamic Society Held Under the Sponsorship of the Advertising Council at the Hotel Waldorf-Astoria," 16 Apr. 1951, 3, 51.

26. Ibid., 7–18; Eric Johnston, "Lifeblood of American Capitalism," 29 Sept. 1953, in *Vital Speeches of the Day,* vol. 20 (1954), 126–28; and Lizabeth Cohen, *A Consumers' Republic: The Politics of Mass Consumption in Postwar America* (New York: Alfred A. Knopf, 2003)., 6; and Advertising Council, "Condensed Record of a Round Table Discussion."

27. Moore, "The National Association of Manufacturers," 726; and Chamber of Commerce Records, Accession 1960, Series I, Box 21, Hagley.

28. NAM Records, 1917–1970—Accession 1411, Series III, Box 842 NIIC Records, and NAM Records, 1917–1970—Accession 1411, Series I, Boxes 11, 110, Hagley.

29. "Advertising in Wartime," *New Republic,* 21 Feb. 1944; "Is Anybody Listening?" *Fortune,* Sept. 1950; "The NAM Would Do Better Dead," *Forbes* (15 Aug. 1951); NAM Records, 1917–1970—Accession 1411, Series I, Boxes 147, 110, "Salesletter" (17 Jan. 1949), Hagley; and Moore, "The National Association of Manufacturers," 659, 661, 663, 715–16, 731–32.

30. NAM Records, 1917–1970, Accession 1411, Series XVI, Box 219: "Guide to Church and Industry Cooperation" (1944), and Series I, Box 147; Jasper Crane Papers—Accession 1416, Box 39, Hagley; and Moore, "The National Association of Manufacturers," 715–16.

31. NAM Records, 1917–1970—Accession 1411, Series I, Box 115: NAM, "A Better America" (1944), 30–31, and NAM: NIIC Records, Series III, Boxes 844, 847: NAM, "How Americans Can Earn More, Buy More, Have More: A Practical Guide to Postwar Prosperity"; "Three to Be Served," 23 May 1944, Hagley.

32. NAM Records, 1917–1970—Accession 1411, Series I, Box 115: NAM, "A Long Look Ahead" (1954) and "A Platform for Prosperity and Progress" (Aug. 1956); Series I, Box 147: "The NAM's Goal: New Dimension For American Dream" (9 Dec. 1956), Hagley.

33. National Museum of American History (NMAH), Smithsonian Institution, "Industry on Parade Collection, 1950–1960," no. 507; and Strange and Wendy Shay, "History of the Industry on Parade Film Collection," NMAH, 2001.

34. NMAH, "Industry on Parade Collection, 1950–1960," #507, Reels 117 (5 Jan. 1953), 453 (20 June 1959), and 479 (19 Dec. 1959); and Hagley, NAM Records, 1917–1970—Acc. 1411, Series I, Box 155: scripts, and Series XVI, Box 219: NAM 1963–64 catalogue for high schools.

35. Moore, "The National Association of Manufacturers," 392, 645; and *Business Week,* 17 Dec. 1966.

36. Chamber of Commerce Records, Accession 1960, Series II, Boxes 12–16: "Outlines of 11 Talks on Timely Questions Affecting the American Free Enterprise System" (1940), Chamber, 1944 "Full Employment: Its Politics and Economics"; "Distribution: A Key to High Employment" (1945) "Can Government Guarantee Full Employment" (1945), Hagley.

37. Chamber of Commerce Records, Accession 1960, Series II, Boxes 15–18, 21: "Freedom and the Free Market Inseparable" (Oct. 1944); "Program for American Opportunity Through Advertising" (1947); and "Economic Discussion Group Workbook: How to Organize and Conduct a Successful Program for Developing Spokesmen for the American Free Enterprise System" (1956), Hagley.

38. Ibid., Boxes 20–22, 24, 15: "Free Markets and Free Men" (1953); "It's Everybody's Business" (1954); "The World of Tomorrow . . . What Will It Be Like?" (1955); "How to Double Wages" (1955); "The Story of Creative Capital" (1957); 10 Oct. 1960, Motley speech to the Economic Club of Detroit; and "How to Plan Economic Understanding Projects" (1963); "Can We Depression-Proof Our Economy" (1955); "The Story of Creative Capital" (1957); 22 Sept. 1968 Blount speech; and "1964–65 Progress Report."

39. Conference Board Records, Accession 1057, Series 5, Box 13, "The Conference Board: An Historical Celebration of the Conference Board's 75th Anniversary" (1991), Hagley.

40. Ibid., "Economic Background for Postwar Reconstruction" (May 1943), 3, and "Jobs, Profits, and Economic Growth" (May 1963), 32.

41. Fones-Wolf, *Selling Free Enterprise;* Cohen, *A Consumers' Republic,* 125; and McKee and Moulton, *A Survey of Economic Education.*

42. Karal Ann Marling, "Disneyland, 1955: Just Take the Santa Ana Freeway to the American Dream," *American Art* 5:1/2 (Winter/Spring 1991): 181, 191, 205.

43. Michael Smith, "Making Time: Representations of Technology at the 1964 World's Fair," in *The Power of Culture: Critical Essays in American Culture,* ed. Richard Wightman Fox and T. J Jackson Lears (Chicago: University of Chicago Press, 1993), 223–29, 9; Mary Pillsbury and Catherine Barnes, *A Day at the New York World's Fair with Peter and Wendy* (New York: Spertus Publishing, 1964); and Roland Marchand, "The Designers Go to the Fair II: Norman Bel Geddes, The General Motors 'Futurama,' and the Visit to the Factory Transformed," *Design Issues*

3:2 (Spring 1992) 29; Editors of Time-Life Books, *Official Guide: New York World's Fair, 1964/1965* (New York: Time Inc., 1964), 221–22, 90–92, 110, 74, 99, 81.

44. James M. Lambie Jr. Records, 1952–61, Box 23, DDEL.

Chapter 4: The Big Postwar Story

1. Hedley Donovan, *Right Places, Right Times: Forty Years in Journalism, Not Counting My Paper Route* (New York: Holt, 1989), 136.

2. Fortune, *The Changing American Market* (Garden City, N.Y.: Hanover House, 1954), 7.

3. Walter Heller, "Economy Is Like a Regular .300 Hitter," *Life*, 10 Mar. 1961, 24–25.

4. "Is a New Era Really Here?" *U.S. News & World Report*, 20 May 1955, 21–23; "People's Capitalism," *House Beautiful*, Nov. 1956, 226; "Changed America," *Business Week*, 6 June 1953, 101–4; "Everybody Rich in the U.S.? The 15-Year Trends in Incomes," *U.S. News & World Report*, Oct. 1956, 27–32; "Perpetual Prosperity: Is the Business Cycle Out?" *Nation*, 29 Jan. 1955, 96–98; Sumner Slichter, "Have We Conquered the Business Cycle?" *Atlantic*, May 1955, 51–55; "The Boom-Bust Cycle: How Well Have We Got It Tamed?" *Business Week*, 3 Nov. 1956, 176–78; and Robert T. Elson, *The World of Time Inc.: The Intimate History of a Publishing Empire* (New York: Atheneum, 1968–73), vol. 2, 257–58.

5. Lloyd Wendt, *The Wall Street Journal: The Story of Dow Jones and the Nation's Business Newspaper* (New York: Rand McNally, 1982), 261, 295, 300, 354; Jerry M. Rosenberg, *Inside the Wall Street Journal* (New York: Macmillan, 1982), 75, 214–15; Peter Baida, "The Business of America: 100 Years of the *Journal*," *American Heritage* 39:8 (Dec. 1988): 16–18; James L. Baughman, *Henry R. Luce and the Rise of the American News Media* (Boston: G. K. Hall, 1987), 66; and Arthur Jones, *Malcolm Forbes* (New York: Harper & Row, 1977), 75, 94, 97.

6. "Annual Financial Review," *New York Times*, 2 Jan. 1934.

7. C. D. Jackson Papers and Records of Gabriel Hauge, Dwight D. Eisenhower Library (DDEL).

8. Donovan, *Right Places, Right Times*, 134–35; Time Inc., *Writing for Fortune: 1930–1980* (New York: Time Inc. 1979), 123; Baughman, *Henry R. Luce*, 137; and Galbraith, "The Job Before Us," *Fortune*, Jan. 1943, 65.

9. "The United States in a New World: III—The Domestic Economy," *Fortune*, Dec. 1943, 1–13. Richard Parker, *John Kenneth Galbraith: His Life, His Politics, His Economics* (New York: Farrar, Straus and Giroux, 2005), 157–61; and Galbraith, "Transition to Peace: Business in AD 194Q," *Fortune*, Jan. 1944, 83ff; Davenport, "Baron Keynes of Tilton," *Fortune*, May 1944, 146–47; and Benton, "The Economics of a Free Society," *Fortune*, Oct. 1944, 162–65.

10. Time Inc., *Writing for Fortune*, 128, 189; Elson, *The World of Time Inc.* vol. 2, 196–203; Donovan, *Right Places, Right Times*, 104–5, 129–30; interview with Carol Loomis, 17 June 2004; Eric Hodgins Oral History, DDEL; and Daniel Bell, *The Cultural Contradictions of Capitalism* (New York: Basic Books, 1976), 76.

11. Elson, *The World of Time Inc.*, vol. 2, 199; Baughman, *Henry R. Luce*, 63, 67; Ronald Weber, *Hired Pens: Professional Writers in America's Golden Age of Print* (Athens, Ohio: Ohio University Press, 1997), 240; and interview with Todd May, 21 July 2004.

12. Rosenberg, *Inside the Wall Street Journal*, 75–76; "The Myth of Unlimited Abundance; 'Full Employment' Was to Create Economic Paradise, but America Is Discovering That There Is No Substitute for Freedom and Hard Work," *Wall Street Journal*, 8 Oct. 1946, and "We Have Been Warned: State Planning Means Allocations, Controls, Constant Shortages of Materials, Liberal Advocate Warns," *Wall Street Journal*, 9 Feb. 1949.

13. Wendt, *The Wall Street Journal*, 261, 295, 300, 342, 354, 359, 365; Rosenberg, *Inside the Wall Street Journal*, 75, 214–15; Baida, "The Business of America"; and Francis X. Dealy, *The Power and the Money: Inside the Wall Street Journal* (New York: Birch Lane, 1993).

14. Rosenberg, *Inside the Wall Street Journal*, 78; and *Wall Street Journal*: "Truman's New Soci-

ety," 10 Jan. 1949; "Social Progress—The Record," 31 May 1960; "The New America" and "Joint Congressional Group Opposes Tax Cuts, Curbs on Credit for Now; but Democrats on Economic Report Unit Assail Many Administration Proposals," 2 Mar. 1956; "Governor Rockefeller and the Future," 11 Nov. 1959; and "Merry Gentlemen," 24 Dec. 1959.

15. Arthur Jones, *Malcolm Forbes: Peripatetic Millionaire* (New York: Harper & Row, 1977), 93–97.

16. Leon Keyserling Papers, Box 78, HSTL.

17. Elson, *The World of Time Inc.*, vol. 2, 18–21; Galbraith, "Transition to Peace," *Fortune*, Jan. 1944, 83ff; Time Inc., *Writing for Fortune*, 21–22; John K. Jessup, "America and the Future: I—Our Domestic Economy," *Life*, 13 Sept. 1943, 104–6ff; and Parker, *John Kenneth Galbraith*, 157–61.

18. Henry Luce, "Reformation of the World's Economies," *Fortune*, Feb. 1950, 59–63; John K. Jessup et al., *The National Purpose* (New York: Holt, Rinehart & Winston, 1960); Elson, *The World of Time Inc*, vol. 2, 463–66; Jessup, "How to Make the Troubled U.S. Economy Succeed without Juggling: Choices Ahead for New Prosperity," *Life*, 24 Aug. 1962, 72–78, and *Reader's Digest*, Nov. 1962; "The American and His Economy: About Our $1,300,000,000,000 Economy," *Life*, 5 Jan. 1953, 7–100; "Boom Time," "Luckiest Generation," and "Wizards of the Coming Wonders," *Life*, 4 Jan. 1954, 6–11, 27–29, 92–94; "The Good Life: From 1890–1975—Leisure of the Classes and the Masses," *Life*, 28 Dec. 1959, 12–185.

19. *U.S. News & World Report*, 14 Jan. 1949, 68–95, and 13 Jan. 1950, 64–90.

20. "The Fabulous Fifties: America Enters an Age of Everyday Elegance," *Look*, 2 Oct. 1956 (cover); "If Our Pay Envelopes Are Fatter Now, It's Because Workers Produce More," *Saturday Evening Post*, 3 Apr. 1954, 7, 22, 46, 76; Joanne P. Sharp, *Condensing the Cold War: "Reader's Digest" and American Identity* (Minneapolis: University of Minnesota Press, 2000), 12; "America's Vast New Leisure Class," *Reader's Digest*, Jan. 1954, 12–14; "Fresh View of Capitalism," *Reader's Digest*, July 1956, 137–38; "Continuing Revolution in the U.S.," *Reader's Digest*, Aug. 1955, 72; "Second U.S. Revolution That Shook All Mankind," *Life*, 13 July 1959, 28, 94–96; "Our Gadgets Set Us Free," *Reader's Digest*, Aug. 1953, 33–34; "What Marxism Promises, U.S. Capitalism Delivers," *Reader's Digest*, Feb. 1957, 173–74.

21. Paul Hoffman Papers, Boxes 118, 131, HSTL; Keyserling, "The Boom-Bust Cycle: How Well Have We Got It Tamed?" *Business Week*, 3 Nov. 1956, 176–78; Parker, *John Kenneth Galbraith*, 267; Leon Keyserling Oral History, 3, 10, 19 May 1971, and Leon Keyserling Papers, Boxes 17, 18, 28, 29, 30, 32, Harry S. Truman Library (HSTL); and Frederick Lewis Allen, "This Time and Last Time: Postwar Eras I and II," *Harper's*, Mar. 1947, 193–203; "Unsystematic American System," *Harper's*, Jan. 1952, 21–26; "What Have We Got Here?" *Life*, 5 Jan. 1953, 46–50; and Allen, *The Big Change: America Transforms Itself, 1900–1950* (New York: Harpers & Brothers, 1952).

22. *Saturday Review*: "The American Economy 1959," 17 Jan. 1959, 17–46; "The Challenge of Prosperity," 9 Jan. 1965, 23–32ff; W. Allen Wallis in "The American Economy 1959," 17 Jan. 1959, 17–46; "The Soviet Economy," 21 Jan. 1961; "Collective Bargaining," 13 Jan. 1962; "Education in the Ghetto," 11 Jan. 1969; and Jan. 1959, 18, 24–25, 27, 29.

23. Galbraith, "The Unseemly Economics of Opulence," *Harper's*, Jan. 1952, 58–63; Lekachman, "If We're So Rich, What's Eating Us?" *Harper's*, Feb. 1956, 38–42; "Challenge to Our Economy," *New Republic*, 11 June 1956, 21–26, and "Soviet and U.S. Economic Growth," *New Republic*, 25 June 1956, 3; "Growth Growth Growth" *New Republic*, 7 Nov. 1960, 21–23; "What America Can Afford," *New Republic*, 7 Mar. 1960, 15–23; "Time for a Keynes," *New Republic*, 20 Oct. 1962, 35; "Eisenhower's Second Term," *New Republic*, 6 Nov. 1965, 25–27; and Keyserling, "The Prospects for Prosperity in 1955," *New Republic*, 14 Mar. 1955, 13–17; "How Fast Do We Grow?" *New Republic*, 16 June 1958, 7–8; "Report on the Economy," *New Republic*, 10 July 1961, 13–16.

24. "Prosperity for Whom?" *Nation*, 2 Oct. 1954, 284; "Voodoo Prosperity," *Nation*, 23 Oct. 1954, 358–60; "Perpetual Prosperity," *Nation*, 29 Jan. 1955, 96–98; "What Makes Prosperity," *Nation*, 4 Feb. 1956, 82; "People's Capitalism," *Nation*, 25 Feb. 1956, 151; "Myth of Guaranteed

Prosperity," *Nation,* 3 June 1961, 471–76; and "Economics of Affluence," *Nation,* 2 June 1962, 493–96.

25. Luce, "The American Century," *Life,* 17 Feb. 1941, 61–65; Galbraith, "Transition to Peace: Business in AD 194Q," *Fortune,* Jan. 1944, 83ff; "Ruml Asks U.S. Aid on Postwar Jobs," *New York Times,* 19 May 1943; Hansen, "Wanted: 10 Million Jobs," *Atlantic,* Sept. 1943, 65–69; "AFL and CIO Urge Reconversion Unit; Head of U.S. Chamber Agrees on Need for New Agency to Effect Postwar Transition," *New York Times,* 10 Jan. 1944; "Full Employment," *New York Times,* 19 Oct. 1944; "The Full Employment Bill," *New York Times,* 5 June 1945; Philip Murray, "Road to Freedom," *New Republic,* 24 Sept. 1945, and "The Road to Freedom—Full Employment," *New Republic,* 24 Sept. 1945, 395–415; I. F. Stone, "On Reconversion," *Nation,* 12 Aug. 1944, 175; Hansen, "Planning Full Employment," *Nation,* 21 Oct. 1944, 492; Ezekiel, "Full Employment-Beveridge Model," *Nation,* 3 Mar. 1945, 251–53; Ezekiel, "Road to Postwar Prosperity," *Scientific Digest,* Sept. 1943, 37–42; "Two Types of Crises; We Must Act to Avoid Mass Unemployment and Make Sure Bureaucratic Control at No Time Takes the Place of Individual Creative Effort," *Wall Street Journal,* 30 July 1945; Hansen, "Wanted: Ten Million Jobs," *Atlantic,* Sept. 1943, 65–67; David Cushman Coyle, "Planning a World of Plenty," *Parents,* Jan. 1943, 19ff; Alvin Hansen, "Planning Full Employment," *Nation,* 21 Oct. 1944, 492; and Mordecai Ezekiel, "Full Employment-Beveridge Model," *Nation,* 3 Mar. 1945, 251–53.

26. "Full Speed Ahead," *Time,* 9 Sept. 1946, 83; "Boom: It's Started, but—," *Newsweek,* 1 Apr. 1946, 68; "Boom: A Second Look," *Fortune,* Dec. 1946, 113–19; "Our Production Job During the War Is the Marvel of All Times," *U.S. News,* 9 Oct. 1945; and Donovan, *Right Places, Right Times,* 118.

27. Heilbroner, "Will Our Prosperity Last?" *Harper's,* Dec. 1948, 47–55; "USA: 1950–1960," *Business Week,* 26 Apr. 1947, 55–70; "How Well Can Americans Live?" *Fortune,* May 1947, 124–32; "Economists See 1950–1960 Boom," *New York Times,* 25 Apr. 1947; "U.S. Economic Trends from 1950 to 1960," *New York Times,* 4 May 1947; "Surveying American Economy in Terms of American Needs," *New York Times,* 1 June, 1947; "Good Times A-Comin'," *Life,* 5 May 1947, 30–31; and *Time,* "Everything for Everybody?" 5 May 1947, 85–86.

28. *Business Week,* "Our Postwar Economy—Bigger or Different," 4 Oct. 1947, 116.

29. "Who's Utopian Now? *Fortune,* Jan. 1948, 2–4; Eric A. Johnston, "Labor Should Have a Stake in Capitalism," *New York Times,* 24 Feb. 1946; and Hoffman, "The Great Challenge to Capitalism," *New York Times,* 8 Sept. 1946.

30. Slichter, "Economic Picture: More White Than Black," *New York Times Magazine,* 22 May 1949, 7; Slichter, "Upturn in Business is Not Far Away," *New York Times Magazine,* 17 July, 1949, 7; Slichter, "How Big in 1980?" *Atlantic,* Nov. 1949, 39–43; Slichter "Better Than We Think," *Atlantic,* Jan. 1950, 46–49; Slichter, "Our $416 Billion Future," *Science Digest,* Feb. 1950, 68–73; "We Can Win the Economic Cold War Too," *New York Times Magazine,* 13 Aug. 1950, 7; and Keyserling, "Planning for a $300 Billion Economy," *New York Times Magazine,* 18 June 1950, 9.

31. "Perpetual Prosperity: Is the Business Cycle Out?" *Nation,* 29 Jan. 1955, 96–98; "Where Do We Go from Here?" *Life,* 5 Jan. 1953, 86–92; "I Predict We'll Have Greater Prosperity," *Look,* 1 Jan. 1955, 42–43; "The Good Life," *Life,* 28 Dec. 1959; "How America Feels as It Enters the Soaring Sixties," *Look,* 5 Jan. 1960, 11–12; "Choices Ahead for New Prosperity," *Life,* 24 Aug. 1962, 72–74; and *Reader's Digest,* Nov. 1962, 82–87; "The Challenge of Prosperity," *Saturday Review,* 9 Jan. 1965, 23–32.

32. "Half Trillion," *Time,* 31 Jan. 1955, 12; "Ten Amazing Years: The Official Story of America's Growth," *U.S. News & World Report,* 1 Feb. 1957, 26–29; and "The Big Surge: The New America," *Newsweek,* 12 Dec. 1955, 56–60.

33. "The American and His Economy," *Life,* 5 Jan. 1953, 7–100.

34. "U.S. Growth: Our Biggest Year . . . and Basis for a Bigger Future" (cover), *Life,* 4 Jan. 1954; "Special Report: The Changed American Market—There Are More, Richer, Freer-Spending People in Every Region," *Business Week,* 4 July 1953, 74–76; "Leisured Masses," *Business*

Week, 12 Sept. 1953, 142–43, and 19 Sept. 1953, 144–46; "America's Vast New Leisure Class," *Reader's Digest,* Jan. 1954, 12–14; and "25 Years That Remade America," *Business Week,* 4 Sept. 1954, 74–76; "The Big Land at Mid-'53: Hot, Rich, At Work," *Newsweek,* 13 July 1953, 73; "In a Season of Plenty," *Newsweek,* 12 Sept. 1955, 29–30; and "The New America," *Newsweek,* 12 Dec. 1955, 56–60; "On the Rise," *Time,* 17 May 1954, 106; "In the Pink," *Time,* 9 May 1955, 22; "Year of Plenty," *Time,* 31 Dec. 1956, 26; Arthur Burns, "Good Times Ahead: $400 Billion Economy," *U.S. News & World Report,* 14 Oct. 1955, 48–51; "Everybody Rich in the U.S.?" *U.S. News & World Report,* 26 Oct. 1956, 27–32; "Ten Amazing Years: The Official Story of America's Growth," *U.S. News & World Report,* 1 Feb. 1957, 26–29; "Americans Never Had It So Good," *U.S. News & World Report,* 3 July 1953, 76–78, and "Americans Never Had it So Good," 15 Apr. 1955, 122; "Wonderful Ordinary Luxury Market," *Fortune,* Dec. 1953, 117–19, and "Next Year: $400 Billion," Dec. 1955, 27–28; "This Amazing Boom," *Newsweek,* 26 Mar. 1956, 81–84; "The Fabulous Fifties: America Enters an Age of Everyday Elegance," *Look,* 2 Oct. 1956 (cover); "Trillion-Dollar Country," *U.S. News & World Report,* 30 Jan. 1953, 24; and "Everybody Rich in the U.S.?" *U.S. News & World Report,* 26 Oct. 1956, 27–32.

35. Fortune, *The Changing American Market,* 13; "U.S. Growth: Our Biggest Year," *Life,* 4 Jan. 1954; "How America Feels As It Enters the Soaring Sixties," *Look,* 5 Jan. 1960, 11–12; and "Social Progress—The Record," *Wall Street Journal,* 31 May 1960.

36. "National Financial and Business Review," *New York Times,* 4 Jan. 1954; *U.S. News & World Report,* "New Year to Set Some Records" and "Headed for a New Record in '57," 6 Jan. 1956 and 4 Jan. 1957; *Business Week,* "Nation's Economy Sets New Records," 25 May 1955, 28–29; *Senior Scholastic,* "Economic Records Broken," 27 Oct. 1955, 30; interview with Todd May, 21 July 2004; "The National Financial and Business Review," *New York Times,* 3 Jan. 1955; "What a Country!" *Fortune,* Oct. 1956, 126–30; Fortune, *The Fabulous Future* (New York: Dutton, 1956); David Sarnoff, "Today Is Only a Fumbling Prelude," *Fortune,* Jan. 1955, 82–83.

37. Interview with Todd May, 21 July 2004; Time Inc., *Writing for Fortune,* 171; "The Sixties," *Newsweek,* 14 Dec. 1959, 79ff; "I Predict . . . We'll Have Greater Prosperity, *Look,* 11 Jan. 1955, 42–43; "The New America" (cover), *Time,* 30 Jan. 1953, "In the Pink," *Time,* 9 May 1955, 22 "How America Feels as It Enters the Soaring Sixties," *Look,* 5 Jan. 1960, 11–22; "This Is Living in 2000," *Newsweek,* 28 Sept. 1959, 49–50; "What the U.S. Will Be Like 10 Years from Now," *U.S. News & World Report,* 9 Nov. 1959, 76–83; "U.S. in 1970," *New York Times Magazine,* 17 May 1959, 25ff; "USA in 1970," *Reader's Digest,* Jan. 1961, 25–29; and "How We'll Live 50 Years from Now," *Coronet,* Dec. 1959, 82–86.

38. "What a Country!" *Fortune,* Oct. 1956, 126–30ff; "America: Body and Soul," *House Beautiful,* Nov. 1956, 42; Slichter, "Growth of Moderation," *Atlantic,* Oct. 1956, 61–64; *Business Week,* "The Leisured Masses," 19 Sept. 1953, 142–43; Fortune, *The Changing American Market,* 14 and chapter 3; Fortune, *Markets of the Sixties* (New York: Harper & Brothers, 1960), 89; and *Life,* "The American and His Economy," 5 Jan. 1953, 7–100.

39. "Special Report: The People Who Are Doing Best in the Boom," 28 Oct. 1955, 90, and "Everybody Rich? The 15-Year Trend in Incomes," *U.S. News,* 26 Oct. 1956, 27–32; and the series, "New American Market, *Business Week,* 12 Apr. 1947, 43–52, 31 May 1947, 41–48, 5 July 1947, 55–62, and 20 Dec. 1947, 61–72; Fortune, *Markets of the Sixties,* xi; "Prosperity and Expansion," *Time,* 31 Dec. 1956, 54ff; "Ten Amazing Years," *U.S. News & World Report,* 1 Feb. 1957, 26–29; *Business Week,* "25 Years That Remade America," 4 Sept. 1954, 75–94; "Social Progress—The Record," *Wall Street Journal,* 31 May 1960; "25 Years That Remade America," *Business Week,* 4 Sept. 1954, 75–94; "The Big Surge: The New America," *Newsweek,* 12 Dec. 1955, 56–60; "The Sixties," *Newsweek,* 14 Dec. 1959, 79ff; "The Fabulous Fifties: America Enters an Age of Everyday Elegance," *Look,* 2 Oct. 1956 (cover); "In the Next America, Everyone Will Cook Like a Connoisseur," *House Beautiful,* Apr. 1953, 132–34; "America Body and Soul," *House Beautiful,* Nov. 1956, 42; "How High is Up?" *House Beautiful,* July 1955, 95; and "What a Country!" *Fortune,* Oct. 1956, 126–30.

40. Peter Drucker, *The New Society: The Anatomy of Industrial Order* (New York: Harper & Brothers, 1950), 1, and "Look What's Happened to Us!" *Saturday Evening Post,* 19 Jan. 1952, 30; "U.S.A.: The Permanent Revolution," *Fortune,* Feb. 1951, 62–83; Allen, "The Unsystematic American System," *Harper's,* Feb. 1952, 21–26; "The American and His Economy," *Life,* 5 Jan. 1953, 7–100; "Twentieth Century Capitalist Revolution," *Business Week,* 30 Oct. 1954, 114–15; Fortune, *The Changing American Market* (1954); "The Bull Market with a Business Review and Forecast," *Time,* 10 Jan. 1955, 72–79; "America's Possibilities," *Business Week,* 30 Apr. 1955, 158–62; Slichter, "The Growth of Moderation," *Atlantic,* Oct. 1956, 61–64; A. A. Berle, "Marx was Wrong and So Is Khrushchev," *New York Times Magazine,* 1 Nov. 1959, 9; "Why Marx Failed Here," *Saturday Evening Post,* 20 Aug. 1960, 32–33; and R. L. Bruckberger, "The Great Twentieth-Century Revolution," *Life,* 13 July 1959, 94; "Fresh View of Capitalism," *Life,* 9 Apr. 1956, 58; "Special Report: The Changed America," *Business Week,* 6 June 1953, 101–3; "The Big Surge: The New America," *Newsweek,* 12 Dec. 1955, 56–60; "Perils of Prosperity—How Great?" "Good Times (It's How You Look at Them)," and "Five Economists Set Their Sight, *Newsweek,* 18 Feb. 1957, 27, 77–78ff; "Is 'New' Era Really Here?" *U.S. News & World Report,* 20 May 1955, 21–23; "How You Will Live in the Next America," *House Beautiful,* Apr. 1953, 11–134ff; and interview with Dan Seligman, 29 June 2004.

41. "Too Much Leisure Parts I and II, *Life,* 14 Feb. 1964, 76, and 21 Feb. 1964, 84.

42. "Europeans Fail to Conceive Free Enterprise as We Use It: They Continue to Confuse It with Nineteenth Century Brand of Capitalism Practiced There," *New York Times,* 14 Sept. 1947; Fortune, *The Changing American Market* (1954), 110; "Catch-Phrase of the Day," *Wall Street Journal,* 16 June 1960; "How Long Will World Prosperity Last?" *Look,* 24 Jan. 1956, 92ff; "A Fresh View of Capitalism," *Life,* 9 Apr. 1956, 58; and "Worker Loses His Class Identity," *Business Week,* 11 July 1959, 90–92.

43. Fortune, *The Changing American Market,* chapter 5; "Everybody Can Own a House," *House Beautiful,* Nov. 1956, 42; and "The Great Twentieth Century Revolution," *Life,* 13 July 1959; and "The Rise of Negroes in Industry: Problems and Progress," *Newsweek,* 12 Sept. 1955, 86–88.

44. Ebony, *The Negro Handbook* (Chicago: Johnson Publishing Company, 1966), 214–17; and Ebony, *The Negro Handbook* (Chicago: Johnson Publishing Company, 1974), 264, 7.

45. "Special Report: The Changed America," *Business Week,* 6 June 1953, 101–3; Fortune, *The Changing American Market* (1954), 29; "The Consumer Economy" and "The American Economy: The Great Shopping Spree," *Time,* 8 Jan. 1965, 58–62; "National Financial and Business Review," *New York Times,* 4 Jan. 1954; "The Next America," *House Beautiful,* Apr. 1953, 11–134; and "Money for Fun," *Newsweek,* 12 Dec. 1955, 72.

46. Dulles in "The American and His Economy," *Life,* 5 Jan. 1953, 7–100; Ludwig von Mises, "The Anti-Capitalistic Mentality," *U.S. News & World Report,* 15 Oct. 1956, 110; Heilbroner, "The Uncomfortable Paradise of Full Employment, *Harper's,* Apr. 1947, 336–40; Niebuhr in "The Big Surge: The New America," *Newsweek,* 12 Dec. 1955, 56–60; Hazlitt, "Unstable Paradise," *Newsweek,* 12 Sept. 1955, 93; "The Department of Windy Words," *Wall Street Journal,* 21 July 1961; "People's Capitalism," *New York Times,* 15 Feb. 1956; "U.S. Capitalism Seen as Ideal for the World," *New York Times,* 24 Nov. 1956; "People's Capitalism: This Is America," *Collier's,* 6 Jan. 1956, 74; "U.S.A.: The Permanent Revolution," *Fortune,* 62–83, Feb. 1951; "The People's Capitalism," *House Beautiful,* Nov. 1956, 226; "People's Capitalism," *Nation,* 25 Feb. 1956, 151; and "People's Capitalism?" *New Republic,* 20 Oct. 1962, 16–17.

47. "The People's Capitalism," *House Beautiful,* Nov. 1956, 226; "Inside the Soviet Economy," *Saturday Review,* 21 Jan. 1961, 44; and Sharp, *Condensing the Cold War,* 83–85; "Now the Challenge of an Economic Sputnik," *New York Times Magazine,* 8 Feb. 1959, 7, "Economic War," *Newsweek,* 25 Jan. 1960, 22; "Russian vs. U.S. Growth," *Time,* 14 Dec. 1959, 90; "Inside the Soviet Economy," *Saturday Review,* 21 Jan. 1961, 44; "What Counts: The U.S. vs. the U.S.S.R.," *Newsweek,* 7 Feb. 1955, 20; Fortune, *Markets of the Sixties;* von Mises, "The Anti-Capitalistic Mentality," *U.S. News & World Report,* 19 Oct. 1956, 110; "The Bull Market With a Business Review and Forecast,"

Time, 10 Jan. 1955, 72–79; and "The American Economy 1959," *Saturday Review,* 17 Jan. 1959, 17–46.

48. Heilbroner, "Will Our Prosperity Last?" *Harper's,* Dec. 1948, 47–55; Michael Harrington, "The Myths of U.S. Liberalism," *Commonweal,* 17 Dec. 1954, 303–6; Slichter, "Have We Conquered the Business Cycle?" *Atlantic,* May 1955, 51–55; Slichter, "The Growth of Moderation," *Atlantic,* Oct. 1956; "The Boom-Bust Cycle: How Well Have We Got It Tamed?" *Business Week,* 3 Nov. 1956, 176–78; "How Long Will World Prosperity Last?" *Look,* 22 Mar. 1955, 92ff; Niebuhr, "Ike Committed to New Dealism," *Time,* 2 May 1955, 25; "Fight for the Annual Wage," *Time,* 7 Feb. 1955, 72–73; "Business in 1965: The Keynesian Influence on the Expansionist Economy," *Time,* 31 Dec. 1965, 64–67; Lekachman, "If We're So Rich, What's Eating Us?" *Harper's,* Feb. 1956, 38–42.

49. "Boom Can Go on 10 Years," *U.S. News & World Report,* 23 Feb. 1951; "Special Report: The Changed America You Will Be Living in, Doing Business In," *Business Week,* 6 June 1953, 101–3; "The Boom-Bust Cycle: How Well Have We Got It Tamed?" *Business Week,* 3 Nov. 1956, 176–78; "Soon—An End to the Downturn," *U.S. News & World Report,* 5 Feb. 1954, 20–21; "Managing the Boom," *Newsweek,* 2 Dec. 1955, 68; "Ike's Minister for Prosperity," *Collier's,* 25 May 1956, 32; "Perils of Prosperity—How Great?" "Good Times (It's How You Look at Them)," and "Five Economists Set Their Sights," *Newsweek,* 18 Feb. 1957, 27, 77–78; Fortune, *The Fabulous Future* (1956); "The Bull Market with a Business Review and Forecast," *Time,* 10 Jan. 1955, 72–79; "Eisenhower Report Visions Long-Term Economic Rise," *New York Times,* 21 Jan. 1955; "The American Economy 1959," *Saturday Review,* 17 Jan. 1959, 17–46; "Is Automation Really a Job-Killer? More Automation for the US, Not Less," *Business Week,* 24 Feb. 1962, 46–48; "A Well-Tempered Boom," *Business Week,* 27 June 1964, 27–29; and Donovan, *Right Places, Right Times,* 134.

50. "Business in 1965: The Keynesian Influence on the Expansionist Economy," *Time,* 31 Dec. 1965, 64–67.

51. "The President's Prophets," 4 Jan. 1954, 92–94; "Soon—An End to the Downturn," *U.S. News & World Report,* 5 Feb. 1954, 20–21; Hobart Rowen, "Kennedy's Economists," *Harper's,* Sept. 1961, 25–32; "Business in 1965: The Keynesian Influence on the Expansionist Economy," *Time,* 31 Dec. 1965, 64–67; President's Office Files, Departments and Agencies, CEA, Box 75A, 76, JFKPL; Edwin G. Nourse, *Economics in the Public Service: Administrative Aspects of the Employment Act* (New York: Harcourt Brace, 1953); "Twelve Men Close to Kennedy," *New York Times Magazine,* 22 Jan. 1961, 6–7; Francis Bator, "Money and Government," *Atlantic,* Apr. 1962, 110–18; and "Kennedy's Economic Mixture," *Business Week,* 25 Feb. 1961, 23–26.

52. Jared Bernstein, *All Together Now: Common Sense for a Fair Economy* (San Francisco: Berrett-Koehler, 2006).

Chapter 5: Defining the New America for the World

1. National Archives and Records Administration (NARA), College Park, Md., RG 306-99-008, MLR#1252, Boxes 1–9: Records of the United States Information Agency (USIA), Pamphlets and leaflets produced between 1953 and 1960.

2. David F. Krugler, *The Voice of America and the Domestic Propaganda Battles, 1945–1953* (Columbia: University of Missouri Press, 2000), 24; Oral History Interview with Edward W. Barrett, 9 July 1974, Harry S. Truman Library (HSTL); Laura Belmonte, "Selling Capitalism: Modernization and U.S. Overseas Propaganda, 1945–1959," in *Modernization, Development, and the Globalization of the Cold War,* ed. Michael Latham et al. (Amherst: University of Massachusetts Press, 2003), 109–12; C. A. Thomson and Walter Laves, *Cultural Relations and U.S. Foreign Policy* (Bloomington: University of Indiana Press, 1963), 64, 66, 67; Paul Hoffman, *Peace Can Be Won* (Garden City, N.Y.: Doubleday, 1951), 135ff; Leo Bogart, "A Study of the Operating Assumptions of the U.S. Information Agency," *The Public Opinion Quarterly* 19:4 (Winter 1955–56): 369–79; Dwight D. Eisenhower, *Waging Peace: The White House Years, A Personal Account, 1956–1961* (Gar-

den City, N.Y.: Doubleday, 1965), 132, 136–38, 637; Richard T. Davies, "The American Commitment to Public Propaganda," *Law and Contemporary Problems* 31:3 (Summer 1966): 452–57; Harry S. Truman, "Statement by the President on the Voice of America," The American Presidency Project (TAPP), www.presidency.ucsb.edu/ws/?pid=14053); "Policy Statements" and "The Eisenhower Statement of the USIA Mission," in Agency History Program Subject Files, Box 5, Record Group (RG) 306 (Records of the USIA), NARA; Eisenhower, "Remarks to the Staff of the U.S. Information Agency," 10 Nov. 1953, in TAPP; Eisenhower, "Remarks at Ceremony Marking the Tenth Anniversary of the Smith-Mundt Act," 27 Jan. 1958," in TAPP; John F. Kennedy, "Remarks on the Twentieth Anniversary of the Voice of America," 26 Feb. 1962, and "Remarks Recorded for the Opening of a USIA Transmitter in Greenville, NC," 8 Feb. 1963, in TAPP; Edward W. Barrett Oral History, Interview by Richard D. McKinzie, New York, N.Y., 9 July 1974, Harry S. Truman Library (HSTL); and Psychological Strategy Board Files, Boxes 1 and 3, in Staff Member and Office Files, HSTL; USIA Alumni Association, *United States Information Agency: A Commemoration—Telling America's Story to the World, 1953–1999,* n.d., 30; L. John Martin, "Effectiveness of International Propaganda," *Annals of the Academy of Political and Social Science,* Nov. 1971, 61–70; and Wilson Dizard Jr., "Telling America's Story," *American Heritage* 54:4 (Aug./Sept. 2003): 41–48; and Oral History Interview with Edward W. Barrett, 9 July 1974, HSTL; and Walter L. Hixson, *Parting the Curtain: Propaganda, Culture, and the Cold War, 1945–1961* (New York: St. Martin's Press, 1997), 5.

3. Eisenhower, *Waging Peace,* 132, 637; "Operations Coordinating Board," Sept. 1955, in Historical Program Subject Files, 1953–2000, Box 2, RG 306, NARA; Eisenhower, "Remarks to the Staff of the U.S. Information Agency," 10 Nov. 1953, and "Remarks at Ceremony Marking the Tenth Anniversary of the Smith-Mundt Act," 27 Jan. 1958, in TAPP; U.S. President's Committee on Information Activities Abroad Records, Box 26, C. D. Jackson Papers, Box 62, Dwight D. Eisenhower Library (DDEL); Leo Bogart, *Premises for Propaganda: The United States Information Agency's Operating Assumptions in the Cold War* (New York: Free Press, 1976), 4, 92, 16, 69–90. Laura A. Belmonte, "Defending a Way of Life: American Propaganda and the Cold War, 1945–1959" (Ph. D. diss., University of Virginia, 1996), 334; Theodore Streibert Oral History and U.S. President's Committee on Information Activities Abroad, Box 14, DDEL; Wilson P. Dizard, *The Strategy of Truth: The Story of the U.S. Information Service* (Washington, D.C.: Public Affairs Press, 1961), 58, 60, 96; Hixson, *Parting the Curtain,* 138; Robert H. Haddow, *Pavilions of Plenty: Exhibiting American Culture Abroad in the 1950s* (Washington, D.C.: Smithsonian Institution Press, 1997); and Michael Nelson, *War of the Black Heavens* (Syracuse: Syracuse University Press, 1997), 58–59, 101–2.

4. Lynn Hinds and Otto Windt, *The Cold War as Rhetoric, 1945–50* (Westport, Conn.: Praeger, 1991), 146; Psychological Strategy Board Files, Box 3; and Barrett interview, 9 July 1974, NARA.

5. Publications about the United States, 1945–1999, Entry 1053, *America Illustrated* magazine, 1945–1952, America Illustrated archive, Boxes 40 and 41, RG 306, Records of the USIA, NARA.

6. "The Strength of Democracy," *Amerika,* Issue 55 (1951), 40; "The Fourth of July," *Amerika* 12 (1946), 72; Robert Oppenheimer, "Science and Freedom," *Amerika* 53 (1951), 14–15: "President Truman's Address at the Opening of General Assembly of United Nations," *Amerika* 10 (1946), 2–3, "The U.N. Builds Its Home," *Amerika* 33 (1949), 50–53; "The World Health Organization," *Amerika* 44 (1950), 2–6; "The United Nations Builds," *Amerika* 45 (1949), 2–9; "A Brief Survey of American History Part 1," *Amerika* 24 (1948), 2–13; "A Brief Survey of American History Part 2," *Amerika* 25 (1948), 38–49; "A Brief Survey of American History Part 3," *Amerika* 26 (1948), 63–71; "A Brief Survey of American History Part 4," *Amerika* 27, 28–35; "A Brief Survey of American History Part 5," *Amerika* 28, 18–27; "A Brief Survey of American History Part 6, *Amerika* 29 (1949), 40–49; and "A Brief Survey of American History Part 7," *Amerika* 30 (1949), 48–59, in America Illustrated Archive, Boxes 40 and 41, NARA.

7. Pamphlets and leaflets produced between 1953 and 1960, Boxes 5 and 7, RG 306-99-008, Entry 1252, Records of the USIA, NARA; and Sharp, *Condensing the Cold War,* 84.

8. "Ensuring Stability in the United States," *Amerika* 15 (1947), 2–6, in America Illustrated Archive, Box 40, NARA.

9. Frederick Martin Stern, American Labor and the Classless Society," *Amerika,* Issue 54 (1951), 20–21, in America Illustrated archive, Box 41; Robert Heilbroner, "Wages and Prices in the United States," *Amerika* 46 (1950), 2–7, in America Illustrated archive, Box 41, NARA.

10. Yale Richmond, *Cultural Exchange and the Cold War: Raising the Iron Curtain* (University Park: Pennsylvania State University Press, 2003); "The Meaning of American Labor Day," *Free World* 2:10 (1953): 42–45; and "How a U.S. Labor Union Works," *Free World* 3:3 (1954): 34–37, in *Free World* archive, RG 306, Records of the USIA, NARA.

11. "America 1900–1950: Fifty Years Brings a New Concept of Good Living for Everyone," *Free World* 3:2 (1954): 21–24; "Social Welfare in the United States," *Free World* 3:4 (1954): 12–15; John Foster Dulles, "A Spirit of Justice," *Free World* 3:4 (1954): 42; "The Greatest Success Story in the World," *Free World* 3:12 (1954): 2–5; and "Mutual Capitalism—An American System," *Free World* 3:5 (1954): 12–15, in Free World Archive, NARA.

12. Paul Hoffman, *Peace Can Be Won* (Garden City, N.Y.: Doubleday, 1951), 141.

13. Belmonte, "Selling Capitalism," 113; Pamphlets and leaflets produced between 1953 and 1960, Boxes 2 and 8, RG 306-99-008, Entry 1252, Records of the USIA, NARA; James M. Lambie Jr. Records, 1952–61, Boxes 17, 23, 31, 38, C. D. Jackson Papers, Box 95, DDEL; Hixson, *Parting the Curtain,* 133; Haddow, *Pavilions of Plenty,* 49; and Charles Jackson Files, Boxes 15, 16, HSTL.

14. Fresh View of Capitalism," *Life,* 9 Apr. 1956, 58; "People's Capitalism," *New York Times,* 15 Feb. 1956; "U.S. Capitalism Seen as Ideal for the World," *New York Times,* 24 Nov. 1956; "People's Capitalism: This is America," *Collier's,* 6 Jan. 1956, 74; "The People's Capitalism," *House Beautiful,* Nov. 1956, 226. See also "People's Capitalism," *Nation,* 25 Feb. 1956, 151, and "People's Capitalism?" *New Republic,* 20 Oct. 1962; "A New Name—'People's Capitalism' in America," *Free World* 5:10 and 11 (1956) and 4:1 (1957), in Free World Archive, NARA.

15. "'People's Capitalism' in America," *Free World* 5:10 and 11 (1956) and 4:1 (1957), in Free World Archive, NARA, and "Classless Capitalism," *Free World* 5:11 and 6:1, in Free World Archive, NARA.

16. "People's Capitalism," Pamphlets and leaflets produced between 1953 and 1960, Box 6, RG 306-99-008, Entry 1252, Records of the USIA, NARA.

17. "The Common Man in America," *Free World* 7:10 (1959), in Free World Archive, NARA.

18. John Melby, Foreign Affairs Oral History Project, Association for Diplomatic Studies and Training, Washington, D.C., 16 June 1989; interview with William E. Hutchinson, 10 Aug. 1989; and Publications about the United States, Entry 1053, America Illustrated Archive), Box 47, No. 1, RG 306, Records of the USIA, NARA.

19. "Vacation Time," *America Illustrated,* Box 47, No. 1 (1956), 56; "Up the Labor Ladder," *America Illustrated,* no. 37 (1959), 47–49; "The Day's Work Is Done," *America Illustrated,* no. 26 (1958); "Three Office Workers at Home," *America Illustrated,* no. 26 (1958), 37; and "Four Family Budgets," *America Illustrated,* no. 29 (1959), 12, in Boxes 47–50, America Illustrated Archive, NARA.

20. "Revolution in the Kitchen," *America Illustrated,* no. 17 (1957), 34; "Leisure in a Changing Society," no. 40 (1959), 2; "Vacation Time," no. 1 (1956), 56; "Boats for Everyone," *America Illustrated,* no. 35 (1957), 6; "Teenagers' Economics," *America Illustrated,* no. 26 (1958), 53; "Assembly Line Home Building, *America Illustrated,* 38 (1959), 56–61; "Second Homes for Family Vacations," *America Illustrated,* no. 47 (1960), 27–31; "About Telephones: 65,000,000 of Them," *America Illustrated* (Polish edition), June 1959, no. 6, 139–44; and "The 'Family Vacation,'" *America Illustrated* (Polish edition), Aug. 1959, no. 7, 116–22, in *America Illustrated* Archive, Boxes 47–50, RG 306, Records of the USIA, NARA.

21. The Changing American Society" and "The 1960s: A Forecast of the Technology," *America Illustrated,* no. 48 (1960), 2–7 and 34–39; "Ten Amazing Years," *America Illustrated,* no. 16 (1957),

2ff; "Facts About the United States: Decade of Growth," *America Illustrated*, no. 46 (1960), 16–17; "Facts about the U.S. Income," *America Illustrated*, no. 33 (1959), 6ff, in America Illustrated Archive, Boxes 48–50, NARA.

22. "The Changing American Society," *America Illustrated*, no. 40 (1960), 2–7, America Illustrated Archive, Box 50, NARA.

23. Clinton Rossiter, "Role of the President," *America Illustrated*, no. 6 (1956), 13, "Congress of the United States," *America Illustrated*, no. 16 (1957), 34, and "Supreme Court of the United States," *America Illustrated*, no. 17 (1957); Dennis S. Feldman, "150th Anniversary," *America Illustrated*, no. 29 (1959), 2; "Congress at Work," *America Illustrated*, no. 40 (1960), 22, in boxes 48 and 50 in America Illustrated Archive, NARA.

24. *People's Capitalism, American Capitalism: The Economic Progress of a Free People* (1956); *The People: The Real Sinews of the U.S. Economy* (1956); *Primer of the American Economy* (1958); *Thomas Brackett: American Capitalist* (1957); *The American Economy: Prospects for Growth to 1965 and 1975* (1958); *The American Consumer: Key to an Expanding Economy* (1960); and David Potter, *The American Economy*, pamphlets and leaflets produced between 1953 and 1960, Boxes 1–9, RG 306-99-008, Entry 1252, Records of the USIA, NARA.

25. U.S. President's Committee on Information Activities Abroad Records, 1959–61, Box 14, DDEL; Claudio Gonzales-Chiaramonte, "What Is Americanism Anyway? Exporting an American Identity," paper delivered at Dickinson College, 7–9 Apr. 1999; "The U.S.A. Goes to the Fair," *Reader's Digest*, Dec. 1955; and Haddow, *Pavilions of Plenty*, 52, 15.

26. Haddow, *Pavilions of Plenty*, 63, 65, 113, 123, 147, 156, 169.

27. Ibid., 181–88; and Marling, *As Seen on TV*, 246–48.

28. Eastern Europe Region; Soviet Union; Cyprus (Washington, D.C.: GPO, 1993), in U.S. Department of State, *Foreign Relations of the United States*, 1958–1960, vol. 10, part 1; U.S. President's Committee on Information Activities Abroad Records, 1959–61, Box 14, DDEL; Marling, *As Seen on TV*, 243, 277; Foner, *The Story of American Freedom*, 271; Haddow, *Pavilions of Plenty*, 214–17; *Consumer Society in American History: A Reader*, ed. Lawrence B. Glickman (Ithaca: Cornell University Press, 1999), 8; and Richard W. Fox and T. J. Jackson Lears, *The Culture of Consumption: Critical Essays in American History, 1880–1960* (New York: Pantheon, 1983), ix.

Chapter 6: Beyond Civics and the 3 R's

1. Joint Council on Economic Education (JCEE). *Education for the Economic Challenges of Tomorrow: A Report of a Symposium in Conjunction with the 10th Anniversary of the JCEE, 1949–1959* (New York, 1959), 28–30.

2. James D. McCabe, *The Centennial History of the United States* (Philadelphia: National Publishing Co., 1875), 4; McGuffey cited in *The American Nation, National Identity, Nationalism*, ed. Knud Krakau (New Brunswick, N.J.: Transaction Publishers, 1997), 39; David H. Montgomery, *The Leading Facts of American History* (Boston: Ginn and Co., 1900); and Charles Morris, *Young Student's History of the United States* (Philadelphia" J. B. Lippincott, 1900), 3, 250.

3. Morris, 53, 59, 63, 65; and David Saville Muzzey, *An American History* (Boston: Ginn and Co., 1920), 537.

4. Willis Mason West, *American History and Government* (Boston: Allyn and Bacon, 1913), iii, 642, 703, chapters 1–11; Charles and Mary R, Beard, *History of the United States: A Study in American Civilization* (New York: Macmillan, 1921), 186, 297, 401, 620; Frances Fitzgerald, *America Revised: History Schoolbooks in the Twentieth Century* (Boston: Little Brown, 1979), 114; and Mabel B. Casner and Ralph H. Gabriel, *Exploring American History* (New York: Harcourt, Brace & Co., 1933), 750, 560, 625.

5. Robert Lerner, Althea K. Nagai, and Stanley Rothman, *Molding the Good Citizen: The Politics of High School History Texts* (Westport, Conn.: Praeger, 1995), 107; Joseph Moreau, *Schoolbook Nation: Conflicts over American History Textbooks from the Civil War to the Present* (Ann Arbor: Uni-

versity of Michigan Press, 2003), 37, 210ff, 241, 243, 248; Fitzgerald, *America Revised*, 37; and Harold Ordway Rugg, *A History of American Civilization: Economic and Social* (Boston: Ginn and Co., 1930), 596, 606, 615–24.

6. Fitzgerald, *America Revised*, 105, 109; Ralph Volney Harlow and Ruth Elizabeth Miller, *Story of America* (New York: Henry Holt, 1947), v, 391–92, 664.

7. Fremont P. Wirth, *The Development of America* (New York: American Book Company, 1950), 1, 225, 811; and P. Wirth, *United States History*, rev. ed. (New York: American Book Company, 1957), introductory section, 3, 139, 437, 661–62; chapters 29–40.

8. David Saville Muzzey, *A History of Our Country: A Textbook for High School Students* (Boston: Ginn and Co., 1945), 109, 137, 164, 313, 320–21, 806, 897.

9. Howard B. Wilder, Robert P. Ludlum, and Harriet McCune Brown, *This Is America's Story* (Boston: Houghton Mifflin, 1954), xi, 2, 7, 442, 481, 535, 664, 507, 509, 467.

10. Henry W. Bragdon and Samuel P. McCutchen, *History of a Free People* (New York: Macmillan, 1954), ix, 3, 672, 644.

11. Gertrude Hartman, *America: Land of Freedom* (Boston: D.C. Heath, 1959), 577–78, 583, vi–vii.

12. Edna McGuire and Thomas B. Portwood, *Our Free Nation* (New York: Macmillan, 1954), v; Wilder, Ludlum, and Brown, *This Is America's Story*, 507; Philip Dorf, *American History in Review* (New York: Keystone Education Press, 1954), 231; and Howard Eugene Wilson and Wallace E. Lamb, *American History* (New York: American Book Company, 1955), 589, 577–80.

13. Lewis Paul Todd and Merle Curti, *The Rise of the American Nation* (New York: Harcourt, Brace and World, 1966), 810, 556, 545, 815, 797; John D. Hicks, George E. Mowry, and Robert E. Burke, *A History of American Democracy*, 3rd ed. (Boston: Houghton Mifflin Co., 1966), 788–89; and Arthur Link, *The Growth of American Democracy: An Interpretive History* (Boston: Ginn, 1968), 725, 676, 669–73, 573.

14. *Senior Scholastic:* "What Economics?" (10 May 1956), "Task Force Reports on Economics" and "Study Materials for Economic Education in the Schools" (20 Oct. 1961), and the issues of Feb. 1950 and 9 Feb. 1956.

15. NMAH, Ayer Collection, Series 3, Box 36.

16. "America's Economic System," *Senior Scholastic*, 15 Mar. 1950; and Hoffman Papers, Box 118, HSTL.

17. *Senior Scholastic:* "Business, Labor, and the Good Citizen" (11 Apr. 1951), "Our Economic Picture Today: Changing Face of America" (17 Mr. 1954); "Economic Records Broken" (27 Oct. 1955); "1956: Another Boom Year?" (9 Feb. 1956); "U.S. Boom Keeps Rolling" (8 Feb. 1957); "Are We Having Too Much Prosperity?" (8 Mar. 1957); and "U.S. Charts its Course for '62" (7 Feb. 1962).

18. *Senior Scholastic:* "America: The Middle Way" (8 Dec. 1955), "Democratic Capitalism" (19 Apr. 1956), "Watchdogs on Wall Street" (7 Nov. 1958), "Special Issue: The American Economy 1962—From Main Street to Wall Street," 18 Apr. 1962, and "Economic Prosperity," 23 Sept. 1964, 16.

19. NYU Workshop on Economic Education, "Problems of Our American Economy" (1948), JCEE Papers, Hagley; CED, *Improving Economic Understanding in the Public Schools* (1950), 3; Hill, "The Joint Council on Economic Education: A Program For Curriculum Change," 17–21; CED, *Improving Economic Understanding in the Public Schools* (1950), 15; interviews with Stowell Symmes, 2 Oct. 2004; Mark Schug, 7 Feb. 2005; and Leon Schur, 15 Feb. 2005; NYU Workshop on Economic Education, "Problems of Our American Economy" (1948); G. Derwood Baker, "The Joint Council on Economic Education," *Journal of Educational Sociology* 23:7 (Mar. 1950).

20. Harold J. Bienvenu, "Economic Education: Problems and Progress," *Elementary School Journal* 59:2 (Nov. 1958); "Program of the JCEE," *Journal of Higher Education* 30:2 (Feb. 1959); CED, *Improving Economic Understanding in the Public Schools* (1950), 8; and JEC, Subcommittee on Economic Progress, *Economic Education*, vol. 2, "Related Materials" (1967).

21. M. L. Frankel, Hearings Before the Subcommittee on Economic Progress of the Joint Economic Committee, *Economic Education,* 21 Apr. 1967, 58; interviews with Charles L. Schultze, 3 June 2005, Todd May, 24 July 2004, and Stowell Symmes, 2 Oct. 2004; and Hill, "The Joint Council on Economic Education: A Program for Curriculum Change," 111, 62, 107, 115–16.

22. JCEE, *Bibliography of Free and Inexpensive Materials for Economic Education* (1955).

23. Carskadon and Modley, *U.S.A. Measure of a Nation,* foreword, 1, 97, 98; Carskadon and Soule, *U.S.A. in New Dimensions,* 120–24.

24. JCEE, *Bibliography of Free and Inexpensive Materials for Economic Education* (1957).

25. Moore, "The National Association of Manufacturers," 659; Hagley, NAM Records, 1917–1970, Accession 1411, Series 6, Box 219, and JCEE Papers; CED, "Study Materials for Economic Education in the Schools" (Oct. 1961); and CED Annual Report, 1960.

26. NAM Records, 1917–1970, Accession 1411, Series 6, Box 99, Hagley; and McKee and Moulton, "A Survey of Economic Education."

27. CED Study Materials for Economic Education in the Schools," Oct. 1961; Laurence E. Leamer and Dorothy Lampen Thomson, *American Capitalism: An Introduction* (New York: Council for Advancement of Secondary Education, 1958, 1968), 2, 62, 77, 89, 22; and Personal Papers of Stowell Symmes; JCEE, *Our Growing America,* JCEE Papers, Hagley; and CED, *Study Materials for Economic Education in the Schools,* Oct. 1961.

28. JCEE, *Education for the Economic Challenges of Tomorrow: A Report of a Symposium in Conjunction with the 10th Anniversary of the JCEE, 1949–1959* (New York, 1959), 21.

29. CED, *Economic Education in the Schools* (National Task Force on Economic Education, Sept. 1961), 7, 9, 15, 22, 43, 64–78; Karl Schriftgiesser, *Business and Public Policy: The Role of the Committee for Economic Development, 1942–1967* (Englewood Cliffs, N.J.: Prentice-Hall, 1967), 209–10; G. L. Bach, Paul R. Olson, and Howard S. Ellis; "Economic Education: Challenge to Our Profession," *American Economic Review* 51:2, Papers and Proceedings of the Seventy-third Annual Meeting of the American Economic Association (May 1961); John R. Coleman, George J. Stigler, and Lewis E. Wagner; "Economic Education," *American Economic Review* 53:2, Papers and Proceedings of the Seventy-fifth Annual Meeting of the American Economic Association (May 1963); and interviews with Leon Schur, 15 Feb. 2005, and Stowell Symmes, 2 Oct. 2004.

30. Coleman, "Economic Literacy: What Role for Television?" *American Economic Review* 53:2 (May 1963); Learning Resources Institute, *Prospectus for "The American Economy,"* Dec. 1961 and 20 Mar. 1962, John F. Kennedy Presidential Library, CEA, Box 73; Statement of M. L. Frankel, Hearings Before the Subcommittee on Economic Progress of the Joint Economic Committee, *Economic Education,* 21 Apr. 1967, 59; Schriftgiesser, *Business and Public Policy,* 209–10; interview with Stowell Symmes, 2 Oct. 2004; and *Vital Speeches of the Day,* vol. 29 (5 Jan. 1963), 288.

31. Personal papers of Stowell Symmes; and Statement of Lawrence Senesh, Hearings, JEC, *Economic Education,* 17 Apr. 1967, 41; William B. Walstad and John C. Soper, *Effective Economic Education in the Schools* (JCEE, 1991), in JCEE Papers, Hagley.

32. JEC, Hearings of the Subcommittee on Economic Progress, *Economic Education,* 14, 17, 21 Apr. 1967, vol. 2; and Related Materials 29–31.

33. Interviews with Mark Schug, 7 Feb. 2005, and Stowell Symmes, 2 Oct. 2004; William B. Alstad, "Economic Instruction in the High Schools," *Journal of Economic Literature* 30:4 (Dec. 1992); and Hill, "The Joint Council on Economic Education."

34. Interviews with Mark Schug, 7 Feb. 2005, Leon Schur, 15 Feb. 2005, and Stowell Symmes, 2 Oct. 2004.

Chapter 7: A Flawed Measure: Critics and Realities

1. Jackson Lears, *Fables of Abundance: A Cultural History of Advertising in America* (New York: Basic Books, 1994), 2, 2, 38, 127, 139, 235; Werner Sombart, *Why Is There No Socialism in the*

United States? (White Plains, N.Y.: International Arts and Sciences Press, 1976), 106; Vance Packard, *The Hidden Persuaders* (New York: Pocket Books / David McKay Company, 1957), 1–5; Daniel Horowitz, *Vance Packard and American Social Criticism* (Chapel Hill: University of North Carolina Press, 1994), 103, 124–25; Stuart Ewen, *Captains of Consciousness: Advertising and the Social Roots of the Consumer Culture* (New York: McGraw-Hill, 1976), 13–14, 18, 33, 41, 191; Jean-Christophe Agnew, "Coming Up for Air: Consumer Culture In Historical Perspective," in *Consumer Society in American History: A Reader,* ed. Lawrence B. Glickman (Ithaca: Cornell University Press, 1999); and C. Wright Mills, *The Power Elite* (New York: Oxford University Press, 1956).

2. David Riesman, "The Nylon War," *Individualism Reconsidered and Other Essays* (Glencoe, Ill.: Free Press, 1954); Riesman, *Abundance for What and Other Essays* (Garden City, N.Y.: Anchor Books, 1964) 100–101; Howard Brick, *Transcending Capitalism: Visions of a New Society in Modern American Thought* (Ithaca: Cornell University Press, 2006), 172, 178; Thomas L. Hartshorne, *Distorted Image: Changing Conceptions of the American Character since Turner* (Westport, Conn.: Greenwood Press, 1968), 174; Richard Pells, *The Liberal Mind in a Conservative Age: American Intellectuals in the 1940s and 1950s* (New York: Harper & Row, 1985), 189; Dwight Macdonald, *Against the American Grain* (New York: Random House, 1962); Daniel Boorstin, *The Image: A Guide to Pseudo-Events in America* (New York: Alfred A. Knopf, 1961), 61, 183, 205; Holly George-Warren, ed., *The Rolling Stone Book of the Beats: The Beat Generation and American Culture* (New York: Hyperion, 1999), 6, 59, 233; Ann Charters, ed., *Beat Down to Your Soul* (New York: Penguin, 2001), 220–21; and Norman Mailer, "The White Negro," in *The Conquest of Cool: Business Culture, Counterculture, and the Rise of Hip Consumerism,* ed. Thomas Frank (Chicago: University of Chicago Press, 1997), 12.

3. "Grab Bag of Goals," *Wall Street Journal,* 30 Nov. 1960; John K. Jessup / Life, *The National Purpose* (New York: Holt, Rinehart & Winston, 1960), 41, 133; John W. Jeffries, "The Quest for National Purpose of 1960," *American Quarterly* 30:4 (Autumn 1978): 451–470; *Life,* 30 May 1960; and Fortune, *Markets of the Sixties,* xiii–xiv.

4. "The Challenge of Abundance," *Commonweal,* 20 May 20 1955; Betty Friedan, *The Feminine Mystique* (New York: W. W. Norton, 1963); and John Gottheimer, ed., *Ripples of Hope: Great American Civil Rights Speeches* (New York: Basic Civitas Books, 2003), 234, 260, 268, 299; Robert E. Weems Jr., *Desegregating the Dollar: African-American Consumerism in the Twentieth Century* (New York: New York University Press, 1998), 3; University of Michigan, Survey Research Center, Economic Behavior Program, *Survey of Consumer Attitudes and Behavior, 1965* (Ann Arbor: Inter-University Consortium for Political and Social Research).

5. Habermas, *The Structural Transformation of the Public Sphere: An Inquiry Into a Category of Bourgeois Society* (Cambridge, Mass.: MIT Press, 1989); Jean Baudrillard, *The Consumer Society: Myths and Structures* (London: Sage, 1998), 80, 15, 41, 65; and Guy Debord, *Society of the Spectacle* (Detroit: Black and Red, 1970), 17, 1.

6. Richard Parker, *John Kenneth Galbraith: His Life, His Politics, His Economics* (New York: Farrar, Straus and Giroux, 2005), 647; Hal Lindsey with C. C. Carlson, *The Late Great Planet Earth* (Grand Rapids: Zondervan, 1970); E. F. Schumacher, *Small Is Beautiful: Economics as if People Mattered* (New York: Harper & Row, 1973); and The Club of Rome, *Limits to Growth: A Report for the Club of Rome's Project on the Predicament of Mankind* (New York: New American Library, 1972).

7. Christopher Lasch, *The Culture of Narcissism: American Life in an Age of Diminishing Expectations* (New York: W. W. Norton, 1979), 370, 137–40; and Michael Schudson, "Delectable Materialism: Second Thoughts on Consumer Culture," in *Consumer Society in American History,* ed. Lawrence B. Glickman (Ithaca: Cornell University Press, 1999), 342, 351.

8. *Public Papers of the Presidents: Jimmy Carter, 1979,* vol. I, 1562–63.

9. Robert Bellah et al., *Habits of The Heart: Individualism and Commitment in American Life* (New York: Harper & Row, 1986); and Robert Putnam, *Bowling Alone: The Collapse and Revival of American Community* (New York: Simon & Schuster, 2000), 283, 17.

10. Robert J. Ringer, *Looking Out for Number One* (New York: Fawcett, 1977); "John Taylor, "The Decline of Economics," *New Yorker,* 2 Dec. 1996; and Arthur Schlesinger Jr., *The Disuniting of America* (New York: W. W. Norton, 1992).

11. Daniel Bell, *Work and Its Discontents* (Boston: Beacon Press, 1956), *The End of Ideology: On the Exhaustion of Political Ideas in the Fifties* (Glencoe, Ill.: Free Press, 1960, and *The Cultural Contradictions of Capitalism* (New York: Basic Books, 1976), 71, 21, 237; Robert Samuelson, *The Good Life and Its Discontents: The American Dream in the Age of Entitlement, 1945–1995* (New York: Random House, 1995), 50; Godfrey Hodgson, *America in Our Time* (New York: Vintage Books, 1976), 74–75; and Foner, *The Story of American Freedom,* 268.

12. John Kenneth Galbraith, *The Affluent Society* (Boston: Houghton Mifflin, 1958), 190–204, 6–17, 122, and *A Life in Our Times* (Boston: Houghton Mifflin, 1981), 669.

13. William H. Whyte Jr., *The Organization Man* (New York: Simon & Schuster, 1956), 4–6, 50, 347–49; Pells, *The Liberal Mind in a Conservative Age,* 233–35; and John Keats, *The Crack in the Picture Window* (Boston: Houghton Mifflin, 1956), 61, 5, 18, 43, 87.

14. Juliet Schor, *The Overspent American* (New York: Basic Books, 1998), 8–9; James Duesenberry, "The Increase-of-Consumption Part of Economic Growth," *American Economic Review* 46:2 (May 1956); Spiegel and Samuels, eds., *Contemporary Economists in Perspective,* vol. 2, 466–67; Harold F. Williamson, "An Appraisal of American Economic Progress," *American Economic Review* 40:2 (May 1950); Kenneth E. Boulding, "Defense and Opulence: The Ethics of International Economics," *American Economic Review* 41:2 (May 1951); Boulding, "The Fruits of Progress and the Dynamics of Distribution," *American Economic Review* 43:2 (May 1953); Boulding, "A New Look at Institutionalism," *American Economic Review* 47:2 (May, 1957); and Solow, "Technical Progress, Capital Formation, and Economic Growth," *American Economic Review* 52:2 (May 1962).

15. Tibor Scitovsky, "A Critique of Present and Proposed Standards," *American Economic Review* 50:2 (May 1960), "On the Principle of Consumers' Sovereignty," *American Economic Review* 52:2 (May 1962), and *The Joyless Economy: The Psychology of Human Satisfaction and Consumer Dissatisfaction* (New York: Oxford University Press, 1972).

16. Heilbroner, "The Uncomfortable Paradise of Full Employment," *Harper's,* Apr. 1947, and "Will Our Prosperity Last?" *Harper's,* Dec. 1948; and Jan Myrdal et al., "The Triple Revolution" (Santa Barbara, Calif.: The Ad Hoc Committee on the Triple Revolution, 1964).

17. Lekachman, "If We're So Rich, What's Eating Us?" *Harper's,* Feb. 1956; and "Does Economics Ignore You?" *Saturday Review,* 22 Jan. 1972.

18. *Business Week,* 12 Mar. 1955; Keyserling, "Public Weal and Private Too," *New York Times Magazine,* 21 Aug. 1960; Conference on Economic Progress, "The Gaps in Our Prosperity" (1956) and "The Federal Budget and the General Welfare" (1959), Leon Keyserling Papers, Box 65, Harry S. Truman Library (HSTL); and "Democracy Can't Live in These Houses," *Collier's,* 9 July 1949.

19. Michael Harrington, *The Other America: Poverty in America* (New York: Macmillan, 1962), 9; Daniel Horowitz, *The Anxieties of Affluence: Critiques of American Consumer Culture, 1939–1979* (Amherst: University of Massachusetts Press, 2004), 8–16.

20. Mollie Orshansky, " Children of the Poor," *Social Security Bulletin* 26:7 (July 1963); Orshansky, "Counting the Poor: Another Look at the Poverty Profile," *Social Security Bulletin* 28:1 (Jan. 1965); CEA, "The Problem of Poverty in America," *Economic Report of the President* (Washington, D.C.: GPO, 1964); and Robert J. Lampman, "Population Change and Poverty Reduction, 1947–75," in *Poverty Amid Affluence,* ed. Leo Fishman (New Haven: Yale University Press, 1966).

21. Allen Matusow, *The Unraveling of America: A History of Liberalism in the 1960s* (New York: Harper & Row, 1984), 179.

22. Steven D. Leavitt and Stephen J. Dubner, *Freakonomics* (New York: William Morrow, 2005), 13–14; Steven E. Landsburg, *The Armchair Economist: Economics and Everyday Life* (New York: The Free Press, 1993); and Tyler Cowen, *Discover Your Inner Economist* (New York: Dutton, 2008).

23. Organization for Economic Cooperation and Development, "Growing Unequal: Income Distribution and Poverty in OECD Countries" (Paris: OECD, 2008).

24. CEA, Economic Report of the President (Washington, D.C.: GPO, 1990); and *Washington Post*, 1 Feb. 2006.

25. President Bill Clinton, 8 Jan. 1999; 20 Jan. 1997; 12 June 1999; and 26 July 1993, American Presidency Project, www.presidency.ucsb.edu/index.php.

26. Mary Douglas and Baron Isherwood, *The World of Goods: Towards an Anthropology of Consumption* (New York: Basic Books, 1979), 10, 57, 15, 20; Baudrillard, *The Consumer Society*, 6–7; and Baudrillard, *The Mirror of Production* (Saint Louis: Telos Press, 1975), chapter 1.

27. James Twitchell, *Lead Us into Temptation: The Triumph of American Materialism* (New York: Columbia University Press, 1999), 19–20, 27, 44–46, 54; and Schudson, "Delectable Materialism," 354.

28. 26 Jan. 1985, *Public Papers of the Presidents: Ronald W. Reagan, 1985*, vol. 1, 75–76.

29. Gallup-A.I.P.O., *The Gallup Poll: Public Opinion 1935–1971*, vol. 2, 1016; vol. 3, 1749, 2046; and "81% Say U.S. on Wrong Track," CBS News, 3 Apr. 2008.

30. Federal Reserve Board, *Survey of Consumer Finances;* Christian Weller, "Economic Snapshot for November 2008," Center for American Progress (Washington, 2008); "A Reality Check on Debt before Retirement," *Washington Post*, 17 June 2007; "By One Measure, U.S. Home Equity Is Down to 20 Percent," *Los Angeles Times*, 14 June 2009; "Given a Shovel, Americans Dig Deeper into Debt," *New York Times*, 20 July 2008; "Americans Teetering on $14 Trillion Debt Pile," Reuters, 14 Nov. 2008; "Bankruptcy Filing Rise to 6,000 a Day, as Job Losses Take Toll," *USA Today*, 6 June 2009; "U.S. Foreclosures Double as House Prices Decline," Bloomberg, 25 July 2008; Center on Budget and Policy Priorities, "State Budget Troubles Worsen," 9 Jan. 2009; Peter G. Peterson Foundation, "State of the Union's Finances" (Mar. 2009); Andrew L. Yarrow, *Forgive Us Our Debts: The Intergenerational Dangers of Fiscal Irresponsibility* (New Haven: Yale University Press, 2008); *USA Today*, 29 May 2007; "Retiree Benefits Grow into Monster" *USA Today*, 24 May 2006; FASAB, "Accounting for Social Insurance," 23 Oct. 2006; "Public-Sector Pensions," *The Economist*, 18 Nov. 2006; "Economy Made Few Gains in the Bush Years," *Washington Post*, 12 Jan. 2009; Government Accountability Office, "State and Local Government Retire Benefits," (Washington, D.C.: GPO, Jan. 2008); "Credit Card Statistics, Industry Facts, Debt Statistics (Nilson Reports, 2009).

31. Steven Greenhouse, *The Big Squeeze: Tough Times for the American Worker* (New York: Alfred A. Knopf, 2008); Jared Bernstein, Elizabeth McNichol, and Karen Lyons, "Pulling Apart" (Washington, D.C.: Economic Policy Institute and Center on Budget and Policy Priorities, 2006); and Isabel Sawhill and John E. Morton, "Economic Mobility: Is the American Dream Alive and Well? (Washington, D.C.: Brookings Institution, 2007).

32. Pew Research Center, "Trends in Political Values and Core Attitudes: 1987–2007" (Pew, Mar. 2007); Robert Reich, "Secession of the Successful," *New York Times Magazine*, 20 Jan. 1991; and Jared Bernstein, *All Together Now: Common Sense for a Fair Economy (San Francisco: Berrett-Koehler, 2006).

33. Clive Crook, "Rags to Rags, Riches to Riches," *Atlantic,* June 2007; Sawhill and Morton, "Economic Mobility"; and Ron Haskins and Isabel Sawhill, *Creating an Opportunity Society* (Washington, D.C.: Brookings Institution Press, 2009).

34. Frank Levy, *Dollars and Dreams: The Changing American Income Distribution* (New York: Russell Sage Foundation, 1987); Barbara Ehrenreich, *Nickel and Dimed: On (Not) Getting By in America* (New York: Henry Holt, 2001); Jacob Hacker, *The Great Risk Shift: The Assault on American Jobs, Families, Health Care, and Retirement, and How You Can Fight Back* (New York: Oxford University Press, 2006); Derek Bok, *The Cost of Talent: How Executives and Professionals Are Paid and How It Affects America* (New York: The Free Press, 1993); Robert Frank and Philip Cook. *The Winner-Take-All Society* (New York: Free Press, 1995); Frank, *Luxury Fever: Why Money Fails to Satisfy in an Era of Excess* (New York: Free Press, 1999); and U.S. Census Bureau, Historical Income Inequality Tables.

35. Schor, *The Overspent American*, 3–4, 12–13, 19–20, and *The Overworked American: The Unexpected Decline of Leisure* (New York: Basic Books, 1992); and Valerie Ramey and Neville Francis, "A Century of Work and Leisure," NBER Working Paper 12264 (Cambridge, Mass.: NBER, 2007).

36. Elizabeth Warren and Amelia Warren Tygi, *The Two-Income Trap: Why Middle-Class Mothers and Fathers Are Going Broke* (New York: Basic Books, 2003).

Chapter 8: Measuring America in the Twenty-first Century

1. James Oppenheim, "Bread and Roses," *American Magazine,* Dec. 1911.

2. Benjamin Barber, *Consumed* (New York: W. W. Norton, 2007).

3. Erwin Quintan and Jason Saving, "Inequality and Growth: Challenges to the Old Orthodoxy," Federal Reserve Bank of Dallas, Jan. 2008; Theo S. Eicher and Stephen J. Turnovsky, eds., Inequality and Growth: Theory and Policy Implications (Cambridge, Mass.: MIT Press, 2003); Alberto F. Alesina and Dani Rodrik, "Distributive Politics and Economic Growth," Quarterly Journal of Economics 109 (1994): 465–90; and Roberto Perotti, "Growth, Income Distribution and Democracy: What the Data Say," Journal of Economic Growth 1:2 (1996): 149–88.

4. "Kurt Vonnegut and the Longing for a Bygone America," Washington Post, 13 Apr. 2007.

5. Bradley Foundation, "E Pluribus Unum: The Bradley Project on National Identity" (Milwaukee: Bradley Foundation, 2008).

6. Jared Bernstein, All Together Now: Common Sense for a Fair Economy (San Francisco: Berrett-Koehler Publishers, 2006).

Index

Andrew L. Yarrow is a public policy professional and teaches modern U.S. history at American University. Dr. Yarrow is the author of *Forgive Us Our Debts: The Intergenerational Dangers of Fiscal Irresponsibility* (2008) and *Latecomers: Children of Parents over 35* (1991).

A former reporter for the *New York Times,* Dr. Yarrow has published many op-eds and popular and scholarly articles and has a regular column in the *Baltimore Sun*. A resident of Bethesda, Maryland, he has worked for Public Agenda, the Brookings Institution, the U.S. Department of Labor, the Export-Import Bank, the World Bank, UNICEF, the U.S. Department of Education, and the Carnegie Corporation, and he has taught communications at American University.

Dr. Yarrow has a PhD in history from George Mason University, an MPA from the Kennedy School of Government at Harvard University, an MA in history from Princeton University, and a B.A. in history from the University of California, Los Angeles. He has one son, Richard.